ENCYCLOPEDIA OF
NATURE

TREASURE PRESS

Contents

First published in Great Britain in 1979 by
Macdonald Educational Limited

This edition published in 1988 by
Treasure Press
59 Grosvenor Street
London W1

© Macdonald Educational Limited 1979

ISBN 1 85051 279 5

Printed in Czechoslovakia
50690

Contents

Why life exists

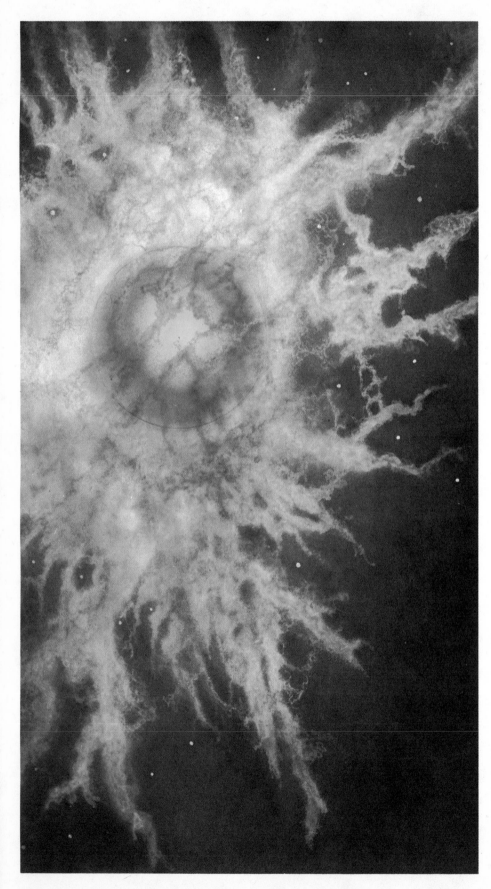

Our sun seems big and important to us. But really it is no different from all the stars that we see as tiny points of light in the night sky. The stars seem so small because they are so far away but some are actually much bigger than our sun. Some are older, and some are younger. By studying the stars scientists can guess how our sun, and the planets that circle round it, were formed.

Formation of stars

They all probably formed about 4,600 million years ago, and started as an enormous spinning cloud of gas. Gradually, the gases at the centre of the cloud condensed together to form the planets. The outer planets, which lie far from the light and warmth of the sun, are cold masses of gas and ice. The inner planets lying closer to the sun are very hot. The earth, too, was very hot when it first formed. It began as a mass of glowing gas which gradually cooled and turned to liquid. Then a solid crust of rock formed on its surface. Even today, the inside of the earth is still hot, and when volcanoes erupt they throw out molten rock which we call lava.

The atmosphere of the earth at first contained gases such as hydrogen, carbon dioxide, methane and ammonia. Water, too, was only a steamy vapour in the air. It took millions of years for the first rain to form. Only then could streams and rivers appear. The seas and oceans formed when pools of water gradually ran together.

The beginning of life

Many types of chemical were dissolved in these warm waters. When lightning from storms struck into the water, electrical energy linked the chemicals together in many different ways. Eventually, a chemical appeared that could make more molecules like itself. That was the beginning of life. Scientists believe that this first form of life appeared about 3,000 million years ago.

Above: The sun began when the central parts of a mass of gas gradually clumped together. The gases started to react. Then they began to glow with heat. So the sun began to shine! The cooler parts of the mass formed the planets which make up our solar system.

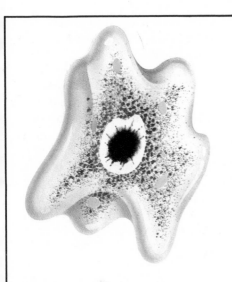

Above: This amoeba is one of the simplest animals alive today. It is so small that you can only see it under a microscope. It can move simply by extending outwards in one direction and pulling the rest of itself along. The amoeba can divide into two smaller amoebae, both of which grow.

Below: At first, the world must have been a very hot and unpleasant place. Volcanoes spouted out streams of molten lava and rained down hot rocks and cinders all around them. They also produced hot, poisonous gases that filled the air.

Living things are made up mainly of water. So life could not have evolved until the earth became cool enough for the water vapour to change from steam into liquid. The first plants were probably just mats of slimy algae which covered the surface of pools of water. Yet all the wonderful variety of life we know today evolved from such simple-celled organisms.

The first living things
The earliest types of life must have been quite tiny and simple, like bacteria. They probably got their energy from breaking down other complex chemicals around them. Some of these early living things evolved a green chemical that absorbed the energy from the sunlight in order to make their own food. These were the first plants, and must have been like microscopic single-celled algae. Animals cannot make food. They get their energy from eating plants or eating other animals. So they could only evolve after the first plants, perhaps 1,000 million years ago. These first animals were tiny single-celled organisms too.

Every living organism must be able to do two things. It must be able to use energy to make more of its own body chemicals so that it can grow. And it must be able to reproduce, making more organisms, each like itself.

Evolution
Each pair of animals or plants can produce very many offspring, but in each generation most of the offspring die before they grow up. That is why scientists speak of a "struggle for survival".

Though each organism is very like its parents, no two organisms are quite identical. Perhaps one plant may be able to grow a little faster, or one animal may be able to run a bit further than its brothers and sisters. Any animal or plant with such an advantage is more likely to be able to survive to grow up and produce its own offspring. In this way, by the "natural selection" of those with advantages, animals and plants gradually change or "evolve" over many generations.

Records of the past

Over the last few hundreds of millions of years, very many different types of animals and plants have lived on earth. Some have left descendants still alive today, but many are completely extinct. We only know about these vanished forms of life because traces of them have been left behind, buried in the rocks. These traces are called fossils and may consist of bones, shells, eggs, seeds, tree trunks or leaves.

How fossils form

Most fossils are the remains of the hard parts of an animal or plant, such as its skeleton or its shell, because the soft parts rot away quickly. After the skeleton or shell has become buried in sand or mud, it slowly turns to stone. This is because the water that gradually seeps through the rock contains various minerals. The water dissolves away some of the chemicals in the bone or shell, and the other minerals take their place. These minerals also fill in any spaces in the fossil, so that it becomes hard and solid. The fossil still shows a lot of the detailed structure of the original bone or shell, even after being cracked and crushed for millions of years in the rocks.

Some rocks are made entirely of fossils. Coal is formed from the remains of plants that grew in a tropical forest. You can sometimes see impressions of the leaves or stems in it. Chalk is the remains of the skeletons of millions of tiny creatures that lived in the sea.

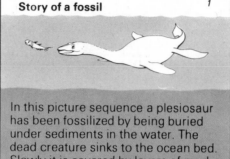

Story of a fossil 1

In this picture sequence a plesiosaur has been fossilized by being buried under sediments in the water. The dead creature sinks to the ocean bed. Slowly it is covered by layers of mud and sand (2). The layers become thick and harden (3). The sea moves back and the land is lifted above the water. Wind and rain wear away the layers and the fossil is exposed (4).

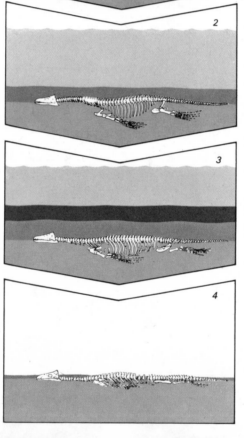

Moulds, casts and impressions

Sometimes, the whole fossil animal or plant is dissolved away. All that is left is a cavity in the rock, shaped like the original fossil. This is called a "mould" of the fossil. The mould may later become filled with another type of mineral, making a natural "cast" of the fossil. Other fossils are the impressions of only parts of the animal or plant, made when perhaps an animal walks on some sand, or a leaf or feather is blown onto some mud. Sometimes the body of a worm or jellyfish is stranded on the seashore and leaves the mark of its body on the sand. If the sand then hardens and turns to stone, it will preserve the impression for millions of years.

Occasionally, the body of an animal becomes covered with snow and ice, so that the flesh does not rot away. As long as the ice remains frozen, it will preserve even the flesh of the animal. The bodies of many woolly-haired elephants, called mammoths, were buried several thousands of years ago and were preserved in this way in the ice of northern Russia. There was no ice millions of years ago when such animals as the dinosaurs were alive, so we shall never be able to find their bodies buried in the ice.

Below left: This well-preserved skeleton of a reptile is over 210 million years old.

Below: This mammoth's flesh rotted away when it was dug from the ice.

Reconstruction of a prehistoric animal

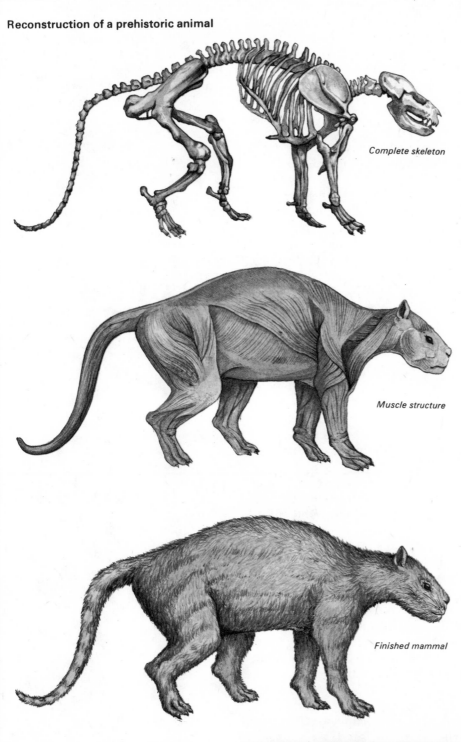

Complete skeleton

Muscle structure

Finished mammal

Reconstructing a fossil animal

The scientist who studies fossils is called a palaeontologist. Sometimes he may find the complete skeleton of a fossil animal buried in rock. He then carefully removes all the rock, mends each bone, and fits all the bones together as they were when the animal was alive. If he only finds some of the bones, he has to study other similar animals to find out what the missing bones were like.

Once we know what the whole skeleton looked like, we can try to reconstruct its original appearance. The bones bear projections or marks where the muscles were attached. By studying these marks, and by studying the bones and muscles in living animals, the palaeontologist can work out where the muscles of the animal were placed, and how big they were. He can also study its joints, and find out how it could move its limbs. By studying its teeth, he can tell whether it ate plants or fed on other animals.

Next, the palaeontologist has to find out how the fossil animal was covered. Fish, lizards and snakes have scales. Birds are covered with feathers, and mammals have a hairy coat. Impressions of some dinosaurs show that they had a leathery skin, sometimes with little bones embedded in it. But nobody can know exactly how any fossil animal was coloured or patterned. We can only look at similar animals living today, and assume that the fossils were of much the same appearance.

Above: Palaeontologists first piece together the bones of a prehistoric animal (*1*). After that, they can work out the positions of the main muscles and draw them in (*2*). The length of the hair and colour of an animal is usually guesswork (*3*).

Right: Every detail of this prehistoric bird feather has been preserved in very fine, soft mud.

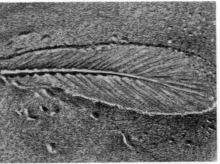

Above: Sometimes the droppings of an animal harden and turn into a stone, which is called a "coprolite". Each animal leaves droppings of a particular shape. Palaeontologists can sometimes tell what the animal fed on by studying the coprolite. But they never know which animal the coprolite was made by.

Variety of life forms

Though it does not seem so to us, the earth's crust is continually altering. Over millions of years the continents are slowly moving and splitting up or rejoining into larger masses. New mountains rise up and old ones are slowly worn down by water and wind. Sometimes the seas flood across the low-lying parts of the land and later draw back again.

The rocks of the earth's surface are a record of all these changes. New rocks are always laid down on top of older ones, which helps us to understand the order of the rocks. But sometimes the rocks are folded and distorted and nowhere is the record complete. As new rocks are being laid down in one area, older rocks are being eroded away in another. Luckily, there are two ways in which the earth scientists, or "geologists", can work out the whole story.

Radioactivity and fossils
One way is by studying the radio-activity that is in some rocks; some for example, contain a mineral called uranium, which gradually changes into lead. Scientists can measure how quickly this happens and can then work out how old the rock is. For example, all the uranium would have changed to lead in 1,400 million years. If only half of the uranium in the rock has changed to lead, then the rock must be 700 million years old. By dating one rock geologists can also date other rocks nearby. Any that lie on top of the radioactive rock must be younger, and any that lie under it must be older.

Geologists can also use fossils to estimate the ages of rocks which do not contain radioactive minerals. New animals and plants are continually evolving and others are becoming extinct. So rocks of different ages contain different types of fossils. By studying many series of rocks, palaeontologists have managed to build up a picture of the order in which the different types of organism appeared and disappeared.

The relative ages of the rocks
The dinosaurs died out before most of the mammals appeared. So most rocks which contain fossil dinosaurs must be older than those which contain fossil mammals. This is how geologists can use fossils to tell them the relative ages of the different rocks. Whenever any of the rocks contain radio-active minerals, they can find out its real age as well.

You can think of the story of the rocks as a book telling you the history of a family, with new members being born and older ones dying. Each layer of rock is a page, and its fossils tell you which chapter of the book you are reading – whether you are near the beginning, the middle, or the end of the book. But the radioactivity method will tell you the number of the page that you are reading.

Changing climates
The climate of the world has not always been as it is today. For most of the earth's history, there have been no sheets of ice near the North Pole and the South Pole. Warmer climates covered much more of the world, and plants could grow much closer to the Poles. Because the continents have gradually moved across the surface of the world, they have sometimes been in hot regions, and sometimes in cold regions. For example, the thick coal deposits of Europe and North America were laid down when these continents lay near the Equator, in a hot tropical climate. Only 50 million years ago, crocodiles and turtles swam near the palm trees that grew where London is today.

Right: The chart shows how geologists divide up the last 600 million years of earth's history. It shows the important types of animal alive during each period of time and explains the main changes which were taking place. We know much less about the older parts of earth's history, because not so many of the older rocks remain to tell us their story.

Era	PERIOD	EPOCH	
CENOZOIC	Tertiary	Pliocene	
		Miocene	Land plants
		Oligocene	
		Eocene	
		Palaeocene	Flowering plants
MESOZOIC	Cretaceous		
	Jurassic		
	Triassic		
PALAEOZOIC	Permian		Fern
	Carboniferous		
	Devonian		
	Silurian		Rhynia
	Ordovician		
	Cambrian		
	Pre-Cambrian		

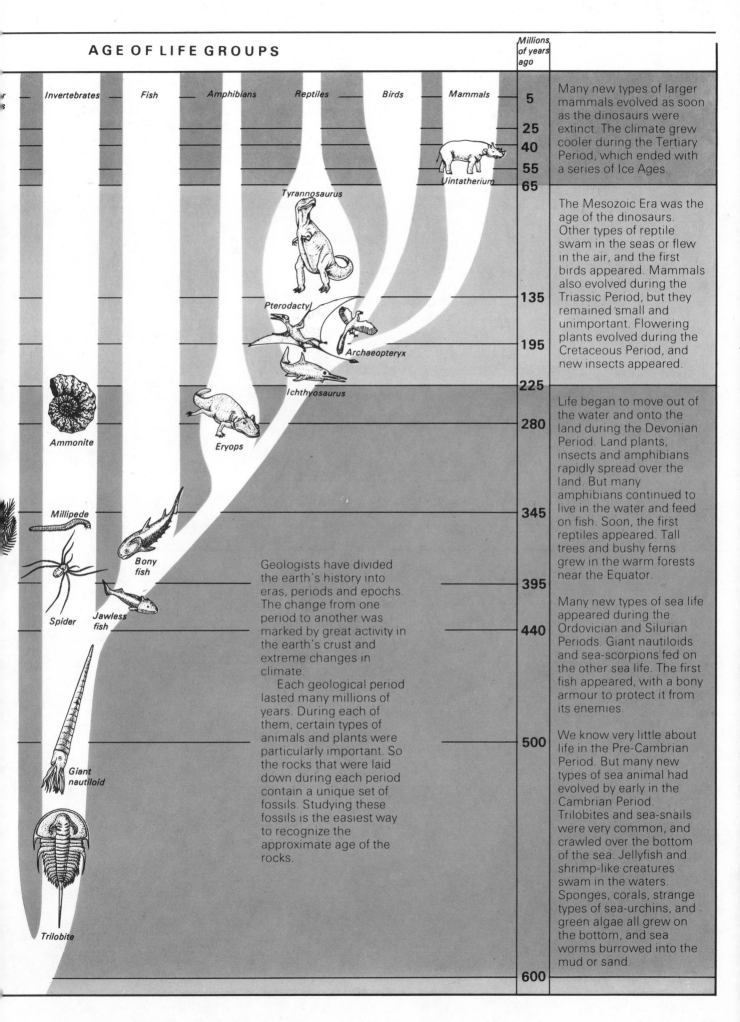

AGE OF LIFE GROUPS

Invertebrates — Fish — Amphibians — Reptiles — Birds — Mammals

Millions of years ago

Tyrannosaurus

Pterodactyl

Archaeopteryx

Ichthyosaurus

Uintatherium

Ammonite

Eryops

Millipede

Bony fish

Spider

Jawless fish

Giant nautiloid

Trilobite

Geologists have divided the earth's history into eras, periods and epochs. The change from one period to another was marked by great activity in the earth's crust and extreme changes in climate.

Each geological period lasted many millions of years. During each of them, certain types of animals and plants were particularly important. So the rocks that were laid down during each period contain a unique set of fossils. Studying these fossils is the easiest way to recognize the approximate age of the rocks.

Many new types of larger mammals evolved as soon as the dinosaurs were extinct. The climate grew cooler during the Tertiary Period, which ended with a series of Ice Ages.

The Mesozoic Era was the age of the dinosaurs. Other types of reptile swam in the seas or flew in the air, and the first birds appeared. Mammals also evolved during the Triassic Period, but they remained small and unimportant. Flowering plants evolved during the Cretaceous Period, and new insects appeared.

Life began to move out of the water and onto the land during the Devonian Period. Land plants, insects and amphibians rapidly spread over the land. But many amphibians continued to live in the water and feed on fish. Soon, the first reptiles appeared. Tall trees and bushy ferns grew in the warm forests near the Equator.

Many new types of sea life appeared during the Ordovician and Silurian Periods. Giant nautiloids and sea-scorpions fed on the other sea life. The first fish appeared, with a bony armour to protect it from its enemies.

We know very little about life in the Pre-Cambrian Period. But many new types of sea animal had evolved by early in the Cambrian Period. Trilobites and sea-snails were very common, and crawled over the bottom of the sea. Jellyfish and shrimp-like creatures swam in the waters. Sponges, corals, strange types of sea-urchins, and green algae all grew on the bottom, and sea worms burrowed into the mud or sand.

5
25
40
55
65
135
195
225
280
345
395
440
500
600

15

Earliest life forms

Life first evolved in the sea, and the body fluids of many animals today differ little from sea water. For many millions of years, living things existed only in the sea.

Early invertebrates

Even today, many groups of animals do not have a backbone. They are called invertebrates. Many strange types of invertebrate animals lived in the sea between 400 and 500 million years ago. Right on the bottom there lived corals. Corals were like sea anemones, with a ring of tentacles which bore tiny poisonous cells so that they could kill smaller sea creatures for food. They made a hard limestone cup to protect their soft bodies and each year grew larger by adding a new, bigger ring to the top.

Sea-scorpions were the largest invertebrates that have ever lived. One type was two metres long and used its powerful pincers to crack open the shells of the early fish and snails. It could swim, or walk along on the bottom of the sea.

Sea-lilies were common, too. They were not plants, but were related to sea-urchins and starfish. They had long stalks, and flexible arms with sticky tentacles for catching their food.

Below: An imagined scene of early sea life. The animal in the centre is a giant nautiloid. It was rather like a squid or octopus, with long tentacles. Nautiloids lived in shells which were full of gas to help them float. Later nautiloids, called ammonites, lived in coiled shells.

Sea lilies

Giant nautiloid

Giant water scorpion

Snail

Coral

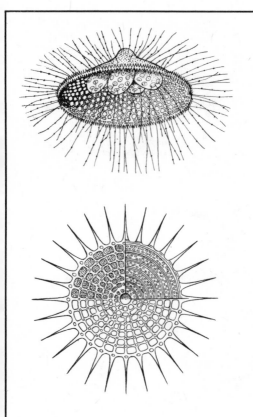

Above left: Simple types of microscopic animal still live in the sea today. They are called radiolarians, and have shells made of silica. Similar radiolarians lived in the seas many millions of years ago.

Above: The early forests were quite unlike those of today. The trees were up to 30 metres tall, but they were related to the little clubmosses and horsetails of today. Other, smaller trees were really large ferns.

The history of plant life

Early plants were small. They lived in the water and were like the slimy algae you find on the seashore or in ponds. Life on land is more difficult for both plants and animals; they need a special covering of waterproof cells or they dry up. Plants have a special system of cells to transport water from the roots to the rest of the plant and, if they are to grow tall, they need hard, woody cells to support their stem or trunk. The first land plants evolved at the end of the Silurian Period, over 400 million years ago.

The coal forests

About 300 million years ago, thick forests grew in North America and Europe. At the bottom of the many swamps and lagoons, dead leaves and plants made thick layers which became compressed. Often the sea flooded the forests, leaving a thick covering of sand and mud over the layers of dead plants which gradually turned into hard coal. Occasionally you can see impressions in the coal of leaves or bones of amphibians and fish.

Several million years later, the first conifer trees evolved. Fir and pine trees are conifers. They have seeds which are borne on cones, and do not have any flowers. Another group of plants called the Bennettitales had big, palm-like leaves. For most of the long reign of the dinosaurs all these plants were the main source of food for herbivores (plant-eating animals).

The beginnings of flowers

Most of the early plants relied on the wind to carry the pollen from one plant to another, to fertilize the ovules. But, about 100 million years ago, a new and important group of plants evolved – the flowering plants. Their beautiful flowers are really only a means of attracting insects to the plant. The flowers also contain sweet nectar, which provides food for the insect. As it goes from flower to flower, the insect carries pollen from plant to plant and fertilizes its ovules. Unlike other plants the seeds of the flowering plants are enclosed and protected.

These new adaptations helped the flowering plants to spread quickly all through the world. The old seed ferns and Bennettitales became extinct, and the ancient types of conifer became much rarer.

Some flowering plants today do not have coloured flowers and the wind carries their pollen. Most plants, even trees and grasses, are types of flowering plant.

New food from new plants

The flowering plants provided many new types of food. Many new varieties of insect evolved to feed on their nectar and fruit. These insects in turn were food for new types of birds and for bats, which evolved to hunt them in the air. Some of the dinosaurs probably fed on the leaves and fruit of the early flowering plants. So did the little early mammals, which climbed about in the trees. Grass is a type of flowering plant that has adapted to live on the dry plains, and many types of mammal evolved to feed on the grass and to run quickly on the hard, dry ground.

The first fish

Most fish today are graceful, agile swimmers. But the early fish were different. Covered with thick, bony armour and with only feeble fins, they must have moved slowly and awkwardly. The reason for their armour was probably the giant sea-scorpions, whose pincers could crack open all but the strongest protection. With enemies like this, the early fish had either to out-swim them or to evolve some defensive armour.

These armoured fish did not swim about much in mid-water, like fish today. Weighed down by their armour, they spent most of their time on the bottom of the sea. They could wriggle from place to place, using their tail and clumsy flippers, but they could not pursue their food. Many of these first fish did not even have any jaws with which to bite. *Cephalaspis* ploughed along the bottom,

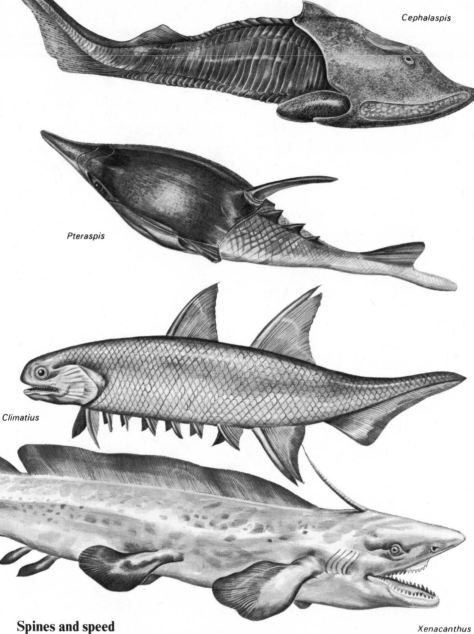

Cephalaspis

Pteraspis

Climatius

Xenacanthus

swallowing the mud and any small worms and snails in it. It was only 20-30 centimetres long, with a flat-tened body so that it did not sink into the mud. On its head, which was a solid mass of bone, it had special sensory areas. These were covered with tiny bones and pro-bably helped it to detect the move-ments of its enemies.

Pteraspis, which was only 15 centimetres long, lived in lakes and streams. It must have swum rather clumsily against the currents to get upstream as it had no fins to guide it. For food it may have scraped plant growth off the rocks with its nibbling mouth plates.

Spines and speed

Some other fish, such as *Climatius,* found that speed was better than armour as a protection from their enemies. They had a cover of thick diamond-shaped scales, but they also had a powerful swimming tail and a series of fins to steer them-selves through the water. At the front end of these fins were sharp spines, like those of a stickleback, which made them hard for other fish to swallow.

To swim faster, some fish evolved lighter bodies in which the skeleton of heavy bones was replaced by one made of cartilage. Cartilage or gristle covers the

Above: Fish evolved in the sea. Though a few are known from impressions in earlier rocks, it is not until the Devonian Period that we find a great variety of fish. By that time, fish were living in freshwater rivers and lakes as well as in the seas. Some of these Devonian fish are shown here.

joints between the bones in all backboned animals (vertebrates). An early fish with a light skeleton of cartilage was *Xenacanthus*. It was 75 centimetres long and had paddle-like fins and many sharp teeth.

The first land fish

The first backboned animal to go ashore was a fish. Though most fish today live in the water and breathe through gills, some do not. Several tropical fish venture into mud near the water in search of food. They breathe air through special cavities near their gills. But a few fish, called lungfish, have lungs just like those of amphibians, as well as gills. They live in tropical regions, where the river often dries up for part of the year. Lungfish dig holes in the mud and use their lungs to breathe air until the river fills up again. Similar burrows dug by ancient lungfish have been found.

Several of the earliest fish also had lungs, which they probably used in a similar way. But, to move on land, a fish also had to have strong fins. One group of fish that had quite strong fins were called the Rhipidistians. One of these was *Eusthenopteron* which may have been the ancestor of all the backboned animals that have lived on land. It was about a metre long, and lived during the Devonian Period.

The body of *Eusthenopteron* was covered with scales, and it had a powerful swimming tail. Its jaws contained many sharp teeth and it must have hunted other smaller fish for food.

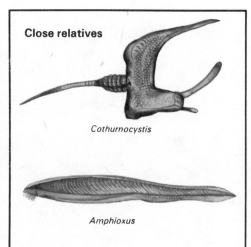

Close relatives

Cothurnocystis

Amphioxus

These sea creatures are the living descendants of the ancestors of the first fish. The backbone of fish forms around a stiff rod, or "notochord", running from head to tail. This notochord is also found in *Amphioxus* and the sea squirt's larva.

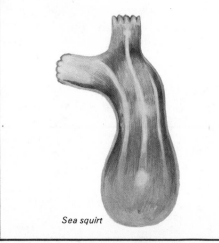

Sea squirt

The development of amphibians

Even if the adult *Eusthenopteron* ate other fish, its young were themselves probably hunted by many other bigger fish. With so much danger in the water, the little *Eusthenopteron* probably kept to the shallow water as much as possible. There, they were safe from the bigger fish, which would have gone aground as soon as they tried to reach them.

Safe in the shallows, the young *Eusthenopteron* must have fed on worms, snails and water insects. But, with their stout limbs, and their ability to breathe air, they would have been able to extend their search for food up onto the moist mud above the edge of the water. They soon found that there was plenty of food there, far from the dangerous waters. Gradually, over several millions of years, these fishes spent more and more of their lives on land. Their fins turned into limbs to support them, and their backbones became stronger to take the weight of their bodies. They had become the first amphibians.

Below: *Eusthenopteron* must have looked rather strange when it scrambled ashore. It pulled itself along with its flippers, looking for worms or snails in the mud around lakes and rivers.

Early land animals

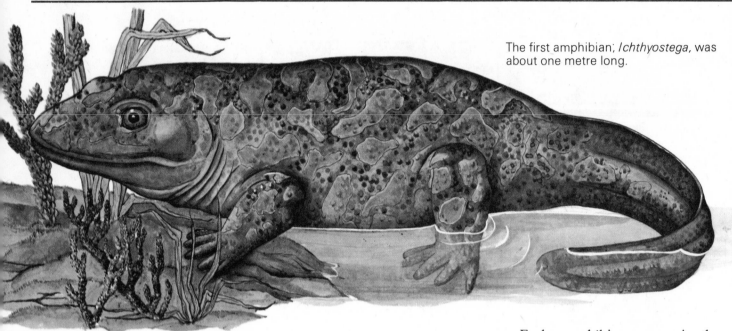

The first amphibian, *Ichthyostega*, was about one metre long.

The amphibians had learnt how to breathe air, how to walk on land, and how to find their food around the edges of the water. But they were still not wholly free from the water in several ways. Some of them, like amphibians today, had moist skins. So they had to stay in the water, or in damp places, or else they would have dried up. Amphibians still had to return to the water to lay their eggs, which were covered only by a layer of jelly.

Also, all the larger early amphibians ate fish. So even if they spent part of their time on land, they had to plunge back into the water every time they felt hungry and needed to search for a meal.

Early amphibians

The very first amphibian is called *Ichthyostega,* and it lived at the end of the Devonian Period. Though it had front and hind limbs instead of fins, it still had a long tail with a fin, which it must have used for swimming. During the next period, the Carboniferous, many types of amphibian are known which lived in the swamps. Some of them were rather like alligators, with big heads armed with many strong teeth. Most of them lived on fish, but some of the bigger amphibians must also have eaten their smaller relatives.

In the Permian Period, too, most of the amphibians that we know lived in the water.

Early amphibians swam in the rivers and lakes that covered part of what is now the state of Texas, in North America, and their bones are found in the deserts that now lie there. Not all of them were large. One, called *Diplocaulus,* had great triangular horns on either side of its head, which must have made it very difficult for enemies to swallow it. By this time, reptiles too were living on land, and some of these Texan amphibians probably ate both small reptiles and other amphibians. *Seymouria,* for example, had quite well developed limbs and could probably move quite well on land. One of its relatives, *Diadectes,* had wide chewing teeth, and was probably the first plant-eating amphibian.

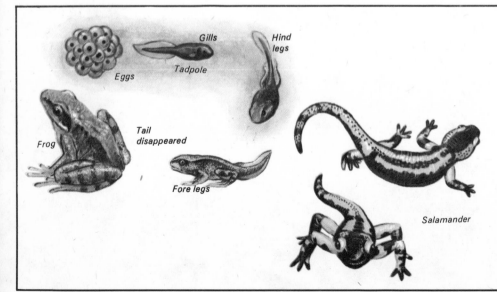

Eggs
Gills
Tadpole
Hind legs
Tail disappeared
Frog
Fore legs
Salamander

Left: Amphibians lay their eggs in a mass of jelly, which keeps each egg separate from the others. It does not contain a lot of yolk, so the young amphibian must soon be able to feed for itself. It spends the first part of its life in the water, as a wriggling tadpole. The tadpole feeds by rasping algae from the surface of the water plants. Later it grows legs, loses its tail and turns into a frog, which lives on land and catches insects for its food. Salamanders are another type of amphibian. They are rather like newts, but they live on land instead of in the water.

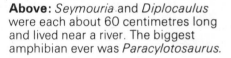

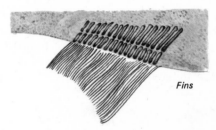

Fins

Lobe fins

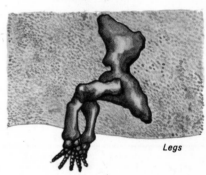

Legs

Above: *Seymouria* and *Diplocaulus* were each about 60 centimetres long and lived near a river. The biggest amphibian ever was *Paracylotosaurus*.

Above: The top drawing shows the long, narrow fins that early fish used to steer themselves in the water. Later, some of them evolved stronger fins with a narrow base, as in the middle drawing. These fins could be used to brake themselves in the water, or to push themselves along the bottom in shallow water. It was from these strong fins that the first clumsy limbs evolved, like the one in the bottom drawing.

Decline of the amphibians

Once the reptiles had evolved, the short reign of the amphibians on land was over. Few of them could compete with the reptiles on land, but some managed to survive in their old way of life, living in the water and catching fish. In fact, one of the very last of the ancient amphibians, *Paracyclotosaurus,* which lived during the Triassic Period, was a monster 420 centimetres long. It must have lurked in the water to pull in even the biggest reptiles when they came down to drink.

After the Triassic Period, the only amphibians to survive were the ancestors of the frogs, toads, newts and salamanders of today. All of them are little creatures, which usually live in or near the water, and feed on insects, snails and other small invertebrates.

The advantages of being a reptile

The reptiles which replaced the amphibians had two great advantages. Their greatest advantage was that they had evolved a much safer way of spending the early part of their lives. Their eggs had evolved a more substantial form of protection. Instead of being surrounded by jelly, the reptile's egg has a waterproof covering that is either horny and flexible, or else hard and brittle like the shell of a bird's egg. The shell is covered with tiny holes, through which air can pass, so that the growing reptile can breathe. The little reptile spends a long time inside the protective shell, gradually growing larger. The rich yolk in the egg provides its food and the egg-white provides the water it needs.

The other great advantage of reptiles is that they have a dry, horny skin. Because of this, their body water does not continually evaporate through their skin, as does that of an amphibian. So they can live in much drier and hotter places – where the wet-skinned amphibians would perish.

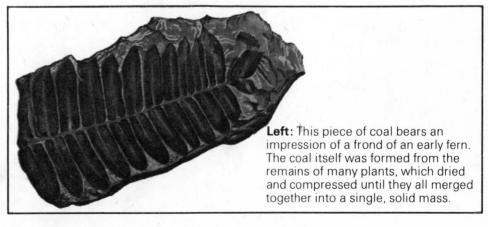

Left: This piece of coal bears an impression of a frond of an early fern. The coal itself was formed from the remains of many plants, which dried and compressed until they all merged together into a single, solid mass.

Prehistoric reptiles

Most of the earliest reptiles were still rather clumsy, lumbering creatures. The most common of them are called "mammal-like reptiles", because they eventually evolved into the first mammals. They were two or three metres long, and lived during the Permian Period. Their limbs projected sideways from their bodies, and when they were not moving they would have rested their bodies on the ground between their legs. Some of them were plant-eaters, or "herbivores". Some such as *Varanosaurus* probably went swimming to catch fish. Others were meat-eaters.

The largest carnivorous (meat-eating) mammal-like reptile was *Dimetrodon*, which grew up to three metres long. It had long, sharp teeth. *Dimetrodon* and some of its relatives also had strange "sails" along their backs. The bones forming the backbone were elongated into spines which projected upwards, and a tough membrane stretched between them.

Palaeontologists believe that the membrane helped the reptile to keep its body at a constant temperature. If it was feeling cold, it could stand so that the sun shone against the big sail. Blood passing along special blood vessels in the sail was warmed by the sun's rays, and then returned to the rest of the body to heat it up. The bulkier the animal, the larger the sail.

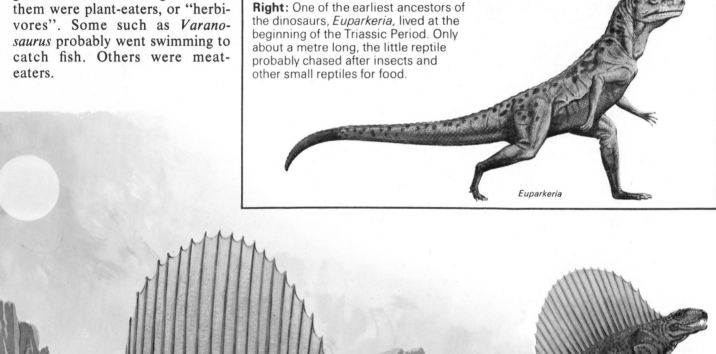

Right: One of the earliest ancestors of the dinosaurs, *Euparkeria*, lived at the beginning of the Triassic Period. Only about a metre long, the little reptile probably chased after insects and other small reptiles for food.

Euparkeria

Dimetrodon

Above: *Varanosaurus* may have searched for fish in the Permian rivers, but *Dimetrodon* was a powerful carnivore that hunted smaller land animals.

Varanosaurus

Right: *Ornithosuchus* was a carnivore. Like many of the dinosaurs, it probably rose onto its hind legs to run quickly, but used its front legs as well when feeding or moving slowly.

Ornithosuchus

The first dinosaurs

During the Triassic Period another group of reptiles became common. These newcomers are called the thecodonts, and they were the ancestors of the dinosaurs. They were probably able to replace the old mammal-like reptiles because they could move very rapidly. Their hind legs were often longer and more powerful than their front legs. When the thecodonts wanted to run quickly, they rose up onto their hind legs, with the long heavy tail balancing the weight of the head and body. Little *Euparkeria* was one of the first of these fast-moving thecodonts. Its descendant, *Ornithosuchus,* a fierce two-metre-long carnivore, preyed on the early herbivorous dinosaurs, and on young, small dinosaurs.

Within about ten million years, nearly all the mammal-like reptiles were extinct. Only the first

Right: *Ornithomimus* was two or three metres long. It had rather weak jaws and front legs, and it must have eaten small animals or broken open the eggs of other reptiles and fed on the yolk.

mammals survived as little furry animals that scuttled about in the undergrowth or scrambled up trees. For over 150 million years, the world was now dominated by the dinosaurs. There were many different types adapted to different ways of life.

"Warm-blooded" dinosaurs?

One of the big differences between mammals and the little reptiles of today is that reptiles have no body covering of hair to keep themselves warm in cold weather. So if the weather does become colder, their body temperature falls too, and they become slow-moving. Nor can reptiles sweat away their body heat if the weather is too hot or if they have been very active. So they cannot run quickly for long, or their bodies become over-heated.

But, although dinosaurs were reptiles, their body temperature probably changed very little, because of their great size. Even if they lost some heat through their skins, this was very little in comparison with the great amount of heat which was contained in their vast bulk. So although they could not run quickly for long without becoming too hot, they could keep warm and active during short cold spells.

Towards the end of the Cretaceous Period, the climate started to change. Instead of being warm all through the year, the winters became colder and the summers became hotter. It would have become more and more difficult for the dinosaurs, without any warm insulation, to keep warm and stay active. Many scientists now believe that that was why they suddenly died out at the end of the Cretaceous Period.

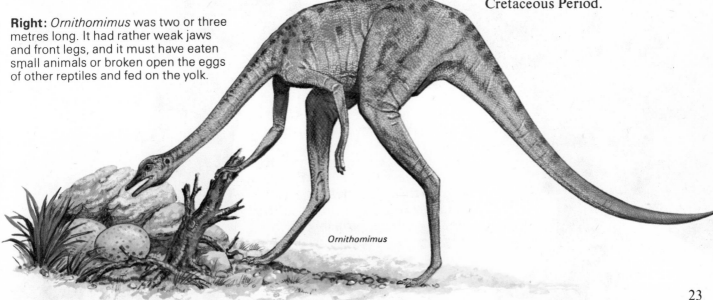

Ornithomimus

The age of the dinosaurs

If we could go back in time to the Jurassic or Cretaceous Periods, we should find the world a strange and frightening place. Today, a rhinoceros or an elephant seems big but they would seem small and harmless in comparison with most of the dinosaurs.

The king of dinosaurs

The biggest and most awe-inspiring of the carnivorous dinosaurs was *Tyrannosaurus*. It did not use its front limbs even for slow walking, and they had become small and useless. When reared up on its hind limbs, *Tyrannosaurus* was about six metres high, so it could see its prey from a long distance away. After quietly stalking the un-suspecting herbivore, *Tyrannosaurus* would have been able to run it down, moving fast on its hind legs. Then, using its sharp teeth, each 15 centimetres long and set in powerful jaws, *Tyrannosaurus* would have quickly killed its prey. It would have held the carcass down with its hind feet, while it pulled lumps of flesh from the body.

Tyrannosaurus Rex

Left: Nearly 15 metres long, six metres tall and weighing ten tonnes, *Tyrannosaurus* was the largest and most frightening carnivore that has ever lived.

With enemies like *Tyrannosaurus* hunting them, the herbivorous dinosaurs had two alternatives. Either they could stand and protect themselves with bony armour and horns, or they could become light and fast, hoping to escape their enemies by running even more quickly than them. Some of them probably tried to stay together in herds, so that they could all help protect each other.

Stegosaurus

Polacanthus

Below: All these dinosaurs were peaceful herbivores. *Stegosaurus* and *Apatosaurus* lived during the Jurassic Period, the others lived during the Cretaceous. *Corythosaurus* and *Styracosaurus* fed on the flowering plants that had recently evolved.

Plates and spikes

The series of plates that ran along the nine-metre-long backbone of *Stegosaurus* was one of the first protective devices. No carnivore could bite into its backbone to kill it. *Stegosaurus* could also protect itself with flailing sweeps of its tail, which ended in spikes 30 centimetres long. But its sides were unprotected and *Stegosaurus* did not survive after the Jurassic Period. Its place was taken by dinosaurs such as *Polacanthus,* which had spikes along the sides of its body, as well as bony armoured plates sunk into its skin.

The most impressive of all the herbivorous dinosaurs were the giant four-footed animals like *Apatosaurus.* They were the biggest land animals that have ever lived. *Apatosaurus* itself was 25 metres long and weighed over 30 tonnes. It is often drawn with its neck stretched out horizontally. But *Apatosaurus* probably used its long neck to reach high up into the trees to feed on the leaves that other animals could not reach. It had no armour or spikes, but was so large that except when it was young, it was safe from attack.

Protoceratops was protected by a bony shield which projected backwards over its neck. Its descendants, such as *Styracosaurus,* also had sharp, bony spikes on their heads, like those of a rhinoceros. They must have been able to defend themselves very well. *Corythosaurus* had no armour or spikes but could run well.

Apatosaurus

Protoceratops

Corythosaurus

Styrocosaurus

Prehistoric birds

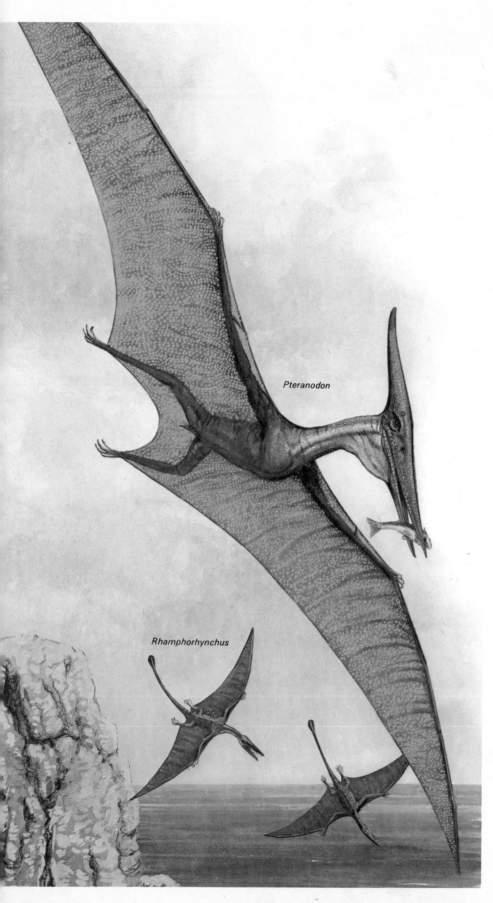

Pteranodon

Rhamphorhynchus

While dinosaurs fed and fought on the ground, the skies above them were also full of strange creatures. Though they were not dinosaurs, the flying "pterosaurs" were reptiles which were closely related to them. Their wings were made of a leathery membrane stretched around the body, rather like a bat's. Its front edge was held by the arms and the fourth fingers of the hands, which were very elongated. The membrane was also attached to the hind limbs and the tail. Their bones were hollow so that the body would be as light as possible.

The skeletons of pterosaurs have often been found inside the skeletons of the big reptiles that swam in these prehistoric seas. Their bones are also found in the chalk layers on the bottom of the sea. Pterosaurs had very weak hind legs; another way in which they were similar to bats. So they would not have been able to jump up into the air to get off the ground and fly. Their wings, too, would not fold up neatly like those of a bat or bird. So pterosaurs would have found it very difficult to move on the ground, and they would quickly have been snapped up by any passing dinosaur. To protect themselves, they probably lived on ledges on steep sea cliffs. Then all they had to do was drop off the ledge, spread their wings and glide on air currents.

Some of the pterosaurs were as small as sparrows. *Rhamphorhynchus* had a wingspan of about one metre. But some of the last pterosaurs, which lived towards the end of the Cretaceous Period, were enormous. *Pteranodon* had a wingspan of over nine metres. It had a crest on the back of its head. This balanced the force of the wind on its long beak, so that it could turn its head in all directions in search of its prey. The largest pterosaur may have had a wingspan of 16 or 17 metres.

Palaeontologists have recently found that pterosaurs had a covering of hair on their wings and bodies.

Above: *Rhamphorhynchus* caught its prey on its long teeth which jutted forward. It had a rudder on the end of its tail to guide it in the air. *Pteranodon* had a sharp, horny beak instead of teeth, and no tail.

Archaeopteryx

Hand bones

Head

Tail

Wing

Feathers for flight

It was the evolution of feathers that made it possible for birds to become much more skilful at flight than the pterosaurs. Feathers are thin and light, easily replaced if they are damaged and easy to fold over one another. A bird's wings are not attached along the sides of its body, or to its legs, and they can be folded away when not in use. As a result, the hind limbs of birds remain strong and powerful so that they can walk or run, or leap into the air to fly.

The first bird, *Archaeopteryx,* lived near the end of the Jurassic Period. Its skeleton is very like that of a little dinosaur. In fact, we only know that it was a bird because, all round its skeleton, we can see the impression of the feathers on its wings. It also had feathers down the sides of its long, reptile-like tail.

Archaeopteryx probably could not fly as strongly as birds today. It must have flapped and glided in the Jurassic forests, catching the insects that fluttered there. Its wings also bore three clawed fingers, which helped *Archaeopteryx* to scramble about in the trees. Its claws and teeth were more like those of a reptile than a bird.

Above: The wing and tail feathers are clearly visible around this *Archaeopteryx* skeleton. In size, *Archaeopteryx* was like a crow.

Phororhacos

Right: Though most birds learned to fly both to escape their enemies and also to catch their prey, a few returned to live on the ground. They could use their strong legs to run very fast, and could kill quite large animals with their powerful beaks. *Phororhachos* was about two metres tall.

Prehistoric mammals

Above: Early mammals were little mouse-sized creatures like these.

About 65 million years ago, when the dinosaurs suddenly died out, the tiny mammals were safe at last from the great reptiles. They were free to evolve into all sorts of different, bigger creatures. New, large herbivorous mammals soon developed along with larger carnivores that preyed on them.

These new mammals belonged to two main groups, both of which still survive. The young of the "marsupials" are born when they are still very tiny and continue growing in their mother's pouch. Kangaroos are marsupials. Most mammals are called "placentals". Their young are not born until they are bigger and are soon able to run about with their parents.

The world was also changing in another way. Its great land mass was splitting up into continents. Australia became separate first, soon after the marsupials arrived there. So the placental type of mammal only reached Australia recently. That is why so many unusual marsupials evolved there. A few types of placentals reached South America where they lived with the marsupials. Everywhere else, though, the pouched marsupials soon became extinct.

New types of mammal evolved in Africa. One of the first was a big, rhinoceros-like herbivore called *Arsinoitherium*, which had two horns side by side on its nose. Elephants first evolved in Africa, and only spread to other parts of the world much later.

Below: *Arsinoitherium* lived about 40 million years ago. Wolf-sized *Pterodon* must have found the fully-grown *Arsinoitherium* too dangerous, but they would have attacked the young ones.

Arsinoitherium

Pterodon

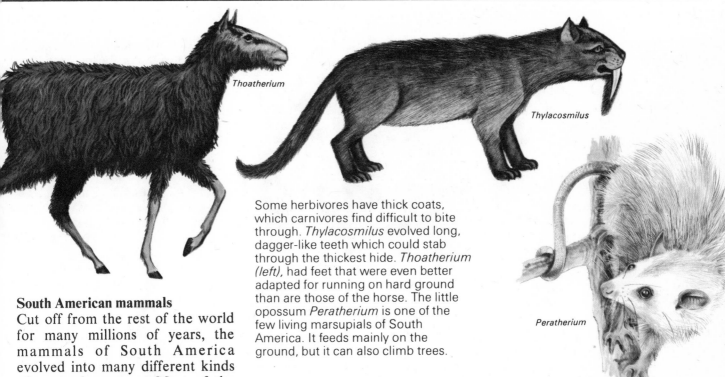

Thoatherium

Thylacosmilus

Peratherium

South American mammals

Cut off from the rest of the world for many millions of years, the mammals of South America evolved into many different kinds of unusual creature. Most of the marsupials were rather like today's opossum, which feeds on smaller animals and on fruit. But some of the prehistoric marsupials included fierce carnivores such as *Thylacosmilus*, which preyed on the strange herbivorous mammals.

As in other parts of the world, the climate in South America gradually became cooler and drier. Great grass-covered plains appeared and new types of mammal evolved that could eat the grass. This way of life was taken up by horses in North America, but in South America the plains were the home of animals such as *Thoatherium*. This was like a horse in size

Some herbivores have thick coats, which carnivores find difficult to bite through. *Thylacosmilus* evolved long, dagger-like teeth which could stab through the thickest hide. *Thoatherium (left)*, had feet that were even better adapted for running on hard ground than are those of the horse. The little opossum *Peratherium* is one of the few living marsupials of South America. It feeds mainly on the ground, but it can also climb trees.

and shape, and it had hooved feet.

Perhaps the strangest of the South American herbivores are the sloths, which hang upside down from the branches of trees. They are still alive today but, millions of years ago, some of the sloths took to living on the ground. They moved rather awkwardly, and they still had the long, curved claws which their ancestors had used to hang onto the branches. Some ground sloths, like *Megatherium*, became gigantic creatures six metres long.

The northern invaders

About five million years ago, South America became connected to North America. This meant that many of the mammals that had evolved in the north could now invade South America. Bred in the colder climate of the north, these new mammals were hardy and fierce. Many of the South American mammals became extinct at this time, but a few of them survived. Some, such as the opossum and the armadillo, even spread into North America and still live there.

Megatherium

Left: *Megatherium* fed on the leaves of the trees. It would squat on its haunches, rear up against the trunk of a tree, and use its hooked claws to pull down the branches so that it could reach the young, tender leaves. *Megatherium* weighed almost as much as an elephant. It could only move slowly, and it must have used its sharp claws to defend itself against its enemies. *Megatherium* spread northwards into North America, and it only became extinct a few thousand years ago.

Animals that died out

Any animal can only survive as long as it has adapted to the world around it. It has adapted to the climate where it lives, such as how hot or cold it is, how much rainfall there is, and whether there is a dry season. It also has adapted to the other animals and plants that live around it. There must be enough of its animal or plant food to keep it alive all through the year, and it must be able to escape from its enemies.

If any of these conditions change, an animal may be doomed. A hotter or colder climate, a longer dry season, new plants replacing old ones, or new animals that share its food or prey upon it, mean that an animal must alter its way of life. Only if it can do so, will it survive. The fossils that we find in the rocks are the memorials to animals that were unable to change their way of life, and became extinct.

The biggest crisis in prehistory was, of course, when the dinosaurs died out, probably because the climate became cooler. The changing climate even affected the sea animals. The great squid-like ammonites became extinct, and so did many tiny sea creatures called plankton which provide food for other, bigger animals. When they, in their turn, died out, even some of the biggest sea creatures found that their food had disappeared. That may be why many large sea reptiles, including the dolphin-like ichthyosaurs, became extinct about 65 million years ago.

Chilling ice and killing man
Since the age of the dinosaurs, the climate had been growing cooler. Eventually it became so cold that sheets of ice formed around the North and South Poles, and glaciers started to appear in the mountains. About two million years ago, the ice started to spread down from the Poles. The Ice Ages had begun.

Scientists now believe that there have been 20 or more different Ice Ages. The climate became colder

Woolly mammoth

Nasal opening

Left: Woolly mammoths lived in the cold northern lands. They scraped away the snow to find their food. Early man hunted them and drew pictures of them on the walls of the caves in which he lived.

during each one, and then warmed up in the intervals. The last Ice Age ended only about 12,000 years ago. We still do not know when the next one will begin.

The Ice Ages made life very difficult for all the animals in the northern parts of the world. As the climate became colder, animals which preferred the warmth had to migrate southwards to stay in the

Right: *Archelon* was an early turtle that lived about 100 million years ago. It was about four metres long and was probably a very good swimmer.

Below: The dodo was a clumsy bird that could not fly. Bigger than a turkey, it was a popular food with early sailors. It finally became extinct 200 years ago.

Dodo

Right: *Teratornis* was a giant eagle which lived in North America. With a wingspan of over five metres, it is the largest known flying bird. One of the biggest flightless birds was the moa. It stood four metres tall, and lived in New Zealand.

Moa

Teratornis

sun. But new types of animal evolved to take their places in the snowy wastes. Instead of ordinary elephants or rhinoceroses, which are almost hairless, woolly animals evolved. It is the bodies of these woolly mammoths and woolly rhinoceroses that the scientists have found preserved in the ice of the northern lands.

Archelon

These animals might still be alive today if the climate had not become much warmer at the end of the last Ice Age. But the days grew warmer, and the animals had to retreat northwards to find the climate and food they preferred. At the same time, mankind was increasing and becoming more skilled at killing other animals for food. So it may have been both the changing climate and man himself that led to the extinction of these great creatures.

As man spread through the world, he found many animals that were almost defenceless against his hunting skills. Some birds that had lost the ability to fly were especially easy to kill. The ostrich-like moas that lived in New Zealand soon became extinct. So did the dodos that lived on Mauritius, an island off the coast of Africa.

Ichthyosaurus

The ichthyosaurs were very successful sea reptiles that lived during the age of the dinosaurs. They were up to three metres long and fed on the squid-like ammonites and on fish.

31

The evolution of man

Gathering food

By studying the fossil record, scientists have been able to show how man evolved from his now extinct ancestors. Man belongs to a group of mammals that also includes apes and monkeys. His closest living relatives are the apes, but that does not mean that he evolved from any of the apes that we see today. Instead, apes and men had a common ancestor that lived about 25 million years ago. After that time, apes remained heavily-built animals that lived mainly in the trees, feeding on fruit and leaves.

Man himself became adapted to a different way of life. He came to spend more and more of his time on the ground. There he could move more quickly by running on his hind legs instead of using his arms to support his body. Standing more upright also helped him to see further around him, in search of his enemies. His hands, too, were now free to become adapted to grasping objects. Early man-like creatures were certainly able to use sticks or bones as weapons. They could use them to kill animals to eat, or to defend themselves from other hunting animals.

The group of mammals to which man belongs also have unusually large brains. Man became the most

Earliest man gathered plant food to eat, as well as hunting animals for meat. Wild fruits and leaves formed an important part of the diet, and edible roots and tubers were dug out of the ground for food. Gradually, man became more and more successful at hunting, often tracking and killing very large animals. Teams of hunters learned to work together to corner their victim and kill it with their stick-like spears and clubs. Mammoths were probably caught in pit-fall traps. Meat was eaten raw at first, but when fire was discovered, people started to cook their food, as it was easier to digest.

intelligent of all. He learned how to make tools for hunting or for cutting up the animals he had killed. Early mankind found that it was better to hunt together in groups. They learned to use different sounds to tell each other what to do, or to describe different objects. That was the beginning of language.

One of the earliest ancestors of man is called *Australopithecus*. He lived in Africa about five million years ago, and was about 120 centimetres tall. He was able to walk almost upright, and used sticks, stones and bones as tools and weapons.

By about one and a half million years ago, *Australopithecus* had evolved into the first type of true man. Called *Homo erectus*, this earliest man was a little taller than *Australopithecus*. He also had a larger brain, and he had learnt to use fire to keep warm and to cook his food. He gathered plant food to eat, as well as animals.

The road to civilization

The next stage in the evolution of man was Neanderthal man, who evolved about 250,000 years ago. Though he had a low, sloping forehead and heavy ridges above his

Hunting food

Growing food

Left: Neolithic man learned to grow his own crops. Man no longer had to live a wandering life to find his food.

Below: *Homo erectus*, the first true man, learned to use fire for cooking and for warmth during the winter nights.

Making fire

eyes, his brain was as large as ours. Neanderthal man lived during the Ice Ages. He lived in caves in the cold northern lands. He learned to make many more types of stone tools, and used these to make clothing from animal skins.

The first type of modern man appeared about 40,000 years ago, during the last Ice Age. He is called Cro-Magnon man, and he probably looked very much as we do today. He led a very simple life, wandering about gathering plant food and hunting animals. He had learnt to make very fine drills and arrow heads from flints. On the walls of his caves Cro-Magnon man also painted the figures of the animals that he hunted. This was the beginnings of man's artistry and culture.

Though man's physical evolution was complete, his skill at making tools continued to improve. Mesolithic man made even finer stone tools, and he also knew how to make tools out of bone. His descendant, Neolithic man, no longer wandered in search of plant food. He had learnt to grow his own crops. For the first time, man could settle in one place. It was the beginning of civilization.

Below: The drawings that Cro-Magnon men made on the walls of their caves may have been used in magical ceremonies, to bring them luck in their hunting.

Painting

Animal characteristics

The animal kingdom includes hundreds of thousands of different types of creatures. They range in size from microscopic single-celled creatures at one end of the scale to giant blue whales at the other. Animals can be found in almost any environment—at the bottom of the sea, on the top of a mountain, in hot deserts or Arctic wastelands. Over millions of years, each type of animal has evolved its own life-style to suit its particular environment. This is why there is such a tremendous variety of life forms within the animal kingdom. But however unalike two types of animal may seem, they always have several characteristics in common which make them animals and not plants.

Animal movement

Perhaps the most obvious difference between plants and animals is that animals can move about. Plants are literally "rooted to the spot", but animals can travel through water or air or over land. There are, however, one or two exceptions. The barnacle, for example, usually remains in one spot for the whole of its adult life. Other animals, such as jellyfish, depend mainly on sea currents to carry them from one place to another.

Many animals can swim, but they do not all swim in the same way. Fish and whales propel themselves forward by their powerful tails. Smaller sea-dwelling animals swim in the water by waving "cilia" which are hair-like structures along their bodies.

Some animals can fly. Nearly all the known species of insects can fly and most birds fly too. Bats are the only mammals that have true wings and can fly.

But the most usual way animals move about is by walking. Advanced vertebrates (animals with

Left: The frilled lizard, sensing danger, responds by erecting a large frill around its neck. This has the effect of making its head appear very large, so frightening off attackers.

backbones) usually have very strong muscular legs which are excellent for walking. Amphibians have legs which are less well adapted for walking on land. Frogs, for example, cannot walk or run but they can jump superbly well by using their long hind legs. Slugs and snails do not have limbs. They only have a single fleshy foot and they pull themselves along.

Many animals are not restricted to one method of getting about. Ducks, for example, can fly, swim and walk.

Feeding

Animals and plants feed in different ways too. Green plants make their own food, whereas animals have to eat plants or other animals for food.

Carnivores (meat-eaters), such as lions, have sharp claws and teeth to tear lumps of flesh from their prey after they have killed it. Birds of prey have powerful beaks which do the same job.

Most animals are herbivores (plant-eaters). Plant food is very tough, and has to be chewed thoroughly. Larger herbivores, such as elephants, have long rows of ridged teeth which grind up their food. Some animals feed on both animal and plant material and are called omnivores. All animals have to rid themselves of solid waste food which they are unable to digest. Plants do not do this.

Senses

All living things react to changes in their surroundings, but among animals there is a more acute awareness of change. This is because animals have very well developed sense organs. Most animals can see, hear, smell, feel and taste. Each sense is developed to a different degree in different animals. For example, insects have excellent eyesight, whereas bats cannot see very well. To compensate, bats have very acute hearing. They can find their way through the air by listening for echoes from their own high-pitched squeaks.

35

Feeding

There are three main feeding groups of animals. These are the plant-eaters or herbivores, the carnivores which feed on other animals, and the omnivores, which will eat almost anything. Each of these main groups have smaller groups within them.

Herbivores

Among the herbivores there are animals that eat mainly grass and vegetation on the ground. These are the grazers. Some invertebrates, like many molluscs and echinoderms, are grazers. They feed on algae and other types of vegetable matter.

Familiar farm animals, like sheep, horses and cattle are better known grazers. Among the wild grazers are gazelles, zebras and buffaloes.

Other species feed on leaves, twigs and fruit. These animals are called browsers. They include giraffes, goats, elephants and giant pandas.

Grazers and browsers have different types of teeth. Grass is tough and often gritty and must be well chewed. Grazers have long teeth that do not wear down quickly. Browsers chew their food less. Their teeth get little wear and although they are short, they do not wear out.

Below: The giraffe, gerenuk and dik-dik do not compete with each other for food. They are browsers. Although they may eat the same species of trees, they eat at different levels. The giraffe eats the top leaves, the gerenuk stands up to reach the middle branches while the dik-dik can reach only the lower ones.

Dik-dik   *Gerenuk*   *Giraffe*

Left: The praying mantis is a greedy predator. Its fore legs are made like strong pincers. These have deadly spines which are used to grip the prey.

Carnivores

Carnivores, or meat-eaters, feed on herbivores, other carnivores and omnivores. They include many kinds of animals – from microscopic creatures to complex and efficient hunters such as sharks, eagles and lions.

Hunters

Many carnivores are active predators. They use a number of different methods to catch their prey. The method depends upon the way the prey defends itself.

Many predators hunt their food by speculation. They guess that the food will be in a certain place and use their senses to help find it. Some wading birds probe the mud below shallow water, expecting to find the worms and other small animals which they eat. The raccoon reaches under the water with its forepaws for shellfish.

Other species stalk their prey. They move towards their prey hoping they will not be seen or heard until they are within striking range. The big cats, such as lions and cheetahs creep very slowly, with their bodies crouched so they are hidden in long grass. The kestrel hovers motionless. Then, when the victim is not looking, it attacks.

Above: Most species of mice are herbivores. They feed on many kinds of seeds, nuts and berries.

Right: Zebras are grazing animals. They are hunted by many predators, such as lions, hyaenas and wild dogs.

Ambush is a common method of hunting, often used by animals which also stalk their prey. The hunter will hide, lying in wait, until its prey approaches. Many animals which hunt like this use camouflage patterns to disguise themselves. Some spiders blend with the colour and texture of the branch on which they wait for an unsuspecting insect. The tiny *Hydra* ambushes passing water fleas by extending its sticky tentacles.

Below: The cheetah is an active predator. It hunts grazing animals such as the gazelle. The cheetah stalks its prey until it is quite close, picking out a weaker member of the herd. Then it charges very fast.

Omnivores
Animals that eat both plants and other animals are known as omnivores. Invertebrates such as starfish that feed on debris containing many kinds of organic matter, can be called omnivores. Others include some birds, bears and man.

Balance of nature
Many different factors make up the balance of nature. All life depends on water, air and minerals, which are not living things, and in some way on all other living things in the environment.

Food chains
Plants, such as grass, are eaten by herbivores, such as zebras, which are eaten by carnivores, such as lions. This relationship between dependent food species is called a food chain.

Food web
Many species are involved in one or more food chains. Grass is eaten by many different grazing herbivores. Each of these is prey for one or more carnivores. These complicated inter-relationships of food chains make a food web.

Cheetah

Gazelles

Parasites and partnerships

Animals normally live together as separate families, or in groups, such as a herd of deer, a flock of sparrows, or a shoal of fish. Sometimes there is a partnership between two quite different animals. There are many reasons for forming a partnership, but it almost always benefits both animals.

For example, a sea anemone sometimes attaches itself to the shell of a hermit crab. The crab is then protected by the anemone and the anemone picks up spare food which is wasted by the crab.

In tropical areas, several kinds of birds settle on the backs of large animals such as antelopes, buffalo and giraffes. The birds feed on ticks and other nuisances in the animal's skin and at the same time help to keep the animals clean. Other birds find food by entering the open mouths of crocodiles to clean worms from their teeth. In return the birds raise the alarm when there is any danger.

Symbiosis

In some cases the partnership is so close that one partner cannot live without the other. This is called symbiosis. Lichens are made up of two closely knit plants—an alga and a fungus. The green alga makes the food, and the fungus re-produces. Lichens are often found growing on bare rocks and gravestones.

Animals like cows which chew the cud have minute animals living inside their stomachs. They carry out a very important function for the cows by breaking down the cellulose which occurs in plant cells. Cows cannot do this. They rely on the microscopic animals in their stomachs to soften the plant food when it is first swallowed. Later, the cows cough up lumps of food (the cud) into their mouths, chew it thoroughly, then swallow it for the second and last time. In this way, all cud-chewers, including many farm animals, obtain the maximum goodness out of their food.

Another partnership occurs in the simple freshwater animal called a *Hydra* which is a kind of miniature anemone. Tiny algal plants live inside its tissues. The *Hydra* gives shelter to the algae, and the algae provide the *Hydra* with oxygen.

Parasites

In other partnerships life is very one-sided. Only one partner benefits. The partner that thrives is called a parasite and it lives at the expense of its host. Many worms live inside animal bodies and live

Above: This hungry baby cuckoo looks far too large for this tiny reed warbler's nest. Although it has lost all its offspring, the warbler continues to feed the cuckoo as if it were part of its family.

Left: The large grouper fish in the centre is about to be attended by small "cleaner" fish. They will enter its mouth and gills in order to remove any parasites that live there.

off the animals' food. Fleas feed on blood. Some toadstools and mistletoe are parasitic tree-dwellers.

As long as there are not too many parasites living off the one host, no harm is done. If they become too numerous, or even enter the wrong host, sickness may result, even death. Germs spread by the malaria mosquito and the rat flea may become killers. Yet the mosquito and flea are usually unharmed.

A parasite may spend all its life inside the same host. Its body is usually pale and it has no legs. It attaches itself to its host with hooks or suckers and is constantly bathed in food. It lives only to feed and lay eggs. Many parasitic worms live this way.

Several hosts
With some worms there may be more than one host. A tapeworm inside a human lays eggs which pass out of his body. A pig may happen to pick up an egg along with its food and swallow it. The egg turns into a larva which grows in the flesh of the pig. Later, the

Greenfly produce large families of young and cause damage to plants. Sometimes they carry germs which are passed on as they feed. If this happens the plant may wilt and die.

pig may be killed and eaten by another human who in turn acts as host to another tapeworm. And so the cycle continues.

Today, few humans have tapeworms because our waste is disposed of through the toilet. Also, government health agencies check samples of the meat we buy from shops to make sure it does not carry worms.

The liver fluke also has two hosts. It attacks the liver of sheep,

where it lays eggs. As each egg is passed out of the sheep's body, it turns into a swimming larva which enters the body of a water snail. There, the larva passes through several stages in development before it leaves the snail, climbs up a grass stem, and forms a hard covering or cyst. A sheep may eat this grass and, once again, a fluke will attack the sheep's liver. The way to control the spread of liver flukes is to get rid of the second hosts—the snails. Sheep should also be kept away from wet pastures.

Cuckoos
Among birds the cuckoo behaves as a parasite. The female cuckoo seeks out the nests of other birds where eggs have already been laid. When the parents are away it slips down, lays an egg, and removes one of the others. The baby cuckoo will eventually get the nest to itself, by tipping out all the eggs and any young that have already hatched. Although the cuckoo is far bigger than its foster parents, they will continue to feed it as if it were their own offspring.

Each parent cuckoo chooses the same kind of bird's nest for its egg, such as that of a hedge sparrow, robin or warbler. The interesting thing is that the cuckoo's eggs usually match the colour and markings of the other eggs in the nest.

Several kinds of birds form a partnership with much larger animals. The birds in the picture are in no danger from the crocodile. They can enter the crocodile's open mouth quite unharmed to look for worms. Oxpeckers are a common sight on the backs of antelopes and other animals that roam the African plains.

Senses

The senses of animals have evolved to suit the way they live. Sometimes an animal's life-style makes one sense particularly important, and this may be developed at the expense of the others.

Sight

Sight is one of the most important senses that animals have. There are many kinds of eyes, ranging from the simple light-sensitive cells of some invertebrates to the more complex and highly specialized eyes of the vertebrates.

Simple eyes are only able to detect changes in how much light there is, while more complex eyes can see images clearly in three dimensions, and often in colour. Sight helps an animal to find its food or to see if it is being hunted.

The eye of a vertebrate is a very complex structure. There is a transparent "window" at the front called the cornea. Light passes through this to the lens, where the amount allowed into the eye is controlled by the coloured part called the iris. The lens focuses the light on to the light-sensitive cells at the back of the eye, which are called the retina.

Left: Birds of prey like the peregrine falcon have very good sight. Even while flying, they are able to spot their prey, which is usually small animals.

Below: Many predators like this lynx have large ears, which help them to hear their prey or their mates from a long way off.

Hearing

For most animals, the sense of hearing is just as important as sight. It helps them know not only that something may be approaching, but how quickly, and even its probable size.

Ears

The sense organ used for hearing is the ear. These are two flaps of skin on the outside of the head.

Most animals have two ears, one on each side of the head. This helps to locate the direction the sound is coming from. The flaps channel sounds, as vibrations in the air or water, into the ear, where they hit the ear drum. Behind the ear drum is the middle ear cavity, where the vibrations are sent through a series of little bones to the inner ear. From the membrane of the inner ear the vibrations are then sent through a spiral cavity called the cochlea. This is where nerve cells pass on the signals to the brain.

Blind people are often more aware than sighted people of the differences in sounds. They use echoes to judge their distance from objects.

Below: Many species of bats are able to navigate by producing very high frequency sounds. They use the echoes from these sounds to detect objects in their way.

Touch, taste and smell

Nearly all animals are sensitive to being touched. More primitive creatures like the amoeba respond to touch by simply moving away. More advanced animals can interpret the feeling and alter their behaviour accordingly.

The senses of taste and smell are very closely related. The range of tastes that can be judged by the taste buds on the tongue is very limited, but the sense of smell adds to it. Smell helps animals recognize their territories and members of their own social group.

Above: A chameleon can rotate each of its eyes independently. This means it can look around without even having to move its head, and can look in two directions at once. When one eye spots an insect, the other will look too.

Defence and attack

All animals have some means of defending themselves. Each species has evolved special adaptations and behaviour patterns for protection from their enemies.

Many animals use camouflage colour patterns to help them blend in with their surroundings. Others have a strong, contrasting colour pattern, like the black bars on angel fish. This breaks up the animal's outline and makes it difficult to see. Yet other animals can disguise themselves as shapes that mimic certain features of the place where they live.

Many species have also developed weapons. They use their weapons as a means of defence as well as to attack other animals.

A large number of different species can produce poisons to protect themselves against their enemies. These species are often brightly coloured with warning patterns.

Below: When wolves attack a herd of musk oxen the bulls form a circle around the cows and calves. They will fight back using their sharp horns or trample the wolves with their hooves.

Colour patterns

Colour patterns play a very important part in helping animals protect themselves. Colour patterns that allow an animal to blend in with its surroundings are called "cryptic". Cryptic colour patterns make animals less visible to their enemies and to their own prey.

Some fish like flounder or plaice, the eggs and chicks of many shore birds and several lizards have dull, speckled colour patterns that resemble their sandy habitats.

Quick change

Some animals can change colour quickly. The animal best known for this is the chameleon. It can change colour from brown to green and become dark or light in only a few minutes. In this way, the chameleon is able to blend in with almost any background.

One of the most dramatic displays of rapid colour change for

Above: Some moths, butterflies and their caterpillars have large "eye spots". These frighten any would-be predators.

defence is used by the common squid. When frightened it can change its colour from a pale, mottled yellow to deep red in a matter of seconds. It then squirts out a jet of dark ink and just as quickly turns pale again as it darts off to safety.

Seasonal changes

Animals that live in the sub-Arctic regions may change from a brown or grey summer colour to winter white. These species have adopted a "protective coloration".

To be less conspicuous in the snowy landscape of winter they lose their cryptic summer colours and turn white for the winter months. In polar areas certain species stay white all year round. These include the polar bear, snowy owl and beluga whale.

Disguise

Many animals, particularly insects, have evolved a bewildering variety of disguises.

A great number of insects look like parts of the plants on which they feed. Some look like twigs, while others look like flowers, leaves or even thorns. Some even have jagged edges to give the appearance of a leaf that has been chewed by another insect.

Weapons

Many larger animals are equipped with weapons. These may be in the form of sharp teeth, claws or horns. Hoofed animals often live in large herds. Many herds have a dominant male as their leader. He often has to fight other males for the leadership and is therefore usually the strongest.

Although animals that have antlers or horns use them for ritual display and in courtship battles between rivals they are also used for defence against their enemies. Predators like cats and dogs use their sharp teeth for biting.

Behaviour

One of the most common means of defence is simply to stay in a large group. Some animals will try to escape from danger by swimming, running or flying away.

Other species, usually those which have camouflaged colour patterns or mimicking disguises, keep very still and hope they will be overlooked.

Many animals try to make them-selves look bigger than they are to confuse their enemies. The common toad blows itself up and stretches up on its back legs. This makes it look too big for a grass snake to eat. Some species like pill bugs, hedgehogs and armadillos roll themselves up into a ball for protection. A few animals pretend they are dead.

Hunting methods

In order to be successful a predator must be able to take its prey by surprise. Predatory animals have developed various methods of hunting. Some species hunt in packs, like wolves, while others hunt alone, like cheetahs.

Right: The European grass snake pretends it is dead when it is threatened. It turns over onto its back with its mouth open and its tongue hanging out.

Above: When an elephant is angry it will raise its ear flaps. This makes its head and face look much bigger and may frighten off opponents.

Community living

The complex relationship between plants and animals is referred to as an ecosystem. It is largely the climate and the habitat which determines a particular ecosystem.

Within every community there is a complex interaction between plants, animals and other organisms. Plants and animals are dependent upon each other for food. Plants convert energy from the sun into starch and sugar. The plants are eaten by grazing and browsing animals. These animals are then eaten in turn by the meat-eating animals.

Their waste products, and dead animal and plant matter are left behind. This is all broken down first by animals like insects and worms. Fungi and bacteria finally decompose the decaying matter completely into simple raw materials. These, together with minerals from the non-living environment, are used by growing plants.

This cycle is known as the food chain. When plants and animals are part of more than one food chain the complex relationship is called a food web. The food web is the basis of community structure.

Competition

Food webs are made up of plants and animals which compete at different levels. Plants compete with each other for space which gives them access to sunlight. They also compete for the raw materials like water and minerals they need for growth. Herbivores compete with each other for plants on which they feed. Carnivores compete for the animals they eat.

Community structure

A community is made up of different levels of organization. These include solitary individuals (trees or snails), the immediate family with parents and offspring, and the total populations of each species.

Within most of these levels there is a more or less strict social order. This is maintained by a constant struggle between the members of each group.

Solitary individuals

Plants are not usually considered as living in social groups. However, they are nonetheless very important in the community structure. As solitary individuals, trees provide both food and shelter for other plants and animals.

Some animals like snails and snakes also live solitary lives.

Right: Seals will gather in large numbers during their breeding season. The adult males fight each other for dominant positions on the beach. The successful males mate with the most females.

Family groups

Many animals live in family groups. These may be small and include only the parents and their offspring. Larger family groups include several breeding females.

In species that live as families the sexes are always separate. They usually mate only in their breeding season. Species that live in family groups often have a strict social order. This usually involves at least one dominant male and a number of subordinate females.

Mature males usually fight for the dominant position. This makes sure that only the strongest males will mate. They are therefore more likely to have the most offspring.

All individuals of a single species that live within the same community are called a population. Many animals lead more or less solitary lives coming together only during their breeding season.

Keeping together

Some populations stay together most of the time. Many species of birds, hoofed mammals and fish find it a good method of defence against their predators. They usually move around a great deal and therefore are part of a constantly changing community. However, their predators will follow them so that certain elements of their food chains do not change. Several other species have evolved complex social structures. These include insects like bees and ants and mammals like rabbits and man.

Below: Some mammals like the rabbit live in a large complex society Several family groups live together in a communal home called a warren. Some individuals will keep a look-out for predators like the hawk and foxes.

Finding a mate

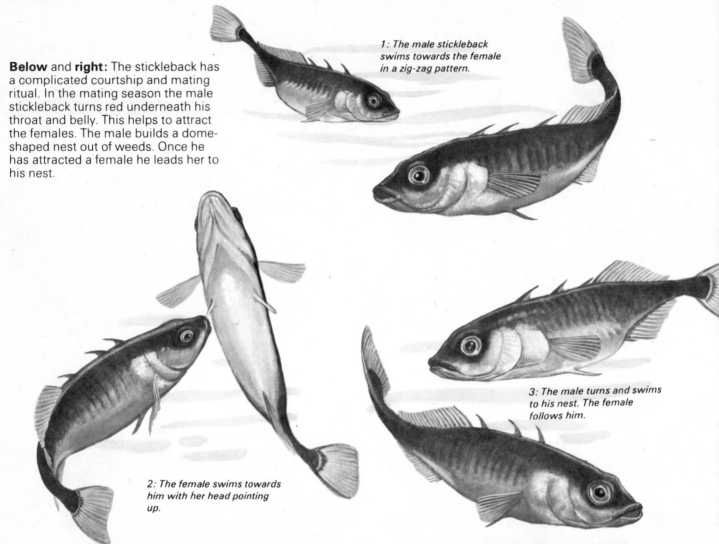

Below and **right:** The stickleback has a complicated courtship and mating ritual. In the mating season the male stickleback turns red underneath his throat and belly. This helps to attract the females. The male builds a dome-shaped nest out of weeds. Once he has attracted a female he leads her to his nest.

1: The male stickleback swims towards the female in a zig-zag pattern.

3: The male turns and swims to his nest. The female follows him.

2: The female swims towards him with her head pointing up.

All living things must reproduce if their species is to survive. There are two basic kinds of reproduction: asexual and sexual.

Asexual reproduction means the animal does not need to find a mate. Many single-celled animals reproduce asexually. When they are mature, they divide into two identical parts. Reproduction like this usually means the animals are all very alike. Each adult can only produce two replicas of itself, and these actually replace it.

Sexual reproduction

The main type of reproduction is sexual. This involves two separate cells fusing together. Each cell contains only half the amount of genetic material needed to make a new animal.

One cell is larger than the other and does not move. This is the egg cell. The other cell is much smaller and has a long whip-like tail called the flagellum. This cell is the sperm.

Egg cells are usually produced by the female animal. Sperm cells are usually produced by the male.

When the sperm and egg cells fuse, all the genetic material needed to make a new animal is there. This new individual will be unique, and will have some characteristics from each of its parents.

Some animals use both of these ways of reproducing. Coelenterates, such as corals and hydroids, may alternate between an asexual and a sexual phase during their life-cycle.

During the asexual phase the animal produces a "bud" on its body wall. This develops into a new individual. These new individuals may stay attached to their parent so that there is a whole colony of them.

In the sexual phase they produce tiny jellyfishes called medusae.

Above: The male frigate bird has an inflatable red sac on his breast. In the breeding season he inflates it, spreads his wings and calls to the females.

These carry eggs and sperms which unite in the water and grow into larvae which settle, and grow into new individuals.

Earthworms, land snails and some other animals are herma-

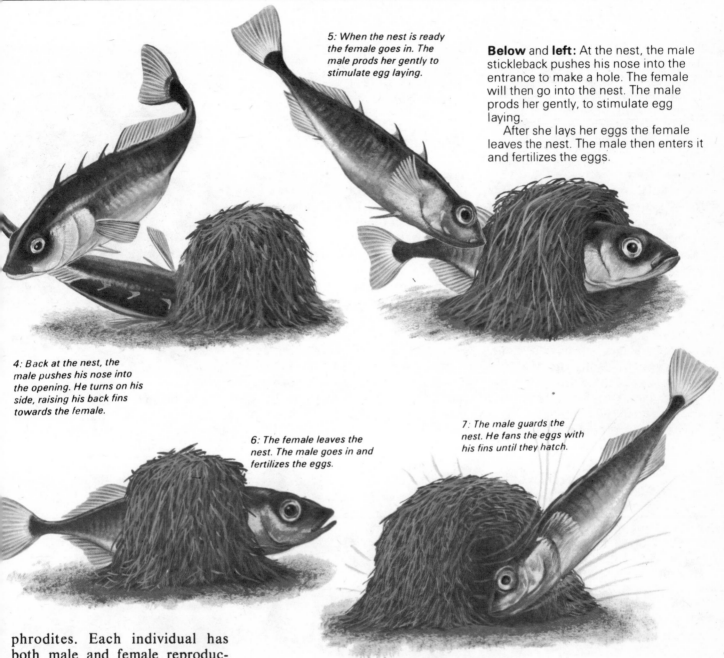

5: When the nest is ready the female goes in. The male prods her gently to stimulate egg laying.

Below and **left:** At the nest, the male stickleback pushes his nose into the entrance to make a hole. The female will then go into the nest. The male prods her gently, to stimulate egg laying.

After she lays her eggs the female leaves the nest. The male then enters it and fertilizes the eggs.

4: Back at the nest, the male pushes his nose into the opening. He turns on his side, raising his back fins towards the female.

6: The female leaves the nest. The male goes in and fertilizes the eggs.

7: The male guards the nest. He fans the eggs with his fins until they hatch.

phrodites. Each individual has both male and female reproductive organs, and both can make eggs and sperms. Any two adult animals can mate.

Courtship

Many animals breed only at certain times of the year. This time is called the breeding season, when the animals gather together and those who are sexually mature will look for a mate. Animals often have complicated courtship rituals.

It is usually the males who compete for the females. The males are often larger and more brightly coloured than the females. The peacock has a long tail of brilliantly coloured feathers. He spreads this to form a huge fan, to impress the peahen, who is less colourful. Animals also use different noises to attract mates. Frogs croak and birds sing.

Some animals use scents to help attract their mates. The scents many insects produce can be detected from a long way off by the insects that could be their mates. Many mammals also produce scents in the mating season. These scents are usually produced by both the male and the female, to show that they are ready to mate.

Most animals use a combination of either special breeding colours and scents with a special ritual behaviour pattern. This may be a "dance" or a fight between rival males for the right to the females.

There are a number of reasons for courtship. It shows which individuals are sexually mature and ready to mate. It also shows how fit an animal is. The most important use of courtship is possibly to stimulate mating.

In some predatory species, such as praying mantis and many spiders, it is very important for the male to follow the correct courtship pattern. If he does not, the female may mistake him for her prey and eat him.

Caring for the young

The reason for parental care is to make sure that at least some of the offspring survive to maturity.

Animals do not all devote the same amount of time and attention to their care of the young. The amount of care given to the young depends on many things. Animals that have a short life-span may spend little or no time looking after their young. Also, the number of young produced can affect the amount of parental care. Animals that produce lots of offspring each season will spend less time looking after them.

Many or few

Animals may abandon their eggs at different stages of development. The eggs of many marine and freshwater animals are left to be fertilized and to develop without any care from the parents.

They may produce many thousands of eggs during each breeding season. Most of the young will be eaten by predators. Those that are left will have to compete to survive. But, producing vast numbers of offspring ensures that at least a few will survive.

The better developed the young are when they are born (or hatch), the greater their chances of survival.

Right: Chimpanzees, like most other primates, devote a lot of attention to the care of their young. Baby chimpanzees cling to their mother and are carried wherever she goes.

The animals that produce only a few offspring will be able to devote more attention to each of them. The parents can collect only a certain amount of food. The fewer offspring there are to feed, the more food each of them will get.

Parental care over a long time may reduce the number of young that will be produced. However, more of the offspring are likely to survive and reproduce.

The environment may also influence the number of offspring produced. In cold, harsh climates where food is more difficult to find, animals may only have one or very few offspring each season. They need a lot of care, but develop quickly.

In some species of fish the male plays an important part in looking after and protecting the eggs. The male stickleback builds a nest in which the female will lay her eggs. After fertilization the male guards them.

The male seahorse also looks after his young. The female lays her eggs into the male's brood pouch where they develop. When the young are ready, the pouch opens and they swim out.

Above: In caring for their young many mammals lick them. This keeps them clean and helps to increase the bond between the mother and her offspring. These puma cubs are licking their mother back.

Many animals that have evolved complex social life-styles take great care in raising their young.

The female Nile crocodile lays her eggs in a hole she has dug in the sand well above the banks of the river. The eggs will develop at a more or less constant temperature buried in the sand.

When they are ready to hatch the young crocodiles will call from inside the eggs. Their calls are loud enough to be heard by their parents, often a few metres away. The mother digs away the sand to get out the hatching babies. Both parents will pick them up very gently in their huge mouths and carry them down to the nursery area in the river.

Nile crocodile families may stay together for as long as a year. The way the young behave usually makes the parents provide either food or care.

Most baby birds open their beaks very wide and "cry". This behaviour stimulates the parents to feed them.

Right: The baby whale suckles milk from its mother while swimming under water. Many toothed whales suckle their calves for nearly a year.

Below: Adélie penguins take turns sitting on their eggs. The eggs hatch in five weeks. The parents also share in feeding and guarding their chicks.

Colonies

Some groups of insects like wasps, bees and ants have evolved a very complex social structure. They live in colonies. All the members of the colony are usually the offspring of a single giant "queen" and her mate. Their eggs develop into infertile "workers". Some workers build up and clean the nest. Others take care of the eggs and the grubs.

Larger animals, for example many mammals, spend a lot of time feeding and caring for their young.

They also teach them to look after themselves.

The young of many mammals are born blind and helpless. They depend on their mothers to provide them with milk and protection from danger.

Marsupial mammals like kangaroos have a pouch in which their babies develop. The "joey" grows inside the pouch for several months suckling its mother's milk. For a short while after it leaves the pouch it may jump back in at the first sign of danger.

Hibernation and life-cycles

Above: Hedgehogs are found in most parts of Europe, except the northern-most parts. They spend the winter sleeping in a burrow thickly lined with dry plant material. Hibernation usually starts around mid-October, but sometimes you still find hedgehogs foraging in December or January.

The habits and life-cycles of animals vary greatly, but there are certain needs which are common to all of them. Unlike plants, animals cannot make their own food, so they have to find it. To do so they need to move about and be aware of their surroundings. They have senses in order to see, hear, touch, taste and smell.

Staying alive

Some animals feed on plants, others eat flesh, some eat both. Those which eat dead material or "left-overs" are called scavengers.

Food passes through a mouth into the food canal where it is broken down, or digested, then spread through the body by a blood system. Food is stored in the body to make it grow, or to repair any damage.

The energy needed for living and moving also comes from food. It is used or "burned" by oxygen. Oxygen is a gas found in air and water. It is breathed into the lungs of land animals, or taken from the water through gills in water animals.

The most important function of any animal is reproduction. Sooner or later an animal's life ends, so it must be able to produce children if the species is not to die out.

Single-celled animals

The simplest animals are called Protozoa. The whole body is a single cell. A common protozoon which lives in ponds is called the amoeba. It creeps among the water plants by pushing out parts of its tiny body. To feed, it wraps itself around its prey and forms a hollow inside which acts as a kind of stomach. Inside this the food is digested and absorbed. Waste products collect in another hollow, called a "contractile vacuole". This bursts from time to time to get rid of any waste.

An amoeba senses its surroundings, and will move away from bright light. To reproduce it simply divides into two separate cells. These cells divide into four, then eight, and so on.

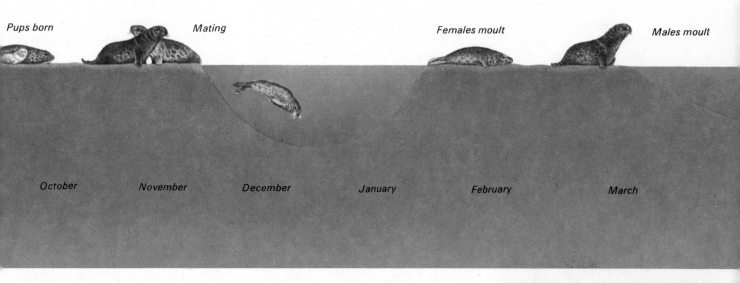

Pups born | Mating | Females moult | Males moult

October | November | December | January | February | March

Above: A year in the life of the grey seal. Shortly after the pups are born, the cows mate with the bulls. After they have moulted, the adults spend most of the summer at sea.

Right: This tadpole is just about to turn into a baby frog. The tail is slowly used up as food. The froglet will wait for some rain before it leaves the pond.

Below right: Some families of caterpillars will stay together in groups as they feed on the same plant.

Sexual reproduction

In higher animals there are two sexes—male and female. The male produces sperm cells which join with the egg cells of the female during mating. Each fertilized egg grows into a new animal. It is provided with food (the yolk) by the mother before it leaves her body.

Eggs are laid by most insects, worms, crustaceans, spiders and shellfish. Among higher animals such as fish, amphibians, reptiles and birds, egg-laying is also the rule. However, some of these animals keep the eggs inside their bodies until they are about to hatch, then lay them.

Most animals grow up looking like their parents. Insects pass through a larval stage (the caterpillar) before turning into the adult. Amphibians such as frogs have a tadpole stage.

The lower animals usually produce large families because few actually survive. The young must fend for themselves as soon as they are born. An insect can lay thousands of eggs. So do some fish. A single clump of frog-spawn may contain 4,000 eggs.

Birds and mammals produce much smaller families. To make sure that enough of them grow up they are given some kind of protection. Birds lay eggs in nests and feed the young until they leave. Mammals feed their young on mother's milk and they look after their babies for quite a long time after birth.

Animal behaviour

Many animal actions are governed by instinct. A spider can make a web, and a bird build a nest without being taught. A young cuckoo finds its way to Africa without help from its parents. However, higher animals such as chimpanzees are capable of learning.

Some animals hibernate, which means they go into a deep sleep during cold weather. They are cold-blooded creatures and cannot control their body temperature. If they did not sleep, their body temperature would sink so low that they would die.

Usually, warm-blooded animals do not need to hibernate, but there are a few exceptions. The dormouse, hedgehog and some bats and bears, although warm-blooded, will hibernate.

Migration

Migration is a movement of animals, sometimes over vast stretches of land, which takes place regularly every year. It is a journey to a place where the animals can breed and where there is enough food to raise a family. This usually coincides with the change of seasons. After breeding, the animals make the return journey and rest until it is time to travel again to the breeding area.

Bird migration

Migration has been studied most closely in birds. Swallows nest in Britain and Europe during the summer. Then, as winter approaches and the young are strong enough to fly, the swallows make their way south to Africa where they remain until the following spring. Some swallows may even return to the same nests the following year.

In the Northern Hemisphere cuckoos, nightingales and warblers are called summer visitors. There are also winter visitors such as ducks, geese and waders which spend the summer in the Arctic region where they nest.

In the Southern Hemisphere it is the other way around; the birds

Left: Herds of wildebeeste slowly make their way across the dry African plain towards the foothills where they will remain and feed until the rains return again.

travel south to breed, and return north to rest.

Some bird journeys are quite remarkable. The longest distance covered by a migrating bird is 17,600 kilometres. This record is held by the Arctic tern which travels south from the Arctic to winter in the Antarctic. Migrating birds usually travel in flocks. Swallows gather together before they leave for Africa. Geese arrive in the Arctic in large numbers flying in V-formation.

Finding the way

Experts believe that migrating birds are guided by the sun during the day, and by the stars at night. A few birds get blown off course by storms and lose their way.

To increase their knowledge of migration, scientists catch birds, place marked rings on their legs, and release them. Those birds which are later recovered can indicate to scientists what routes they take, and how far they travel. One sea bird released in America flew back 4,800 kilometres across the Atlantic to its nest on an island off the Welsh coast.

The urge to migrate may have something to do with the length of daylight. As spring approaches birds feed more and store up fat in readiness for their long journey.

Shorter journeys are made by some insects, amphibians and fish. Every year butterflies like the cab-

Right: This flock of snow geese has just arrived at the breeding grounds in the far north. There, the birds will find enough food to raise a family.

bage white, the painted lady and the red admiral arrive in Britain from the Continent. Some kinds of moths also migrate. For the death's head and hummingbird hawk moths this is only a one-way journey. They arrive in Britain, lay their eggs and die.

Among amphibians the common toad migrates every year to the same pond. It spends the summer in the countryside, often in gardens, then hibernates. The next spring, usually on mild and damp evenings, it travels back to the pond, ignoring other ponds on the way. One marked toad travelled nearly two kilometres.

Migration at sea

Salmon (*see page 102*) come in from the sea to migrate upriver to spawn. The common eel does the same, but in reverse. Eels lay their eggs in deep water in the Sargasso Sea. The eel larvae which hatch come to the surface and are carried by the current across the Atlantic towards the European coast, on a journey of some 3,200 kilometres. Shoals of elvers (young eels) can be seen along the coast in early summer. Eels grow up in rivers and ponds. Some five to seven years later, they return to the sea.

Extreme weather

Land mammals which migrate do so to avoid cold weather or the dry season. Red deer spend the summer up in the mountains, and come down to the sheltered valleys for the winter. Reindeer travel north in spring, then move south for winter. On the East African plains huge herds of game animals such as antelopes and zebras move to better feeding grounds. They journey from the open grassland where everything is dried up, and travel towards the foothills where feeding is still possible.

Left: One of the most spectacular insect migrations is that of the American monarch butterfly. Huge flocks travel south for the winter along the east and west coasts of North America. They gather on trees until spring, then return north. Occasionally, some monarch butterflies arrive in Britain, but they have been carried across in ships.

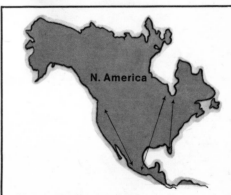

Above: This map shows the routes the monarch butterflies follow

Communication and intelligence

Animals do not have to be taught to do most things. They have an inborn ability to find the right food and protect themselves from danger. This ability is called instinct. Many animals live entirely by following their instincts. Virtually all the invertebrates and several groups of vertebrates simply react to what is going on around them.

Learning

A large number of animals have the ability to learn. One basic way of learning is by "trial and error". If an animal tries to do something and fails, it will try again.

Animals can also learn by watching and copying others. They may also be taught how to do things. Young animals will be taught many skills by their parents. They also learn from each other.

Left: Many animals, such as dogs, can be trained to perform tricks or to do things they would not do in the wild. Dogs learn quickly when rewarded. They have good memories and are very reliable.

Reasoning

Some animals have the ability to figure out how to do things. This ability is known as reasoning. Animals that have the ability to reason are considered to be intelligent. Intelligence varies greatly among animals. An experiment with octopuses has shown that they are capable of solving simple problems. If an octopus sees a crab inside a covered glass jar, it will try to take the cover off and get the crab out and eat it.

Sea gulls cannot break the shells of cockles and mussels with their beaks. They have learned to fly up and drop the shells onto rocks.

Some birds and animals like chimpanzees and man use objects to help them solve problems.

A finch from the Galapagos Islands uses a cactus spine to pick insects out of holes in the bark of trees. Chimpanzees can solve more complex problems like placing several boxes on top of each other to climb on in order to reach a bunch of bananas.

Only man has the ability to work out really difficult problems such as building a machine like a computer to help solve his problems.

Communication

Communication is the passing of information from one animal to another. The information may be just the identity and sex of the individual or an indication of its mood and intentions.

Virtually all animals communicate in some way with both the members of their own species and with other species.

Animals communicate for a number of different reasons. Members of the same species will warn each other if there is danger. They will also exchange information about food and show when they are ready to mate.

Left: Some birds can solve simple problems. A jackdaw was taught to associate food with the number of spots on the "key card". It would choose a box by spots on the lid.

Above: Facial expressions form a very important part of communication. They are signals that may show how the animal is feeling. Chimpanzees use similar facial expressions to people. Four of these are *1:* alertness, *2:* happiness, *3:* fear and *4:* excitement.

Left: Dolphins communicate by making a noise like whistling. This whistling changes in length and pitch. There is a pattern to their sounds that suggests that they are "talking" to each other.

Right: Many deer have scent glands just below their eyes and also between their hooves. These produce a smelly liquid that they rub onto trees to mark their territory. They also rub their bodies against regular "rubbing trees"

Animal languages

Animals communicate in two ways. Information is passed from one animal to another by the way it acts. The messages it sends are referred to as "active" or "behavioural messages". When they provide information about themselves without actually doing anything, the messages are said to be "passive" or "non-behavioural" messages.

Non-behavioural messages

The physical appearance of an animal will provide some information. Its shape, colour, markings and size identify the animal as belonging to a particular species. They may also indicate its social rank.

Within each species there are often physical differences between males and females. These differences may be noticeable only when the individuals are sexually mature.

Many animals have a characteristic smell. These are often produced by special scent glands which secrete a smelly liquid. These secretions are used by animals to mark their territory and even each other. The scent may be slightly different for each family or group within the larger population.

During the breeding season animals may also use their scent to attract and excite their mate.

Behavioural messages

Behavioural messages are much more complicated than non-behavioural messages. Everything an animal does will communicate some kind of information.

Most of these "active" messages may indicate either how an animal feels or that he is about to act in some way. The information may be expressed either as signals or displays.

In all forms of communication the information must be received and understood. The interpretation of messages involves one or more of the senses.

Animals can use most parts of their bodies when they communicate. For many vertebrates the head is the most important part of the body. The use of facial expressions is the way most mammals show how they are feeling. They are usually able to recognize different moods even in species other than their own.

The ability to make noises is one of the most important means of communication. It allows animals to pass messages without seeing each other.

Naming and grouping

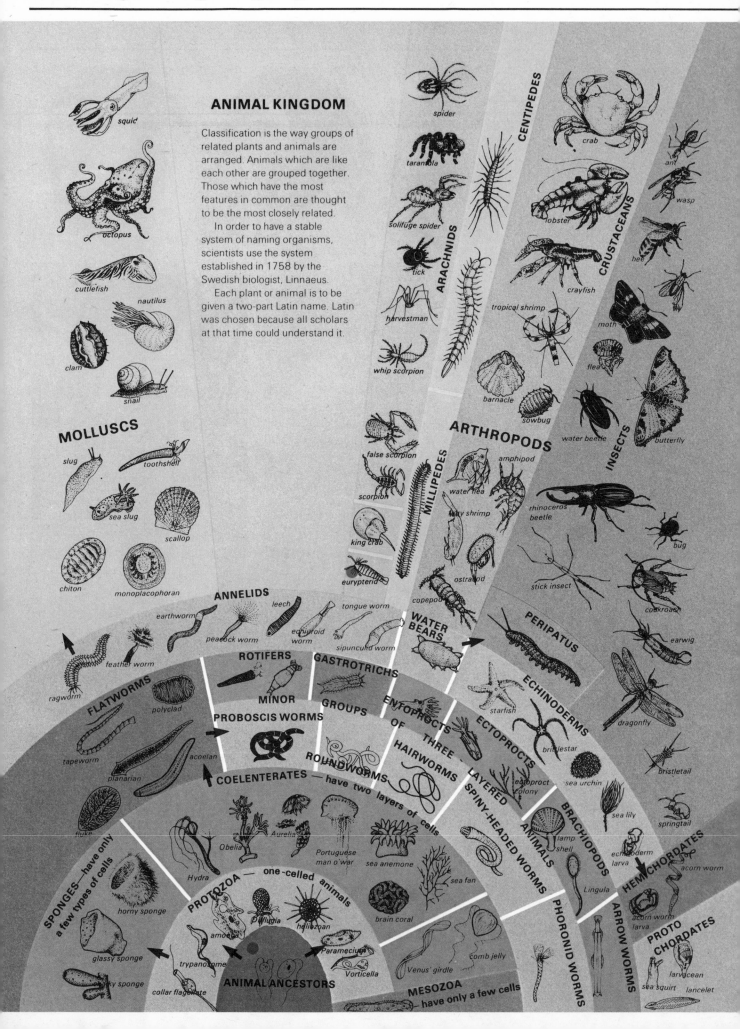

ANIMAL KINGDOM

Classification is the way groups of related plants and animals are arranged. Animals which are like each other are grouped together. Those which have the most features in common are thought to be the most closely related.

In order to have a stable system of naming organisms, scientists use the system established in 1758 by the Swedish biologist, Linnaeus.

Each plant or animal is to be given a two-part Latin name. Latin was chosen because all scholars at that time could understand it.

squid
octopus
cuttlefish
nautilus
clam
snail

MOLLUSCS

slug
toothshell
sea slug
scallop
chiton
monoplacophoran

spider
tarantula
solifuge spider
tick
ARACHNIDS
harvestman
whip scorpion
false scorpion
scorpion
king crab
eurypterid

CENTIPEDES
MILLIPEDES

CRUSTACEANS
crab
lobster
crayfish
tropical shrimp
barnacle
sowbug
water flea
amphipod
fairy shrimp
ostracod
copepod

ARTHROPODS

ant
wasp
bee
moth
flea
water beetle
butterfly
INSECTS
rhinoceros beetle
bug
stick insect
cockroach
earwig
dragonfly
bristletail
springtail

PERIPATUS

WATER BEARS

ANNELIDS
earthworm
leech
tongue worm
peacock worm
echiuroid worm
sipunculid worm
feather worm
ragworm

ROTIFERS
GASTROTRICHS

MINOR GROUPS
PROBOSCIS WORMS

ENTOPROCTS
ECTOPROCTS

ECHINODERMS
starfish
brittlestar
sea urchin
sea lily
echinoderm larva

HEMICHORDATES
acorn worm
acorn worm larva

FLATWORMS
polyclad
tapeworm
planarian
acoelan
fluke

COELENTERATES — have two layers of cells

ROUNDWORMS
HAIRWORMS

THREE-LAYERED
SPINY-HEADED WORMS

ANIMALS
ectoproct colony

BRACHIOPODS
lamp shell
Lingula

ARROW WORMS

PROTO CHORDATES
larvacean
sea squirt
lancelet

SPONGES — have only a few types of cells
horny sponge
glassy sponge
ky sponge

PROTOZOA — one-celled animals
Hydra
Obelia
Aurelia
Portuguese man o' war
sea anemone
sea fan
brain coral
Difflugia
amoeba
heliozoan
trypanosome
Paramecium
Vorticella
collar flagellate

ANIMAL ANCESTORS

MESOZOA — have only a few cells
Venus' girdle
comb jelly

PHORONID WORMS

Protozoa

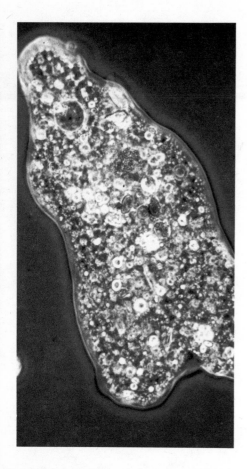

Above: A highly magnified view of an amoeba clearly shows its structure.

Below: Daphnia are minute water-fleas that live in fresh water. They are commonly sold in dried form as a foodstuff for aquarium fish. This is a photomicrograph of a cluster of daphnia.

Protozoa, meaning the "first animals", are the simplest members of the animal kingdom. They are world-wide and exist in the soil, in water and in living things. Each protozoon consists of a single cell. Like all cells which make up the bodies of larger animals, a protozoon consists of living matter, called protoplasm, and a nucleus. The nucleus controls the cell, and carries the inherent characteristics of the protozoon. That is why all the offspring look the same. In all there are some 30,000 different kinds of protozoa.

Protozoa are divided into four main groups. The first group, the Sarcodina, have a flexible cell wall. They move about by changing the shape of their cells. A part of the cell is pushed forward to make a kind of false leg, or pseudopodium, and the cell contents (protoplasm) flow into it. The animal can change direction by pushing out another false leg. This movement is well illustrated in the familiar amoeba which is found in ponds and puddles.

Amoebae reproduce simply by dividing into two. The nucleus separates into two identical nuclei, a "waist" forms in between, and the parent divides into two identical "daughter" amoebae.

Shelled amoebae

Some kinds of amoebae have shells. *Arcifera* is a pond amoeba covered by a shell which has holes. The pseudopodia push through the holes to gather any nearby food.

There are swarms of shelled amoebae in the sea forming part of the plankton which drifts near the surface. They are a valuable source of food for all kinds of sea life. One group, the Foraminifera, have a limy shell, and sink to the bottom when they die. In the past, whole seas have filled up with their shells and formed into thick layers of chalk. These layers can be seen along sea cliffs. Another group, the Radiolaria, have shells covered in spines of silica.

Flagellates

The second main group of protozoa are the Mastigophora, sometimes called the flagellates. These have a whip-like thread, called a flagellum, which helps to move them through the water. *Euglena* is a common flagellate which sometimes makes water appear green. The green is caused by the presence of chlorophyll which also enables *Euglena* to manufacture food by photosynthesis *(see page 172).*

Noctiluca, the little "night-light", lives in the sea. When disturbed it gives off a white light. If a ship passes through a swarm, the sea lights up in its wake. This happens mostly in warmer seas.

Ciliates

The third group, the Ciliophora, are covered in little hairs, called cilia. These beat backwards and forwards in a wave action, and drive the ciliate forwards, or even backwards. The slipper-shaped *Paramecium* is a typical ciliate which can catch food in a kind of mouth. A row of special cilia waft particles of food into this "mouth", which is the only place on the surface of *Paramecium* where food can be taken in.

Cilia are also found in the human body, especially in the

wind-pipe, where they help to pass food into the stomach.

Vorticella lives on a stalk attached to a plant or a stone, and usually lives in colonies. The cell is bell-shaped and has a ring of cilia around its upper edge. This causes a small whirlpool which drags in food. If disturbed, *Vorticella* suddenly pulls in its stalk, and the whole colony may collapse completely.

Another colonial creature is *Volvox,* which consists of a ball-shaped colony of cells rolling slowly through the water.

Most of the protozoa so far mentioned live in water or damp places. As a safeguard against drying up or freezing they can come to rest, compress their bodies and form a hard covering, called a cyst.

Disease-carrying parasites

The fourth group, the Sporozoa, can barely make any movement at all. They live inside other animals as parasites. Usually they are harmless, but some can cause disease. One disease-carrying parasite is *Plasmodium,* which spreads malaria. *Plasmodium* lives a kind of double life, part in a mosquito, and part in a human. In the human the parasite attacks the blood-cells. The *Plasmodium* cells then multiply and make further attacks. This causes fever and high temperature in the human, a condition which used to be described as having the "ague" or shivering disease. Another name for the disease is malaria, which is the Italian word for "bad air". People at one time believed the illness came from the air, when in fact it is spread by the mosquito. Mosquitoes breed in foul-smelling swamps.

Inside the mosquito there are both male and female kinds of *Plasmodium* which unite to form many more parasites. These gather in the mosquito's mouth, and are injected into the human blood-stream when the mosquito bites.

Malaria cannot be transmitted from one human to another – only mosquitoes spread the disease.

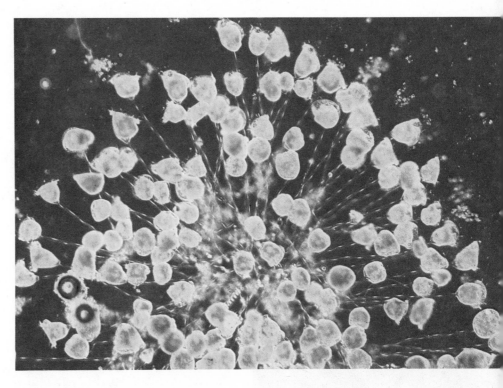

Above: A colony of *Vorticella*, as viewed under a microscope. *Vorticella* are commonly found in ponds where they attach themselves to stones.

Below: *Paramecium* is a ciliate. This magnified photo shows the cilia which beat backwards and forwards to drive it through the water.

One method of control is to drain swamps to stop the mosquitoes breeding so rapidly.

Another parasitic protozoon called *Trypanosoma* causes sleeping sickness. This can be a fatal disease and is a very serious problem in parts of Africa. Gingivitis, a less serious but uncomfortable disease of the gums, is caused by a particular kind of amoeba.

Curing disease

The invention of the microscope has been a great boon to medicine. Minute, disease-carrying protozoa can be magnified to many times their actual size so that we can find out exactly how they live and reproduce. Drugs are then developed which can be used to treat sick patients. More and more efforts are being made to control the insects which help to spread these protozoan diseases. Many countries which once suffered from malaria and sleeping sickness are now rid of them, although we must be constantly on guard to make sure they never return.

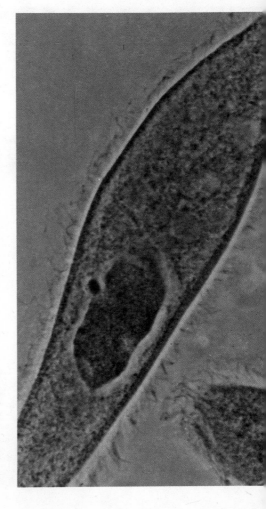

Simple water animals

Jellyfish, sea anemones and corals are among the simplest multicellular animals. There are about 9,000 different species and fossil records date from the Cambrian Period.

These animals are collectively called coelenterates, a word which comes from the Greek meaning "cavity" and very aptly describes their basic body shape. All coelenterates are simply a hollow sac with a mouth at one end surrounded by tentacles.

The body wall of coelenterates is made up of three layers. The inner layer lines the cavity and performs the function of a gut. The middle layer is jelly-like and varies con-

Left: In tropical waters, corals form brightly coloured, underwater forests where many other marine animals live.

Below: Sea anemones, despite their delicate flower-like appearance, are voracious predators catching and devouring any small creatures which swim near their tentacles.

siderably in thickness; in jellyfish it forms the bulk of the body. The outer layer contains the special stinging cells called cnidoblasts. These cells are only found in coelenterates and are one of the reasons why these primitive animals have survived and developed so successfully. They are found in greatest concentrations around the mouth and on the tentacles; when the hair-like trigger of a cnidoblast is touched by a likely food item – a small fish or shrimp – a thread is shot out. Some threads impale the prey with their barbed tips, others inject a minute drop of poison, while another variety entangles the animal. Once the food is caught it is pushed into the mouth by the tentacles.

Coelenterates can be divided into three classes. There are the hydrozoans made up of the hydroids and the siphonophores; the scyphozoans or jellyfish, and the anthrozoans which include sea anemones and corals.

Coelenterates also have two very distinct shapes. There is the sedentary anemone-type animal known as a polyp, and the free-swimming jellyfish-type called a medusa.

Hydroids and siphonophores
Hydrozoans live mainly as the polyp stage, although their life-cycle alternates from polyp to medusa and back. *Hydra,* one of the few coelenterates which has invaded fresh water, lives as a solitary polyp attached to water plants or rocks. Most of the time *Hydra* remains in one place but it can move along by a slow, creeping motion or, more effectively, by actually somersaulting over itself. Other hydroids, such as *Obelia,* form branching plant-like colonies. Close examination of each branch reveals many tiny polyps.

Siphonophores are also colonial hydrozoans. Although looking like jellyfish, their tentacles and digestive unit are made up of thousands of polyps. Some, such as the notorious Portuguese man o'war, have large gas-filled floats up to 30

Top: Corals are colonies of many thousands of polyps in a hard skeleton, while a sea anemone (**middle**) lives a solitary life as a single polyp.

Above: Jellyfish exist in the medusa form and swim freely about the oceans.

centimetres long which give them buoyancy and enable them to drift about the oceans. The floats are often brightly coloured, and are thought to consist of specially adapted medusae.

Jellyfish

This class contains the true jellyfish which rhythmically pulsate their way through the seas. Jellyfish live almost entirely as the medusa form, a tiny polyp stage only occurring during reproduction. They range in size from a few millimetres to the largest, *Cyanea capillata*, which can reach a size of two metres across. The stinging cells on the tentacles of tropical jellyfish sometimes contain deadly poisons, and even the two species found in British waters can cause painful stings.

Sea anemones and corals

Antherozoans exist entirely in the polyp form and are either solitary, such as the sea anemone, or live in colonies like corals. They look very similar to hydrozoans but the body is usually shorter and stouter and the cavity inside is divided into sections.

Sea anemones are extremely widespread, ranging from intertidal rock pools to the great depths of the Philippine Trench some 12,000 metres down. Most sea anemones attach themselves to rocks but some species live on the shells of hermit crabs.

Coral is simply a colony of anemones, each protected by a hard calcareous cup. The stony skeleton is secreted by the polyps and is almost pure calcium carbonate. Some colonies of stony corals are 70 million years old and have slowly grown to form the vast coral reefs and atolls of the Pacific and Indian Oceans.

Not all coral is hard. In south-west England a coral with the rather unfortunate name, dead man's fingers, is found. The skeleton of this coral is made up of a tough jelly-like substance and contains many hard spicules.

Above: The long stinging filaments of the Portuguese man o' war may be over 20 metres long. This siphonophore lives mainly in tropical seas but is occasionally washed up on British shores.

Below: *Hydra* varies in length from a few millimetres to about two centimetres. In favourable conditions, these animals bud off young from the main part of their bodies. When fully developed the young separate off from the parent *Hydra*, and attach themselves to a stone or water plant.

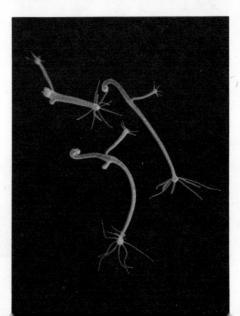

Worms

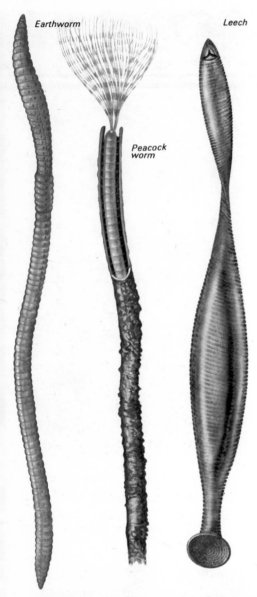

Earthworm

Peacock
worm

Leech

Worms are soft-bodied animals, living either under the ground, in water or as parasites of other animals or plants. They are divided into four main groups – annelids, platyhelminths, nematodes and hirudinids.

Types of worms
Annelids are the segmented worms, their bodies being divided into segments by a number of rings. Many annelids have small bristles or chaetae growing outwards from each segment which help them to move about. Between the outer body wall and the digestive system is a cavity filled with fluid. At one end several segments combine to form the head, complete with mouth, eyes and brain.

There are three types of annelid: polychaetes, oligochaetes and hirudinids.

The polychaetes live either in or near the sea. Although very rarely

Left: Earthworm casts appear as small mounds of coiled earth. The peacock worm is an example of a sedentary polychaete. Leeches have a sucker at either end of their bodies.

Below: The ragworm is a free-moving polychaete found in coastal waters.

seen, these worms are quite common and grow up to two metres in length.

One group of polychaetes is free-moving. They crawl about and burrow amongst the sand and seaweed. They are able to propel themselves around by means of bristly paddle-like "limbs" called parapodia. A pair of parapodia grows out of each segment of the body.

Most free-moving polychaetes have a proboscis or tube through which they feed. The proboscis, with its teeth and strong jaws, is pushed out through the mouth. To swallow the food, the polychaete withdraws the proboscis.

The second group of polychaetes is stationary. They build a permanent home, usually forming a tunnel of lime or sand. Most types feed by catching food with their tentacles which are attached to the head.

The oligochaetes, the second type of annelid, include the earthworms. These too have tiny bristles growing out of each segment of their bodies. Earthworms can grow very long; in South Africa some measure seven metres in length.

Earthworms tunnel under the ground, swallowing the soil as they go. Some species pull leaves and pieces of vegetation into their tunnels for food. The food and soil passes through the body and is deposited as a cast.

The third type of annelid – Hirudinea – comprises the leeches. They have no bristles on their bodies but move along by means of two suckers, one at either end of the body.

In tropical areas leeches live amongst humid undergrowth. When an animal or human host passes by, they attach themselves to them to feed. They feed by sucking blood through the front sucker which contains the mouth.

The medicinal leech has three strong jaws which leave a Y-shaped mark on the skin. As it feeds it pumps an anaesthetic into the opening; this prevents any irri-

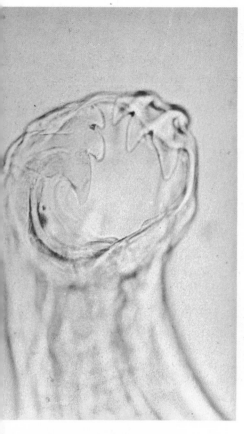

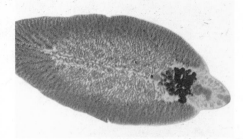

Above: The dark patches on this liver fluke show part of its reproductive and excretory organs. Flukes are very common in China and Japan where people work bare-footed in the damp fields. The fluke enters the body by boring into the foot.

Left: Hookworms attach themselves to the wall of the intestine by their mouths to suck blood. Adult worms grow to about ten millimetres long.

Right: Elephantiasis is a skin disease caused by the parasitic nematode, *Filaria*. Limbs sometimes swell up to a huge size. *Filaria* grows up to ten centimetres long.

tation, so stopping the host from removing the leech.

Flatworms

Platyhelminths are more usually known as flatworms. Their bodies are flat and made up of a spongy substance enclosing the internal organs. In most flatworms, food is taken in and waste food let out through one single opening.

Platyhelminths are mainly hermaphrodite. This means that each worm has both male and female reproductive organs. They are one of the most primitive groups of animals to have a central nervous system, although they have no blood system.

The platyhelminths are divided into four types – turbellarians, two kinds of trematodes (flukes) and cestodes (tapeworms).

Turbellarians vary considerably in size. Some cannot be seen with the naked eye while others measure 500 millimetres long.

The trematodes are parasites which live in or upon other animals. They cling to the host by means of a sucker. Blood flukes enter human blood vessels where they reproduce, causing disease. The liver fluke seriously harms and even kills sheep and cattle.

Cestodes are also parasitic. The head has both hooks and suckers to hold it firmly to its host.

Roundworms

The nematodes are more usually known as roundworms. Except for insects and protozoa, they are the most numerous members of the animal kingdom. They are found in many different environments, but most live in the soil. However, some are parasites of man and animals.

One type of roundworm, *Ascaris*, lives inside the intestine where it produces millions of eggs. These are passed out with waste food. In areas where sanitation is poor, the water becomes contaminated and the eggs infect humans with disease.

An even more unpleasant nematode is the hookworm. Again, it is common where sanitation is poor. The worm enters the bloodstream by tunnelling into the flesh. It then attaches itself to the intestine where it feeds on blood and tissue.

Nematodes are tiny hair-like worms measuring from 0.5 to 1.5 millimetres long, although a few have been known to grow as long as 30 centimetres.

Ribbon worms

Nemertines are more commonly known as ribbon worms and also as proboscis worms. As this name suggests, they have a large proboscis which they can extend to catch and kill prey. When it is not in use, the proboscis lies inside the body in a cavity just above the gut.

Nemertines live mainly in shallow sea water, although some live in fresh water and a few live on dry land. They can grow to surprising lengths. For example, the average length of the bootlace worm, found in the North Sea, is five metres; one, however, measured over 44 metres in length.

Nemertines are very fragile, and can crumble into fragments if knocked or even handled. If this should happen, some of the pieces will develop into new worms.

The starfish family

The starfishes and their relatives belong to one of the major groups of invertebrates, or animals without backbones. The group is called the echinoderms. Echinoderm means having a spiny skin.

Some species live in the parts of the sea shore between the high and low tide mark, while others live off shore or in the deep sea.

They all have a body cavity, or coelom.

Symmetry

The body-plan is the same in all echinoderms. They have the parts of their body arranged in sections around a central point – like a wheel. This arrangement is called radial symmetry. Most echinoderms have five sections.

Five classes

There are five sub-groups or classes of echinoderms. These are the starfishes, brittlestars, sea urchins, sea cucumbers and crinoids. Many members of these five classes have spines either on their shell-like outside, or test, or embedded within the layers of their skin.

Water-vascular system

There is a tube inside the body running close to the surface in each of the radial sections. The main radial tubes, or canals, are connected to each other by a ring canal surrounding the mouth. These canals act as a sort of hydraulic skeleton, helping to support the body. This is called the water-vascular system.

On each side of the radial canals there are two regular series of muscular side branches. These stick out through the body wall to form tube feet. These are used for walking and feeding. Some tube feet are specialized to help clear left-over food from around the mouth. Echinoderms move by pushing their tube feet either through a groove in their arms (starfishes and brittlestars) or through holes in their test (sea urchins). They can form suckers on the end of their tube feet which

help them to hold on to or climb up vertical surfaces.

Sea urchins

Sea urchins, or echinoids, have a ball-shaped or flat bun-shaped body, covered with hundreds of moveable spines.

The spines are attached to the test by a ball and socket joint. The "socket" is on the base of the spine. It fits on to the corresponding "ball" or knob on the test. These knobs are usually arranged in regular patterns. When the sea urchin dies the spines usually break off, and the knob pattern can be seen.

The mouth is on the underside, at or near the centre of the body. Sea urchins eat almost anything. Some prefer plant material while others prefer animal matter. They have a powerful jaw-like structure made up of five shelly "teeth" around the mouth. This is called "Aristotle's lantern", because Aristotle compared it to a lantern.

Starfishes

The starfishes, or sea stars, belong to the class Asteroidea. This name comes from a Greek word that

Above: Sea urchins move by extending tube feet through pores in their test. These feet are in rows between the spines.

Above: Starfish have spiny skins, and many have five arms radiating from the centre of the body. They use tube feet to move. These stick out through a groove on the underside of each arm. Some starfish eat shellfish.

Above: The crown of thorns starfish lives on tropical coral reefs. It has many large, sharp spines on its back. It may grow to a third of a metre in diameter and have 15 arms. Sometimes a "plague" of these starfishes can destroy part of a coral reef.

like a starfish turned upside-down with its arms upwards.

Sea lilies are attached to the sea floor by a stalk. On the bottom of the stalk may be off-shoots called cirri. These help to anchor the animal on the sea bottom.

Feather stars do not have a stalk, but they do have a number of cirri attached to their back. They use these to cling to rocks and corals.

Feeding and breathing

Many echinoderms eat microscopic particles of organic matter in the sea water. They make water currents by beating their hair-like cilia. This moves particles along the food grooves to the mouth.

The water currents also bring a fresh supply of oxygen-rich water to the surface gills for breathing.

Above: The common starfish can easily trap a resting scallop. It wraps its arms tightly around the shell. The starfish then pulls the two valves of the shell apart.

Below: These members of the starfish family all have five or more arms.

means star-like. Most starfish have five arms, but some have more.

Starfish have many shelly plates embedded in their skin. These have spines which stick out through their skin and make a prickly surface. These spines help protect the skin gills through which the starfish breathe. The mouth is on the underside of the body and the digestive tract loops upwards to the anus, which is at the top.

Brittlestars

Brittlestars belong to the class Ophiuroidea. They look like starfish, with longer, thinner arms and smaller more disc-shaped bodies.

Sea cucumbers

Sea cucumbers are animals which look like cucumbers. They belong to the class Holothuroidea. They have no spines, but they have microscopic spicules in their skin to support their soft bodies. Some of their tube feet are modified to make feeding tentacles.

Sea lilies and feather stars

Sea lilies and feather stars belong to the class Crinoidea. They look

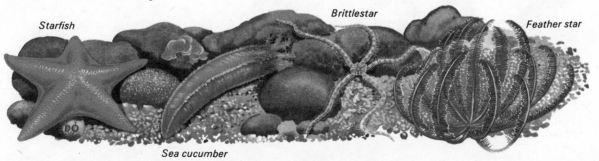

Starfish   Brittlestar   Feather star

Sea cucumber

65

Identifying molluscs

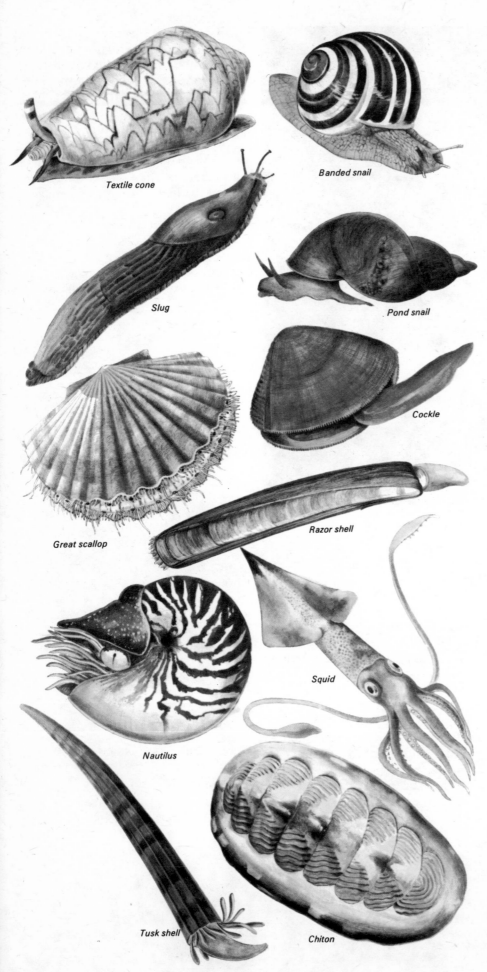

Textile cone

Banded snail

Slug

Pond snail

Cockle

Great scallop

Razor shell

Nautilus

Squid

Tusk shell

Chiton

Another of the major invertebrate groups is the Mollusca. These are all soft-bodied animals and include slugs, snails, scallops and squids. At first it is difficult to see how such different looking animals are related.

There are five major sub-divisions or classes of living molluscs. Most of them form a hard shell. These five classes include the familiar snails, clams, octopuses, chitons and tusk-shells.

Gastropods

The most common molluscs are the snails or gastropods. There are around 20,000 living species. Most gastropods have a one-piece shell which may be cap-shaped as in limpets or coiled as in whelks.

The name gastropod means stomach-footed. Most gastropods have a big flat-bottomed foot, a head with tentacles and eyes. Their stomach and intestines are contained in a part of the body called the visceral mass.

There are many different kinds of gastropods. Many are marine, living either between the tide marks or in the sea. These include the whelks, winkles, cowries, cone-shells and sea slugs, to name a few. These all breathe by means of gills. Other gastropods include the land snails, slugs and freshwater snails which have lungs.

Bivalves

The clams or bivalves are the next class with less than 10,000 living species. Bivalves have a two-piece shell which is held together by one or two muscles. All bivalves live either in the sea or in fresh water and breathe by means of gills. Bivalves do not have a head.

Bivalves may live burrowed in sand or attached to the surface of rocks. Some may even bore into rocks, coral or wood.

Left: Molluscs are the most varied group of animals without backbones. It includes all the familiar seashells, clams, sea-slugs, octopuses, squids and chitons, land snails, pond snails and slugs.

Cephalopods

The cephalopods are the third most common class of molluscs and include the largest and most intelligent invertebrates. The name cephalopod means head-footed. In this class are the octopuses, cuttlefishes, squids and nautilus. Of these, only nautilus has a shell.

All cephalopods live in the sea. Most species are active predators, capturing prey with long tentacles.

Chitons

The chitons have a shell of eight plates held together by a leathery girdle. They have a large foot and a head without eyes or tentacles.

Below: Molluscs come in a variety of different shapes. They are designed to suit their environment. Whelks, winkles, limpets and top shells belong to the largest class of molluscs, the gastropods.

Scaphopods

Scaphopods or tusk-shells are tube-shaped marine molluscs. Their name means plough-footed. The scaphopods live partly buried in mud with the narrow end above the surface. They are predators and catch their prey with thread-like "captaculae".

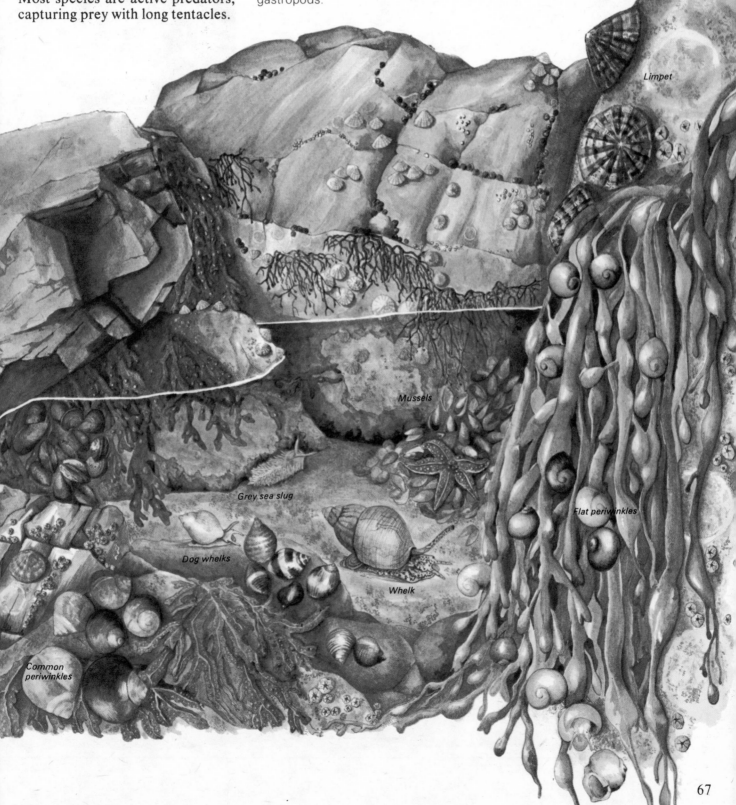

Limpet

Mussels

Grey sea slug

Flat periwinkles

Dog whelks

Whelk

Common periwinkles

Ways of life

There are around 75,000 species of molluscs. They live in most of the major habitats on earth. Although there are many different kinds of molluscs they do have a number of characteristics in common.

Mollusc body

The body of most molluscs has three general regions: the head, visceral mass and the foot. The stomach, the intestines and reproductive organs are contained in the visceral mass.

Internal organs

All molluscs have a thin layer of tissue covering the soft parts of their body. This layer is called the mantle. The gills or lungs are located in the mantle cavity. The shell is built slowly by the mantle.

Most molluscs have a head with a mouth, and a long tongue-like structure called the radula. The radula usually has rows of tiny teeth on it, and is used for feeding. Only the bivalves have no radula.

Most molluscs move by using a very muscular foot. In gastropods and chitons the foot is broad and flat. They use it for creeping slowly or gripping tight to the surface of rocks. Scaphopods and bivalves use the foot for burrowing into sand or mud. Cephalopods, like the octopus, have arms equipped with many rows of suckers which help them to move over rocks.

Visceral mass

The visceral mass contains all the important organs of digestion, the heart and the reproductive organs. Food enters the mouth, moves to the stomach and intestines which end in the mantle cavity. There, the waste products are removed by the water currents from the gills.

In molluscs which live in water the gills are used for breathing. In bivalves the gills are also used in feeding. The food enters the mantle cavity and passes along the gills where it is sorted before entering the mouth.

Below: The body-plan of a gastropod is typical of most molluscs. There is a head with a mouth containing a radula, a muscular foot and mantle cavity containing the gills.

Right: The long tongue-like radula has many rows of tiny teeth. These are of different shapes and sizes depending on the kind of food that is eaten. This is a close-up of a periwinkle radula.

Visceral mass

Gill

Shell

Stomach

Eye

Mouth

Radula

Operculum

Foot

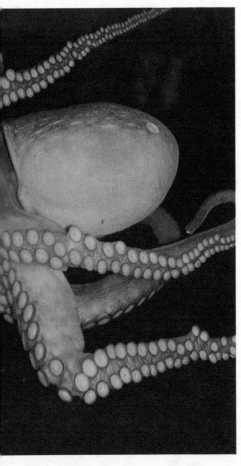

Above: An octopus has rows of
suckers on its arms which help it to
move about easily among the rocks.

Right: Sea slugs that live on tropical
coral reefs are often small with very
bright colours. Irregular patterns help
them to blend with their surroundings.

Colour pattern and camouflage

Some molluscs do not have a shell
to protect their soft body. They
have evolved camouflaging colour
patterns and body forms. Sea slugs
have developed a variety of shapes
and colour patterns that help them
to blend in with their environment.

The cephalopods have some very
complex camouflage and defence
behaviour. Special colour cells in
the skin layers allow them to
change colour rapidly. They can
also squirt out an ink "ghost", then
change their body colour and dart
off.

Some sea slugs also produce a
dark ink similar to that of cephalopods. They also use their ink to
confuse their enemies. Other
species have a bright camouflaging colour pattern.

Senses

Molluscs have much the same
senses as other animals. However,
there are two important senses that
do not occur in molluscs. These
are the senses of hearing and taste.
Molluscs also have no means of
making sounds.

Sight

Mollusc eyes vary from the simple
light-sensitive cells in the mantle of
some chitons, to the much more
complex eyes of the cephalopods
which are able to focus.

Some molluscs do not have eyes.
The scaphopods and most of the
bivalves do not have eyes.
Molluscs that live buried in the
sand do not usually need sight.

Balance

Molluscs are able to maintain their
balance by "statocysts" attached
to the base of the major nerve
ganglia (swellings) in their foot.

Touch and smell

Most molluscs have some sense of
touch. The tentacles on the head of
many snails help to guide them by
feeling the surface as they move.
Tentacles around the edge of the
mantle of bivalves are often exposed on the surface of the
creature. These tentacles sense approaching danger.

The sense of smell is centred in
an organ located inside the mantle
cavity near the gills. This organ
detects changes in salt content,
chemicals and amount of sedi-
ment in the water. In sea slugs this
sense is located in a pair of
tentacle-like structures on top of
the head.

Defence

Molluscs are not usually aggressive creatures. They tend only to
protect themselves by withdrawing into the safety of their
shell or crawling under a rock.

Bivalves can simply clamp shut
the two valves of their shell.

Reproduction

One of the most important activities of all organisms is reproduction. Molluscs have a number of different courtship and mating patterns. Some species undergo elaborate courting rituals before mating. Others just shed their eggs or sperms directly into the water.

In the majority of mollusc species the sexes are separate. However, in many species both sexes are found in each animal. These individuals are called hermaphrodites.

Some molluscs can change their sex during their life. Certain limpets mature first as males. Then they pass through an hermaphrodite stage before their final development into mature females.

Development

Development begins as soon as the egg is fertilized. Many molluscs produce egg capsules in which the young begin to develop.

In a few species the young develop within the mantle cavity of their mother. This is called "brooding". Some molluscs, such as land snails, hatch from eggs directly into the adult form. However, many species which live in water develop from eggs into an intermediate "larval" stage before taking on their adult appearance.

Larval stages

Eggs that are fertilized in water pass through a free-swimming larval stage called a trochophore.

The internal organs and the shell begin to form during the trochophore stage. The next, more advanced stage is the "veliger". It has a band of cilia around two lobes of tissue called the vellum. The veliger swims by beating the cilia and moving the lobes of the vellum.

Torsion

During the veliger stage in gastropods the muscles that attach the body to the shell contract. This twists the body around so that the mantle cavity opens over the head. This new position allows the head to be pulled into the shell before the foot. The gills and sense organs are also brought to the front of the mantle cavity. This process is known as torsion.

Late in the veliger stage the foot grows larger and the vellum is

shed. The veliger then settles.

Growth

Once the larva settles, the animal begins to grow rapidly. Settlement is usually marked by a change in the shell sculpture pattern.

Growth stages are recorded in those species which have a shell. Shell material is secreted at the mantle edge. The blood of most molluscs contains a large amount of calcium carbonate. This is extracted from their food and water. Cells in the mantle are able to concentrate the calcium carbonate and form it into crystals of two minerals—calcite and aragonite. Mother-of-pearl is one of the forms of aragonite.

Molluscs can usually repair injury to their soft parts. If the shell is damaged the mantle will secrete new shell material to fix it.

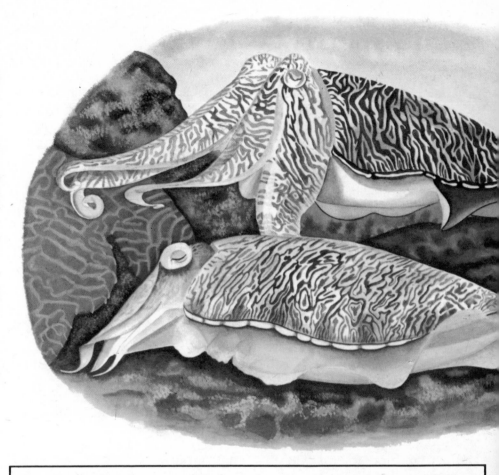

Right: Cuttlefish mate in the spring. During their night-time courtship, the males display their brightly glowing "zebra-striped" patterns. This both attracts the females and frightens away other rival males.

Left: The female octopus lays numerous long egg clusters which she attaches to the ceiling of her cave. She cares for the eggs until they all hatch.

Where molluscs live

Molluscs live in all parts of the world. Some species are very widely distributed, while others are found in only one place. Species like the oceanic squids, the sea snails and a couple of minor groups travel long distances. They swim or drift along with the ocean currents. However, most species do not move far from where their larvae first settled.

Molluscs as food

Molluscs are an important part of many food chains. Bivalves, cephalopods and gastropods are a valuable source of food for many predators, including man.

Molluscs are plentiful and easy to collect. Mounds of oyster and clam shells have been found in many parts of the world.

Many land snails like the large Roman snail perform a very dramatic courtship "dance". They stand up and press their bodies together. The snails then shoot their "love dart" into each other. The "love dart" stimulates mating. After cross-fertilization each snail lays up to 50 eggs in the ground.

What is an arthropod?

The arthropods are invertebrates that have jointed legs and usually a hard outer skeleton. The name Arthropoda comes from the Greek *arthron*, meaning joint, and *podos*, foot. More species of arthropods have been described than all other kinds of animals put together. In fact, over 75 per cent of the known animals, both vertebrate and invertebrate, belong to the phylum Arthropoda, and of these a further 75 per cent are insects.

The major classes of arthropods are the Crustacea, including crayfish, lobsters, shrimps, crabs, water-fleas, woodlice and barnacles; the Chilopoda or centipedes; the Diplopoda or millipedes; the Arachnida, including spiders, harvestmen, scorpions, mites and ticks; and the Insecta, including dragonflies, mayflies, grasshoppers, cockroaches, butterflies, bees, wasps, ants, flies and beetles. The insects are the largest class and they contain about 750,000 species, followed by the arachnids with about 60,000 species and the centipedes and millipedes together, a mere 11,000 species.

Missing link

Arthropods have evolved from marine segmented worms. The animal that comes closer than any other to being the "missing link" between the worms and the arthropods is *Peripatus*, the sole representative of the phylum Onychophora. *Peripatus* is a many-legged caterpillar-like creature about eight centimetres in length which is found mainly in the Southern Hemisphere. It is usually nocturnal and likes moist places under logs in tropical forests.

The Arthropoda are a very ancient group of animals. At the beginning of the Cambrian Period (500 million years ago) there were three well-established classes: trilobites, crustaceans and arachnids. The dominant class was the trilobites which make up over half the fossils known from this period and are the most important group of fossil arthropods. They were at their most numerous in the Ordovician Period (400 million years ago), but finally died out in the Permian (220 million years ago). Their decline and final extinction was probably brought about by the giant Ordovician cephalopods (squids and octopuses) and the Devonian fishes, 320 million years ago. The name trilobite refers to the fact that the dorsal surface of the body is divided into three lobes. The trilobites probably gave rise to no other arthropod groups, but they seem to be most closely related to the Crustacea.

Ancestors

Ancestors of the more primitive crustaceans, like the fairy-shrimps, are well represented in lower Cambrian rocks, but the larger crustaceans, such as lobsters and crabs, do not appear until Jurassic times (150 million years ago).

Eurypterus, a fossil arachnid and the ancestor of the present-day horseshoe- or king-crabs, *Limulus*, occurred in the sea from the Cambrian to Permian Periods, that is from 500 to 220 million years ago. *Limulus* itself has changed little since Triassic times (190 million years ago). *Eurypterus* is the largest known arthropod and at its peak of development it attained a length of three metres.

Although 750,000 species of living insects have been described, only a few thousand fossil species have been found. Many of these were preserved in accumulations of dripping resin over long periods. The resin eventually became fossilized into amber, thus preserving the insect or spider. All of the early insects are now extinct.

The arthropod body-plan is a specialization of the segmented body-plan of annelid worms. The outer layer, or cuticle, serves as a protective armour. Biting jaws, piercing beaks, grinding surfaces, sound-producing organs, walking legs, pincers, wings and many other structures, are made from the cuticle. It is due partly to this hard

Above: A centipede of the genus *Lithobius*. Centipedes have one pair of legs on each segment. They are carnivorous and most are nocturnal and are found in moist places, under stones and decaying logs. They feed mainly on other arthropods which they capture with their strong pincer-like jaws which contain poison glands.

Below: The crayfish (class Crustacea) is a freshwater relative of the lobster, found in temperate countries. It feeds on small water animals such as snails, insects, frogs and fishes.

cuticle that the arthropods have been so very successful. This hard surface is called an exoskeleton, and it is to this that arthropods owe their ability to live on land, for it provides a relatively impermeable outer covering to prevent drying of the watery tissues within, and also provides a rigid framework to support the soft tissues. This exoskeleton enables arthropods to exploit the land with practically no serious competition from the other invertebrate groups, most of which are largely aquatic.

There is no doubt that the arthropods are the most successful of all the animal groups. They have the largest number of species and individuals, and occupy the widest stretches of territory and the greatest variety of habitats. In

the oceans minute crustaceans form the major part of the food chains of whales and the larger fishes. Some arthropods are beneficial to man: crabs and lobsters providing food; bees providing honey; and silkworms (the larvae of silkmoths) providing silk. Others do untold damage, destroying crops, undermining wooden buildings, and transmitting diseases. Where they do not exclude him altogether, arthropods are man's chief competitor for food and shelter.

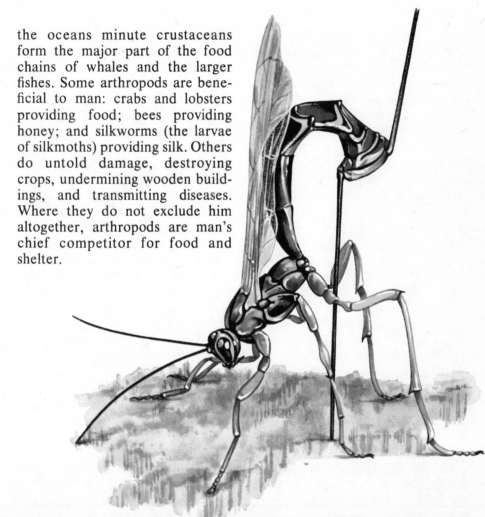

Right: An ichneumon wasp of the genus *Megarhyssa* has inserted its ovipositor (egg-laying tube) into the bark of a tree. Its larva will parasitize the larvae of the woodwasp *Sirex*.

Below: A female spider of the black widow genus *Latrodectus*. Only the females bite, and then only if molested.

Spiders and scorpions

Spiders and scorpions are probably the best-known members of the class Arachnida. There are about 30,000 species of spiders and 700 species of scorpions.

One of the most interesting habits of spiders is their ability to trap their prey with webs. The silk they produce to construct their webs is extremely fine and has been used to mark lines on optical equipment. The large cobwebs that we find in buildings have been produced by the long-legged house spiders of the genus *Tegenaria,* whilst the beautiful orb-webs that glisten with dew or frost in the autumn sunshine are made by members of the family Araneidae, of which the common garden spider *Araneus diadematus* is the most familiar in the British Isles. The spiders that spin silk primarily for lining their retreats, like the trap-door spiders, or for weaving their egg cocoons, like the wolf-spiders, are considered to be more primitive than the orb-weavers. Spider silk helps to disperse the young of some species. The young spider (or spiderling) will climb onto a suitable exposed point, such as a fence-post or a branch, and release its silk from its spinnerets which are situated at the posterior of the abdomen. When the line of

silk is long enough the spider will release its hold and float off to a new area.

Predators

Spiders are preyed upon by other animals, including other spiders. The pirate spiders of the family Mimetidae attack orb-weavers in their webs and, after biting them, suck them dry. Several families of wasps hunt spiders. Social wasps and digger wasps often kill spiders to feed to their larvae, or grubs, whilst some ichneumon wasps lay their eggs on the back of a spider after paralyzing the victim with their sting. Insectivorous mammals eat a large number of spiders and many of the smaller birds feed spiders to their nestlings.

Water spiders

At least one spider, *Argyroneta aquatica,* the water spider, has adapted itself to live in water. It constructs a silken dome-shaped home amongst submerged water plants. The spider captures a bubble of air at the surface and holds it close to the abdomen by the last pair of legs whilst it swims down to its home. The bubble is released and floats up into the dome, displacing some of the water.

The fisher spider of North

Above: A scorpion in typical defensive posture, with pincers outstretched and the tail raised ready to strike forward over its head.

America is covered with tiny hairs which trap enough air to allow the spider to stay submerged for 45 minutes.

Scorpions

Scorpions are far less abundant than spiders and live mainly in hot tropical countries, although several small species are found in southern Europe. Scorpions feed at night on insects and spiders which are themselves nocturnal.

Their prey is caught with the strong pincers and is then stung. Scorpions sting in self-defence, but most stings are not serious to man. However, dangerous species do occur in North Africa, South America and Mexico, and the stings of a number of other species cause considerable pain.

Habitat

Some scorpions live in damp places and are found in tropical forests, whilst others are inhabitants of dry desert areas.

Left: Scorpions have strong maternal instincts and, like some spiders, are to be seen with their young clinging to their backs. They stay with their mother until they cast their first skin.

Above: The nocturnal and swift-running huntsman spiders (family Heteropodidae) are the house-spiders of the tropics. They may have a leg-span of 15 centimetres.

Right: The garden spider *Araneus diadematus* in its dew-laden web.

Apart from man, who has since ancient times maligned scorpions on account of their poison, they have many other enemies. In the tropical rain forests of Africa and America they have been one of the many kinds of animals overrun by columns of marauding driver ants. Several centipedes, spiders, lizards, snakes and birds are recorded as predators, and African baboons have been observed catching large scorpions and tearing off their tails before greedily devouring the rest of the body.

Lobsters and barnacles

Crustaceans form the third largest class of arthropods and are only exceeded in numbers of species by the insects and arachnids. Familiar crustaceans are crabs, lobsters, shrimps, the small shore-hoppers, garden woodlice and barnacles. But there is a large number of lesser known forms that have no popular names.

Midgets and giants

The majority of crustaceans live in the sea, but some inhabit brackish and fresh waters, and a limited number are land dwellers. A few live as parasites on or in other aquatic animals. Adults vary in size – the smallest water flea measures only about 0.25 millimetres whilst the largest known crustacean is the giant spider crab of Japan. It spans 3.6 metres from claw to claw.

Lobsters

The common lobster shows the general features of crustaceans. The external skeleton is thick and rigid. (It is thin and flexible in many smaller crustaceans.) Only the lobster's abdomen is clearly divided into segments. The forepart of the body has a shield (carapace) that protects the delicate gills through which the lobster breathes.

Sensors

The antennules and antennae are used as sensors. The whip-like antennae detect prey, sex partners and obstacles. In addition, at the base of each antennule is an organ of balance. The large claws differ slightly in shape and are used for crushing and cutting food, for defence and during mating. The remaining pairs of legs are used for walking. The lobster's heavy shell prevents it from being a really good swimmer. It much prefers to crawl along over the sea bed in a similar way to its crab-like relatives.

Moulting

The lobster's hard shell must be shed periodically to allow growth. Shell-shedding, or moulting, is hazardous and exhausting. Preparation begins with many changes within the body tissue. Eventually, a new shell is formed beneath the old. As moulting begins, the shell between the abdomen and the thorax splits across its width. The lobster flexes and straightens its body so that the split becomes wider. After a while, the lobster can withdraw its limbs and its soft body through the gap. The shell of a newly moulted lobster is soft. At this stage the animal takes up water that causes it to swell and increase in size. During the next few weeks the shell gradually hardens. Until this has happened the lobster is vulnerable to predators and

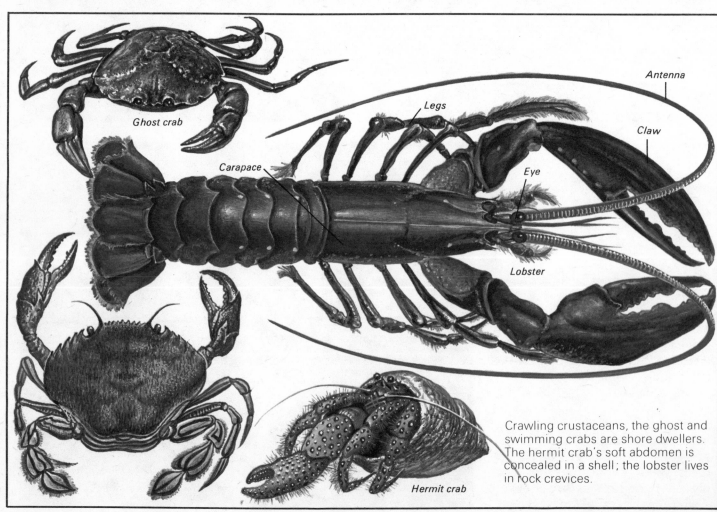

Crawling crustaceans, the ghost and swimming crabs are shore dwellers. The hermit crab's soft abdomen is concealed in a shell; the lobster lives in rock crevices.

usually remains carefully hidden.

Reproduction in lobsters

During the summer newly moulted female lobsters mate with hard-shelled males. Later, the spawned eggs are attached to the hairs on the female's swimmerets. These eggs are carried for nine to ten months and hatch as minute larvae that swim in the upper regions of the sea. As they pass through successive stages they get larger and eventually become tiny lobsters.

Below: Acorn barnacles and their relatives live firmly attached to rock surfaces, often forming dense clusters.

Above: The velvet swimming crab is a large and aggressive species. It usually lives under stones in rock pools, but sometimes burrows into sand.

Barnacles

An example of the smaller crustaceans is the barnacle. A barnacle is attached to a rock surface by its head; its legs are movable "nets" used for collecting small food particles from the water. Common shore species have limy plates surrounding their delicate body. They can close their valves to prevent the body from drying out when exposed at low tide.

Some species of barnacles live high upon the shore and can withstand long periods of exposure to air. Others live in vast numbers in the rocky intertidal regions of the shore. The goose barnacle lives very differently. It attaches itself to driftwood or to submerged parts of ships. Its head is elongated to form a stalk.

The barnacle larva that hatches from the egg is totally unlike its parent in body shape. The minute swimming larva that first emerges gradually develops into a form that has a bean-shaped shell.

This bean-shaped larva seeks out a surface on which to settle. It may make several attempts to attach itself to a surface before using its adhesive "cement" to eventually fix itself in position. Once secure, it develops into the final barnacle-like form.

Acorn barnacles, along with many other marine organisms, attach themselves to submerged parts of ships. Sometimes, the growths are so thickly encrusted that they affect the ship's speed through the water.

Crabs and shrimps

Crabs, hermit crabs, lobsters, crayfish, squat lobsters, mud shrimps, and prawns, all belong to one major group of the Crustacea – the Decapoda.

Crabs

Heavy-shelled crustaceans like crabs, lobsters and their relatives are poor swimmers, and the majority of them spend their lives crawling along the sea bed. Most species of crabs live in the sea, a few in fresh water, and some even come ashore occasionally. Robber or coconut crabs, for example, have been known to climb cliffs and trees.

Hermit crabs live inside empty mollusc shells for protection. When danger threatens, they scuttle back inside the shell. Some crabs are safe because they can run quickly enough to escape predators. An example is the ghost or racing crab found on tropical and sub-tropical sandy beaches. The fiddler crabs of muddy and sandy beaches make burrows in which they can take refuge. The male fiddler crab has a large and often brightly coloured claw. This is used for signalling to females or to other males when he is laying claim to his territory.

Another burrowing crab, the soldier crab, settles itself inside an air-tight chamber in the sand during high tide. When the tide goes out, the crab digs itself free again.

Shrimps and prawns

Krill shrimps, or euphausids, also belong to the same group of Crustacea as crabs. Many species of krill shrimps live in the open sea and swim continuously. Some occur in enormous swarms. They form almost the entire diet of whalebone whales that feed off the dense upper layers of krill in the plankton.

Many species of prawns and spiny lobsters are fished for food. Two of the most popular varieties are the giant tiger prawn of the Indo-Pacific region and the Cape crayfish of south African waters. A number of crab species are also fished; the European edible crab and the American blue crab form an important part of many local fisheries.

Copepods

In contrast to the fixed barnacles (*see page 77*), many of the oar-footed crustaceans (copepods) are active swimmers. They use their

Above: A rock-dwelling barnacle has protective limy plates.

Above: The feet of two of these goose barnacles are stretched out fully to sweep the water for minute food particles. Goose barnacles often form clusters on driftwood.

Left: A female copepod with two clusters of eggs attached to the sides of her body.

well developed legs to propel themselves through the water in a series of jerks. A copepod will not sink if it stops swimming for a moment, because it can move its antennae to stay afloat.

Many species of copepods live in the upper regions of the sea where they form the main component of the zooplankton (floating animal organisms). When large numbers of copepods group together, they provide an important food item for many fish. Sometimes, there are so many copepods crowded together that they colour the water.

A number of copepods inhabit freshwater ponds or lakes. Other species are parasites. They live for at least a part of their lives on fish and aquatic mammals. The body shapes of some of these parasitic forms have become so drastically altered that they hardly resemble crustaceans at all.

Smaller crustaceans
Barnacles and copepods are quite familiar crustaceans, but there are many less familiar ones. There are smaller forms like the marine brine shrimps, or branchiopods, that live

Below: The striking ghost or racing crab of tropical beaches has well developed eyes. Its long legs and light body enable it to run quite quickly.

in land-locked salt water lagoons. There are also the tadpole and clam shrimps that are commonly found in salty and brackish water pools.

The brine shrimps have flattened leaf-like limbs, used for swimming and breathing. They feed upon small green algae. Often brine shrimps occur in such vast numbers all in one spot that they turn the water red. Their eggs can withstand long periods of being dry but only hatch when replaced in strong brine. The minute larvae of one species are used by aquarists for feeding the fry of tropical fish.

Bean shrimps
The small bean shrimps, or ostracods, are common inhabitants of ponds and lakes. Less well known are the large number of marine species that occur in rock pools on

the shore. They are found at depths of over 2,000 metres. The limbs and other organs of an ostracod are enclosed within a hinged shell. At first sight, this makes them look like the small bivalve molluscs (*see page 66*).

Some marine ostracods secrete a phosphorescent substance. This appears as a bright, shining cloud in the water. Other species are able to build tubular houses by sticking together grains of sand. Like many other small crustaceans, female ostracods can produce several generations of offspring without the aid of males. The males of some species have never been found. The females of one group of crustaceans carry their eggs in a brood pouch between their legs. The group includes the garden woodlice, beach hoppers and skeleton shrimps.

Variety of insect life

Insects are among the most numerous of all animals. Nearly one million different kinds have so far been discovered. Apart from the oceans, insects live in all corners of the world, from the Arctic Circle to the tropics.

They are found in ponds and streams, in the soil, on plants, and even in our homes.

There are plant-eaters, hunters and scavengers. Some, like butterflies, we consider beautiful and harmless. Others, like flies and mosquitoes, can be harmful and spread disease.

In all there are nearly 50 different insect groups or orders. They can usually be recognized by the way their wings are built. Most numerous are the beetles or Coleoptera (sheath-wings) which have hard outer wings, or elytra. Flies or Diptera (two-wings) have only one pair of wings instead of the usual two pairs. The bees, wasps and ants belong to the Hymenoptera (membrane-wings), whose wings are supported by a network of veins.

Giant swallowtail

Atlas moth

Bee

Wasp

Above: Bees and wasps, both members of the Hymenoptera, have membranous wings. The front pair are usually larger than the hind pair.

Rhinoceros beetle

Goliath beetle

Hercules beetle

Left: This magnificent giant swallowtail, one of the largest butterflies in the world, has wings nearly 30 centimetres across. It is safe from enemies because of its bright colours and unpleasant taste.

Three of the world's largest beetles are shown in this drawing—the rhinoceros beetle **(top left)**, the Goliath beetle **(top right)**, and the Hercules beetle **(left)**. Their horns may look dangerous but the beetles are quite harmless.

Grasshoppers and crickets, including locusts, belong to the Orthoptera (straight-wings). They have long hind legs for jumping, and can also fly. Fleas are also good at jumping but have no wings. They live on other animals.

Bugs (Hemiptera or half-wing) have half of their forewings hardened, and a sharp, sucking mouth for feeding on plant juices or on blood.

On this page are some of the better known insects. They vary in size from midgets, smaller than a pin's head, to giants like the Goliath beetle and the Atlas moth. The Goliath beetle is ten centimetres long and weighs 100 grams. The Atlas moth has a wingspan of 30 centimetres.

An insect's mouth parts vary according to what it feeds on. A honey bee has a long tongue in order to reach the hidden glands of flowers where the nectar is stored. A hawk moth has an even longer tongue which can be pushed into flowers with deep tubes like the honeysuckle. Flowers with flat heads can be visited by insects with short tongues, such as flies and beetles. Flowers need to attract insects with their bright colours and scents because the insects help them to pollinate.

Inside an insect

Insects can be distinguished from all other arthropods because they have a body divided into three parts—the head, the chest or thorax, and the main body or abdomen.

On the head are the mouth parts, a pair of feelers, or antennae, and the eyes. The antennae are sense organs used in feeling and smelling. The eyes are either simple or compound.

The brain has a nerve cord passing along the lower side of the body. This has a swelling or ganglion in each segment.

Food which is eaten passes into a crop where it can be stored. The gizzard is where it is digested. The kidneys get rid of any waste, which is passed out through the rectum.

The blood system is simple. There are few blood vessels. Instead blood flows freely inside the body cavity, and is kept moving by the pumping of the heart. The blood carries food from the intestine to other parts of the body, and waste products back to the kidneys. Insect blood does not carry oxygen as human blood does. This is done instead by the breathing organs or tracheae (*see page 84*).

How insects fly

Since insects have no inside skeleton of bones in their wings, the way they fly is quite different from birds and bats. Muscles which work the wings are attached to the inside of the body wall. The vertical muscles pull the upper wall of

Above: In this model the wings are raised as the upper body wall is pulled down.

Above: Here the muscles have pulled the upper wall back and the wings are dropped.

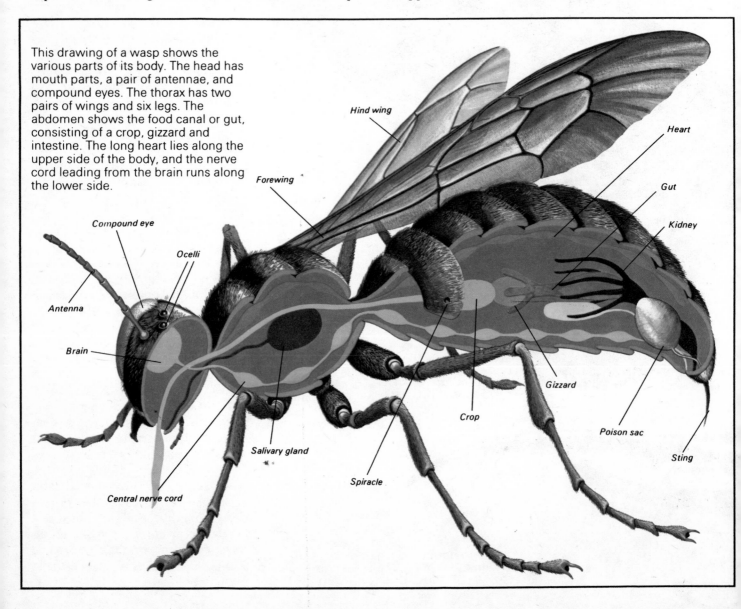

This drawing of a wasp shows the various parts of its body. The head has mouth parts, a pair of antennae, and compound eyes. The thorax has two pairs of wings and six legs. The abdomen shows the food canal or gut, consisting of a crop, gizzard and intestine. The long heart lies along the upper side of the body, and the nerve cord leading from the brain runs along the lower side.

Hind wing

Forewing

Heart

Gut

Kidney

Compound eye

Ocelli

Antenna

Brain

Gizzard

Poison sac

Sting

Salivary gland

Central nerve cord

Spiracle

Crop

the body downwards, and this raises the wings. Then, horizontal muscles pull the upper wall upwards and the wings drop. This can be compared with pulling an oar when rowing a boat.

The up and down wing beats can be as few as five per second in some butterflies, or as many as 1,000 a second in midges. Hawk moths can actually hover in front of flowers as they sip nectar, just as hummingbirds do. Dragonflies and hoverflies are real experts, and can rise and fall, and dart backwards and forwards. The fastest known insect is an Australian dragonfly which can reach 58 kilometres per hour.

Insect eyesight

Eyesight in insects is of a special kind. The simple eyes found mostly in larvae are probably only useful for telling light from dark. The large compound eyes are very efficient in noticing movement. They consist of many separate lenses called ommatidia. These are cone-shaped and each can see a separate part of an object it is looking at. The result is a hazy picture of an image seen in separate parts, rather like a mosaic. However, with so many lenses an insect can spot the slightest movement. If you have ever tried to catch a housefly with your hand you will know how quickly it can see you.

Insects which hunt their prey, such as dragonflies, may have as many as 30,000 ommatidia in each compound eye.

Above: Many experts say that bumble bees do not look as though they have a suitable shape for flying. A bumble bee's body looks too big for its wings! Yet it can of course fly, although not very fast.

The eggs of an insect are formed inside two egg-tubes which lead into the oviduct. As the eggs move down the tube they receive a store of food. They meet the sperms received from the male insect during mating, and become fertilized. Insect eggs vary greatly in shape and appearance, as can be seen when they are under a microscope.

An insect's hard outer skin is made of a dead material called chitin. This is built largely out of waste material, and acts as a support for the body, almost like an outer skeleton. It protects the insect, but more important it prevents the loss of water, without which the insect would soon die. Some insects can live in the driest and hottest places on earth where other animals would soon perish.

Left: This diagram is a section of a compound eye showing the separate ommatidia. Each lens on an insect's eye sees a different part of the object it is looking at.

Right: The result is an ultra-violet image of separate parts. We can see something very similar by looking through frosted glass. This kind of eye helps an insect to detect the slightest movement.

How an insect lives

Insects have many different ways of feeding, depending on what kind of food they eat. The mouth consists of three parts—the mandibles, the maxillae and the labium. Some examples of feeding are shown on this page.

Hunting insects, such as some beetles, wasps and dragonflies, have powerful mandibles, or jaws, with which they can catch and chew up their food. They are usually swift moving in order to catch their prey. Most caterpillars also have strong jaws for eating plants. The grubs of the wood-boring beetle can even chew through wood.

Other insects use their mouths for sucking up soft food, such as plant juices or blood. A bug such as a greenfly, has a sharp labium which pierces a leaf in order to suck up the sap. Water bugs catch and suck out the contents of their prey. Bugs which feed on other animals suck up their blood. A flea feeds in this way, as do gnats and mosquitoes.

The housefly and its relatives have a pad-like tongue, or proboscis, which is pressed on to their food. Since flies feed on filth as well as human food they cause disease by spreading germs.

Butterflies have long tongues which uncoil when they want to sip nectar from a flower, or drink water. A butterfly can be kept alive simply by feeding it on some sugary water. It requires little energy since it does not grow. On the other hand its caterpillar needs constant feeding because it is growing all the time. Many caterpillars will only feed on a certain food-plant and the mother butterfly seems to know just where to lay her eggs. Some moths are even named after the food which their caterpillars eat, such as the poplar and privet hawk moths.

Sometimes when there is a food shortage insects have to go on a hunger strike, or die. Sometimes, if the weather is right, there is a plague of insects. This happens especially with locusts.

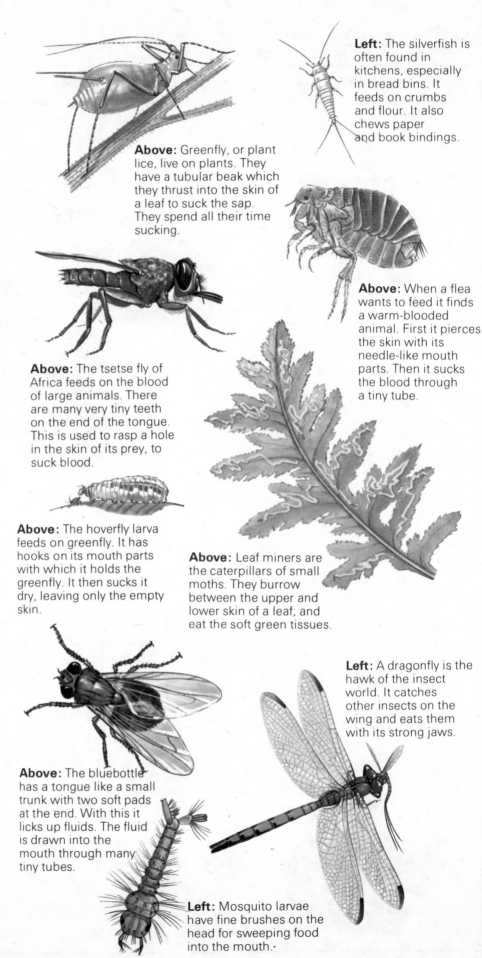

Above: Greenfly, or plant lice, live on plants. They have a tubular beak which they thrust into the skin of a leaf to suck the sap. They spend all their time sucking.

Left: The silverfish is often found in kitchens, especially in bread bins. It feeds on crumbs and flour. It also chews paper and book bindings.

Above: The tsetse fly of Africa feeds on the blood of large animals. There are many very tiny teeth on the end of the tongue. This is used to rasp a hole in the skin of its prey, to suck blood.

Above: When a flea wants to feed it finds a warm-blooded animal. First it pierces the skin with its needle-like mouth parts. Then it sucks the blood through a tiny tube.

Above: The hoverfly larva feeds on greenfly. It has hooks on its mouth parts with which it holds the greenfly. It then sucks it dry, leaving only the empty skin.

Above: Leaf miners are the caterpillars of small moths. They burrow between the upper and lower skin of a leaf, and eat the soft green tissues.

Above: The bluebottle has a tongue like a small trunk with two soft pads at the end. With this it licks up fluids. The fluid is drawn into the mouth through many tiny tubes.

Left: A dragonfly is the hawk of the insect world. It catches other insects on the wing and eats them with its strong jaws.

Left: Mosquito larvae have fine brushes on the head for sweeping food into the mouth.

84

How insects breathe

Unlike humans, insects have no nose with which to breathe in air. Nor do they have lungs. Our lungs pick up the oxygen from the air we breathe in and pass it to the blood. The oxygen is carried by the blood to the various organs in the body.

Insects have little or no oxygen in the blood. Instead, as they breathe, air containing oxygen is passed directly to the body tissue by a complicated system of tubes, called tracheae. These take the place of blood vessels and windpipe. The main tracheae run along and across the body in a ladder-like form, with smaller and smaller branches reaching the different organs. The organs take up the oxygen when it is needed.

The air breathed in enters the tracheae through a number of holes, called spiracles, along the sides of the body. In some insects air can be stored inside the body in special air-sacs.

If you watch an insect it is possible to see a pumping action in the abdomen as a fresh supply of air is pushed in. In hot weather or in dry surroundings the spiracles close to stop the insect losing water.

Breathing underwater

Water insects have two ways of breathing. Some insects come up to the surface for their supply of air while others can breathe underwater. A water beetle or water bug rises to the surface and collects a bubble of air which sticks to its body as it dives under. Many insect larvae have a breathing tube, or siphon, which can be pushed through the water surface to reach the air. A gnat larva will hang on to the surface by its siphon.

There are some insect larvae which have special organs for breathing underwater. These organs are called tracheal gills.

Like fish gills, they can pick up the dissolved oxygen from the water. Rows of gills occur along the sides of a mayfly, and they twitch constantly. This disturbs the water and helps to remove the oxygen from it. The stone-fly larva is another insect which breathes in this fashion.

Dragonfly larvae use two methods. The delicate damselfly nymphs have long gills at the end of their bodies, whereas the larger hunting dragonflies have gills inside, at the end of the food canal.

Unusual mud-dwellers

Bloodworms, really the larvae of certain midges, are coloured bright red because they contain haemoglobin. This is the substance that colours human blood but it is rare in insects. It carries the oxygen around the body. Since bloodworms live in mud where there is little oxygen, the haemoglobin helps to keep them alive.

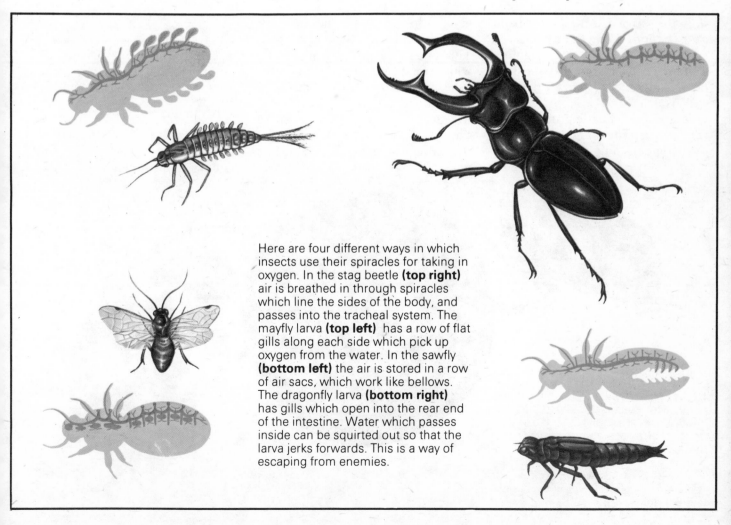

Here are four different ways in which insects use their spiracles for taking in oxygen. In the stag beetle **(top right)** air is breathed in through spiracles which line the sides of the body, and passes into the tracheal system. The mayfly larva **(top left)** has a row of flat gills along each side which pick up oxygen from the water. In the sawfly **(bottom left)** the air is stored in a row of air sacs, which work like bellows. The dragonfly larva **(bottom right)** has gills which open into the rear end of the intestine. Water which passes inside can be squirted out so that the larva jerks forwards. This is a way of escaping from enemies.

Insect life-cycles

Humans, like other mammals, grow up with little change to the body, apart from size. Insects pass through different stages, called metamorphoses. In most orders there are four stages—the egg, the larva, the pupa or chrysalis, and the adult. A butterfly starts as an egg, hatches into a caterpillar, then changes into a chrysalis, and emerges as a butterfly. A housefly lays eggs which hatch into maggots, change into pupae, then become flies. Only adult insects have wings, but they do not grow. It is the larva, the caterpillar or maggot, which grows.

In some groups the metamorphosis is incomplete. In dragonflies the larva, called a nymph, grows up in water. There is no pupa stage. It climbs out and changes directly into a dragonfly. The same happens with grasshoppers, cockroaches and mayflies.

Since an insect has a hard outer skin the larva has to moult from time to time. It crawls out of its old skin by means of a wriggling motion. Then it can grow a little more until the new skin hardens.

It is the larva which lives the longest—some beetle grubs live for three years. The adult stage is very short, lasting only a day for some mayflies.

In warm countries insect life carries on normally throughout the year, but in countries with a cold winter there is a rest period, called hibernation. This is when the insect hides away from frost in a dark corner, sometimes in adult form, sometimes in an earlier stage of development. For example, the tortoiseshell butterfly hibernates as an adult, the cabbage white butterfly as a chrysalis. Other insects such as the greenfly lay winter eggs, and then die.

Home for maggots

The life-cycle of a common insect such as the blow-fly or bluebottle provides just one example of how an insect changes from an egg into an adult. The adult female searches for meat on which to lay her eggs. Hundreds of eggs soon hatch out, and the maggots begin feeding.

After moulting a number of times, each fully grown maggot leaves the food and finds a dark place in which to become a pupa. This is usually in the soil. People who breed maggots as bait for fishermen hang rotten meat in sheds, with a tray underneath. Maggots crawl out and fall on to the tray. In the same way, farmers who want to get rid of maggots place manure over trays of water so that they fall in and drown.

Breeding time

Unlike snails and worms, insects consist of separate females and males which come together in order to mate. Most males find a female either by scent or sight.

Some female moths give off a scent which can be picked up by a male over a long distance. The emperor moth can detect the scent of

Above: The praying mantis on the right shows how this insect gets its name. Here it is displaying before a male with which it will shortly mate.

a female as much as 1.5 kilometres away.

Other insects which have good eyesight will chase after a female in order to mate. Maybe this is where colour helps, as in the case of

Right: Dung beetles belong to a large family which includes the giant Goliath beetle. They are usually found close to animal burrows, or near animal droppings and rotting wood. These two have collected a ball of dung which will be used as a store of food. It is placed in a burrow where the female lays her eggs.

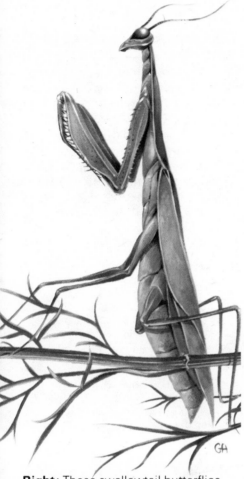

Right: These swallowtail butterflies are joined together during mating. The female will lay her eggs shortly after they separate.

dragonflies and butterflies.

Although insects probably cannot hear as we do, they are very sensitive to vibrations. In flight, the wing beats give off a note of a certain pitch. Experiments have shown that male mosquitoes are attracted to the females by their wing beats.

Whatever the attraction, once a pair of mature insects meet they will mate. With some bees, ants and mayflies this takes place in the air, in a "mating flight".

Mating is usually a straightforward affair, although in some cases there may be a kind of courtship. Some male butterflies appear to dance around a female, other insects may rear up and move their legs, as the praying mantis is doing on this page.

Some insects lay eggs soon after mating, others much later. A queen bee or queen termite can even continue to lay eggs throughout her whole life.

Eggs are laid through an opening called an ovipositor, singly or in batches. The mother chooses a spot where the right food can be found by the young. For example, a blow-fly chooses meat, a cabbage white butterfly chooses a cabbage and a tortoiseshell a nettle. Dragonflies choose a place near or on water where the nymphs will grow.

The number of offspring produced by insects varies a great deal. Many generations a year are born from aphids, such as greenfly. The housefly lays a batch of about 150 eggs six times during her life. A mayfly lays a single family, lives for a day, and then dies.

Right: This lacewing has just laid her eggs and suspended them from slender stalks. They hang from the underside of leaves so that they will be hidden from birds.

Insect defence

An animal can defend itself from enemies by running away, hiding, or imitating something which is unpleasant or looks uninteresting. Insects use all these methods, and the pictures below show examples.

Insects do not move fast, but their darting movements help them to dodge out of harm's way. A grasshopper will leap away, a dragonfly will dart to one side, and a water beetle will dive.

Insects which hide away to avoid enemies are also safe from the frost in winter, or from drying up in hot weather. Under a log, down a hole or in a hollow tree the air is still and moist, and also free from frost. If you disturb insects by lifting the log or opening the hole they will automatically seek cover. This is because many insects avoid the light and search for dark places.

Ways of hiding
Another method of hiding is using camouflage. Although the insect is in full view it is not seen because it blends with the surroundings. Colour is a help. A green caterpillar hides against a green leaf. So does a grasshopper.

Apart from the right colour, many insects also have markings, spots or stripes, which break up the body outline. The brindled beauty moth (*below*) makes a perfect match against the bark of the tree. So does the oleander hawk moth which flies after dark and rests during the day. Compare it to camouflage worn by soldiers in wartime.

Another method of hiding is to look like an uninteresting object. Some moth caterpillars, called loopers, arch their bodies as they crawl. When resting they stand out stiffly from a branch to resemble a twig. Gardeners pruning their plants have even mistaken them for real twigs and cut them off. Stick insects also look like twigs. They tuck their legs close to their long bodies when resting. Other insects look like bird droppings, fruit, thorns and leaves.

Perhaps the most famous example is the Indian leaf butterfly which looks exactly like a dead leaf. It even has spots looking like mildew.

Below: These insects defend themselves from enemies by using colours and shapes which match their surroundings. The oleander hawk moth and the brindled beauty are well hidden when at rest because the colours and markings on their wings blend with the surfaces on which they rest. The looper caterpillar and stick insect both resemble twigs. The famous Indian leaf butterfly is a perfect copy of a dead leaf. The wing tip touches the branch to look like a leaf stalk.

Oleander hawk moth

Brindled beauty moth

Looper caterpillar

Stick insect

Indian leaf butterfly

Clever disguise

Colour has different uses. It may help similar insects to recognize one another, but how do they avoid their enemies? During flight a butterfly looks brightly coloured, but as it alights the colours disappear. This is because only the upper surface of the wings is bright. As the wings close over its back the colours are hidden, and only the dull undersides appear. With moths it is the other way round. The wings close across the back. The upper sides are camouflaged and the bright colours beneath are hidden.

Another method of defence is to

Below: The flashing "eye-spots" of the owl butterfly will startle an enemy, giving the moth a chance to escape. The bombardier beetle makes use of a "gas attack". Wasps are painful to touch and warn us and other animals off by their bright warning colours. The monarch butterfly is unpleasant to eat. These two are copied by the wasp beetle and false monarch, which are both harmless. The ladybird is left alone by birds because it has a very nasty taste, even though its bright colouring makes it noticeable.

scare off an enemy. Bright circles called "eye-spots" can look quite startling. The well-named owl butterfly (*below*) opens its wings as it flies off, and the eye-spots cause the enemy to pause so that the butterfly can escape.

Weapons may also be used as a means of defence. The bombardier beetle squirts an unpleasant fluid in the face of an enemy.

Red for danger

To make these defences more effective, some insects are coloured with the "warning colours" that we use on our roads. A wasp has bands of yellow and black which we soon recognize. They warn us not to touch because of the wasp's sting. A ladybird, coloured red or yellow with black spots is also avoided, especially by birds. This is because of its unpleasant taste.

Many brightly coloured butterflies also taste unpleasant. The monarch (*below*) is an example. The false monarch on the other hand is quite tasty, but because it looks like the true monarch it is left alone. The harmless wasp

beetles, as well as many flies, resemble wasps. Actually, anyone who knows insects can tell the difference. Wasps have two pairs of wings—flies only one pair. This copying is called mimicry, and helps to protect harmless insects.

A walk around the garden, down a country lane, or through a wood, may look empty of wildlife, until something moves. What usually happens is that a resting insect remains very still and uses its camouflage for protection. If it is disturbed it will fly off very quickly. If it has eye-spots it will use them to frighten the enemy off. Insects with warning colours are left well alone.

All these methods of defence are useful to insects. In some cases they work for the enemy as well. The praying mantis (*on page 86*) resembles a leaf and is well camouflaged from birds. On the other hand this helps it to approach its prey without being seen.

In nature camouflage is a serious game of hide-and-seek, and is useful to both the hunter and the hunted.

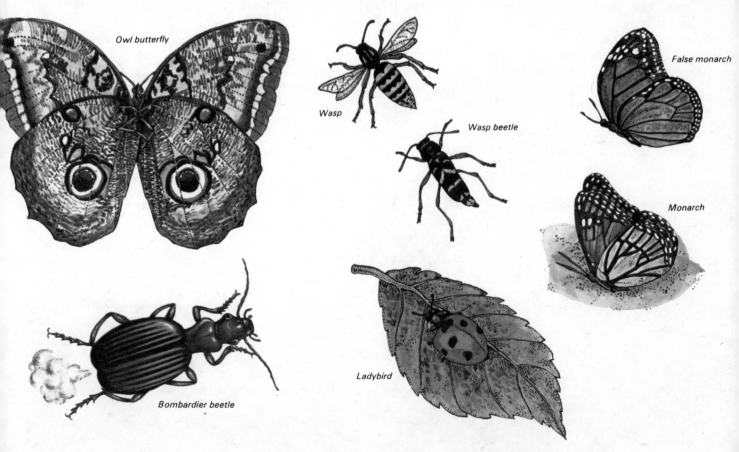

Owl butterfly

Wasp

Wasp beetle

False monarch

Monarch

Bombardier beetle

Ladybird

Water insects and beetles

Beetles are amongst the easiest insects to recognize. They have armoured bodies and appear to have no wings. Actually a pair of hind-wings are folded up beneath the horny fore-wings, called elytra. Most beetles can fly, and are often active at night, but mainly they spend their lives on the ground, or among vegetation. Some beetles also live in fresh water.

Beetles range in size from less than a millimetre long, to giants from the tropics such as the Goliath and Hercules beetles (*page 81*). They can grow to ten centimetres and weigh up to 100 grams.

Beetles belong to the group called the Coleoptera. It contains the largest number of insects and there are some 250,000 different kinds. Most are tiny and harmless, but some do a lot of damage, both to food and to property.

The grub of the click beetle, called a wireworm, damages grass and crops by attacking the roots. So does the grub of the cockchafer or maybug which zooms about the sky on summer evenings.

Bark beetles lay their eggs on the bark of trees. The grub then bores a system of tunnels in the bark which damages the tree. The woodworm damages furniture in the same way, while the timbers of older houses are invaded by the larger death-watch beetle.

Like the "black beetle" or cockroach, many beetles are scavengers and feed on all sorts of rubbish, neglected food and dead animals. Burying beetles cover up a dead body by removing the soil from underneath so that it is covered. They usually work in pairs. The female then lays her eggs and will feed the young on the carcass.

The meal worm is the grub of another beetle which can do great harm to grain in store rooms. But it also has a use to man, and is bred in large numbers as food for cage birds, and other pets.

The violet ground beetle has no wings but can run very fast. It is found in cellars and under logs. It hunts for its food, as does the green tiger beetle which is found in sandy places.

One of the more unusual beetles is the glow-worm. It is the female which is grub-like and able to give off a light. It does not travel much, and small colonies of glow-worms light up in the dark to attract the males which are able to fly. Its favourite food is snails.

Right: The larvae of the maybug and the click beetle live in the soil and can do serious harm to plants.

Below: Different types of ground beetle are found in many parts of the world.

Above: The dung beetle has gathered together a ball of dung which it will store in a hole somewhere. Eggs are laid nearby so that a ready meal is waiting for the grubs when they hatch out. Such beetles are usually found near animal burrows, or close to animal droppings.

Maybug

Click beetle

Maybug grub

Wireworm

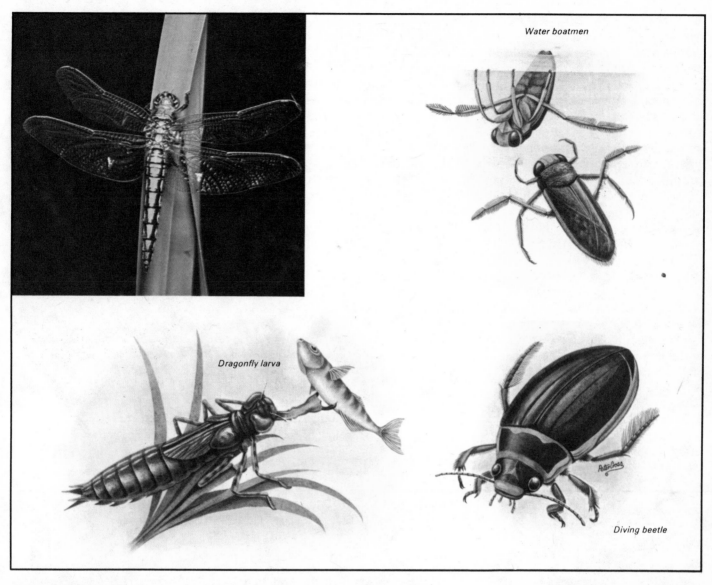

Water boatmen

Dragonfly larva

Diving beetle

Beetles of the pond

Not all insects that live in water spend their whole lives there. Dragonflies live in both water and air. The female lays her eggs at the waterside or drops them on the surface. The eggs which hatch out grow up as nymphs. They usually remain hidden among water plants. They have powerful hinged jaws which can be shot forward with great speed to catch a passing tadpole or fish. When fully grown in one or two years, the nymph crawls up a water plant into the air. The body slowly dries, splits down the back, and the dragonfly can crawl out. At first the wings are crumpled but they slowly spread out as blood is pumped into the veins. It can take an hour or two before the dragonfly is ready to fly away.

Above: A dragonfly pauses on a waterside plant to sun itself, and a water boatman surfaces for air. A dragonfly larva has caught a fish, and a diving beetle swims below the surface of the water. All this activity can be seen by anyone standing quietly at a pond-side during the summer months, when the insects are at their busiest.

The water boatman has an odd habit of swimming upside-down. It swims with jerky movements, using its oar-like hind legs. Now and then it surfaces for air. Water stick insects and water scorpions are named after their shapes, but are also water bugs.

The great diving beetle is a fierce hunter. It is well built for swimming, with a streamlined body. There are few other water animals, including fish, which are safe from its attack.

A common sight in ponds are the whirligig beetles moving in rapid circles on the surface. Here too you can see the pond skaters walking on the surface film.

This film is invisible but it is strong enough to support these water bugs. It also works like a magnet for mosquito larvae which can hang from the surface. There are two kinds of mosquito larvae. Only the larvae that hang horizontal to the surface carry the germs of malaria.

Two dangers which face water insects are freezing and drying up. However, they are safe under the ice during winter since water is always above freezing point. If the pond dries up they must fly away or bury themselves in the mud.

91

Social insects

Bees, wasps and ants belong to the order of Hymenoptera. They are among the most highly organized insects, living in colonies.

Among social wasps only the queen wasp hibernates through the winter. On waking, she starts a new colony by building a "queen nest", about the size of a ping-pong ball. It is usually in a hole in the ground or in the roof of a building. It contains a few cells in which she lays her eggs. The grubs which hatch are fed by her until they hatch into workers. All the workers are female.

Slowly the numbers build up, and in some strange way each worker takes on a different task. Some collect material for enlarging the nest, by scraping off bits of wood or chewing up paper. Others remove the soil to make room for the growing nest, which may end up the size of a football. Yet others attend the queen who does nothing but lay more eggs. There are guards at the doorway, and nurses to feed the grubs.

By late summer the colony may contain 20,000 wasps. But wasps, unlike bees, do not store food, so that with the approach of winter most of the colony dies off. The workers are sterile and cannot lay eggs. What happens now is that some grubs turn into males, or drones, and others into fertile females. These will mate together. The drones then die, but the young queens live through the winter and start fresh colonies the following spring.

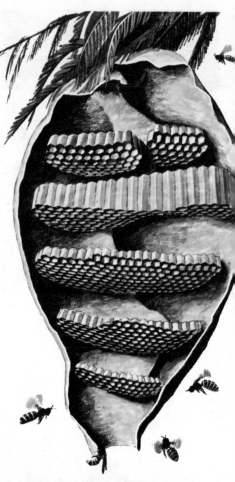

Right: The wasp's nest is entered at the bottom. Notice that the combs are horizontal, with the cells opening downwards.

Below: Termite hills like the one below are a common sight in Australia and Africa. This one has been broken open to show the many tunnels inside.

Below: This queen termite, which has grown to an enormous size, is being attended by her workers who act as nurses. She is just an egg-laying machine, producing thousands of eggs each day.

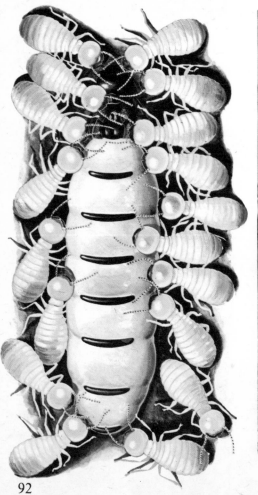

Above: A swarm of driver ants has raided the nest of a solitary wasp and is dragging away the wasp grub.

The life of bees is similar. Those we know best are the hive bees which have been domesticated from wild bees, and are kept by bee-keepers. They too have many workers doing different tasks. In addition they store food as honey and can last through the winter. A hive may contain 50,000 bees.

In a wasp's nest the combs are built horizontally with the cells opening downwards. In a bee's hive they are vertical with openings sideways so that the honey does not fall out.

Fresh cells are built by the worker bees. They are made of beeswax and filled with honey. The queen lays her eggs in the nursery cells. Male or drone bees develop in separate drone-cells, and young queens in much larger queen-cells. It is believed that a worker, a drone, or a queen bee is produced according to the kind of food each bee is given.

One interesting discovery is the way in which a worker will collect the pollen from some flowers and return to the hive to tell the others. By turning round in circles and wiggling his abdomen, the worker can tell the other workers how far off the flowers are, and which direction to take. This is known as the "dance of the bees".

Bees have a habit of swarming when the colony gets too big. The queen takes off and some of the workers follow. They sometimes settle in very odd places, like a car and even on a man's hat. The workers left behind in the hive will choose a new queen.

Tropical colonists

Termites belong to the Isoptera order and live in the tropics. Some burrow into wood and cause damage to buildings. Others nest below ground, then build upwards to form a tall ant-hill full of tunnels. In Australia these mounds can be as high as seven metres.

A termite's hill is made of mud and saliva, which sets almost as hard as iron. It is started by a male and a female. After a mating flight they settle down and produce the first grubs. Some of these do the building and food gathering. Others with large heads and strong jaws act as soldiers to guard the nest. Meanwhile, the queen retires to her "royal" chamber. She grows to an enormous size producing thousands of eggs daily. From time to time young males and females leave the nest and fly off to start fresh colonies.

An interesting fact about these highly organized insects is that some ants and termites will gather fungus plants, and grow them in a "garden" as food for the grubs. Ants will also "milk" aphids for their honeydew.

The lives of insects are very much affected by temperature and weather. For example, when winged ants are ready to swarm they wait for a summer's day when it is warm and still, and all swarm together over a wide area. If the weather changes they all go back to their nests, and wait for another suitable day.

The birth of a bee

A queen bee leaves the hive, followed by the drones, on a mating flight.

After the flight the queen starts to lay eggs in each cell until she dies.

Eggs hatch in about three days and are fed on honey by the worker bees.

The grubs continue to grow. Some will be workers, others drones and queens.

The grub changes shape. The pupa lies facing the open end of the cell.

Finally a young bee emerges from the cell to join the colony.

Insect pests

With so many insects in the world it is not surprising that some are harmful. They can damage our food and property, our crops and garden plants, and also spread disease.

Among plant pests, some of the most serious are the aphids, which include the well-known enemy of the gardener – the greenfly. Apart from feeding on plant sap, some aphids carry minute germs, called viruses, which cause disease to flowers and fruit. Vegetables can also suffer.

Aphids are small insects usually coloured brown or green. Some of them can fly. They breed in enormous numbers over many generations and all the offspring are infertile females. When mature, these females reproduce without mating. As autumn approaches, aphids produce both male and female offspring. The males mate with the females, who then lay eggs which hatch in the spring.

Some aphids produce a fluffy wax. The woolly aphid, seen on apple trees, is a common example.

Other plant bugs, called scale insects or mealy bugs, also breed in huge numbers. One female may lay as many as 1,000 eggs. They attack trees and may kill them. Such insects are often wingless and legless, with a waxy scale.

Far more serious damage to plants is caused by locusts. These live in warm countries and resemble large grasshoppers. Most

Above: This mother aphid is producing a family of young females. Thousands are born every summer, and can cause much damage to plants. This greenfly is commonly found on roses.

Below left: Woolly aphids look like lumps of cotton wool and often appear on apple trees. Here they are being attacked by ladybirds.

Right: A mosquito has settled on somebody's skin and is driving in its sharp tongue to suck up blood. If it should carry a germ the person might catch a disease.

years they go their own separate ways, but then, maybe due to a weather change, they start to band together.

More and more eggs are laid in burrows in the soil. The young locusts which emerge are called hoppers, since they cannot fly. They start on a march, all in the same direction, eating everything in their path. Sometimes they can be stopped by spreading poison bait in their way. With the final moult the wings develop and the locusts take to the air. Poison is sprayed from planes to try to stop them, but it is usually hopeless.

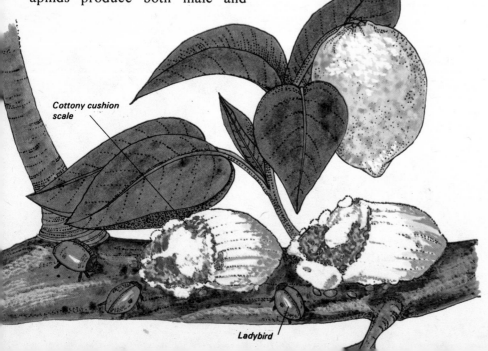

Cottony cushion scale

Ladybird

Swarms may travel across vast distances, and weigh a thousand tonnes. Each locust eats its own weight in plant food in a day.

Diseases spread among humans by insects can be very serious. This is especially true of the diseases carried by mosquitoes. They include malaria, which was once common in England and other developed nations; elephantiasis, which causes huge swelling of the arms and legs; yellow fever, and a worm disease called filariasis.

The malaria germ attacks the blood, and causes high fever. A mosquito bites a person with the illness. The germs multiply in its body and enter the salivary glands. The mosquito then bites another person, and germs in its saliva are squirted into the bite. One human cannot infect another – the germs must pass through a mosquito first. To fight malaria, poisons are spread onto still water where the mosquitoes breed.

Some fleas also spread sickness. The germ carried by the rat flea which lives on black rats, caused an enormous number of deaths during the Middle Ages. The disease was called the Black Death, and in Europe one person in every four died from it.

Sleeping sickness
The tsetse fly of Africa has been a problem for centuries. Its bite can pass on a germ which causes sleeping sickness. It attacks the spinal cord and travels up to the brain, causing the patient to become tired and sleepy. It can end in death. Before it was possible to control the illness, the west coast of Africa was known as the "white man's grave".

The tsetse fly lives in undergrowth close to water, and gives birth to young rather than laying eggs. By the clearing of the banks of lakes and rivers, and the use of sprays, the fly has now been driven away in many places, but not everywhere.

One very common disease-carrier is the housefly. It is a common nuisance in homes and places where it can find food and shelter. The real danger is from any dirt the fly settles on, and the way that it feeds. Its mouth has a sucker-like pad which presses on to food and softens it with a drop of saliva. In this manner germs are spread from dirt to food. There is particular danger from human excreta. Germs that breed there can cause outbreaks of typhoid, dysentery and other stomach

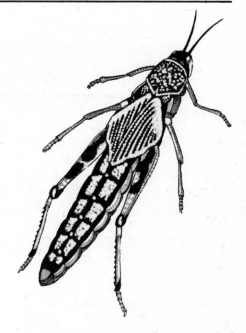

Above: This young locust, still a hopper, has not yet grown its wings.

Above: Fleas can be recognized by their flattened bodies, minus wings.

upsets. This is why we should use the toilet so that all our waste is flushed away, and why it is important that we wash our hands.

Butterflies are usually looked upon as harmless and beautiful. But occasionally, in good summers, swarms of them, especially cabbage whites, will destroy a farmer's vegetable crop. This may also happen with the Colorado beetle from America. It attacks potato fields. It is easy to recognize as its body is brightly striped in black and yellow.

In order to control pests it helps to know about their habits. Sometimes one insect can be used to catch another. In some places where aphids do harm, ladybirds have been bred and set free to attack the aphids.

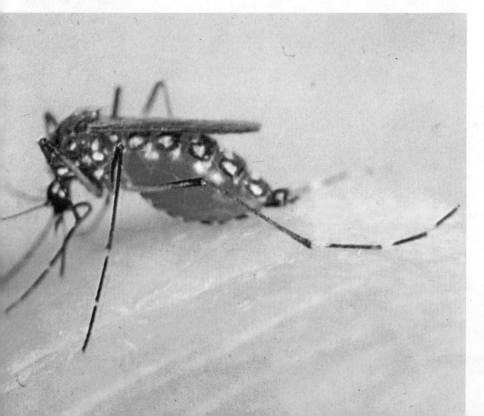

Types of fish

Fish are found wherever there is enough water to live in. They inhabit the seas, freshwater ponds, lakes and rivers, swamps and even puddles. They can exist in warm tropical waters and below ice.

Fish range in size from midgets two centimetres long, to giants like the whale shark, which is up to 14 metres long. Altogether there are 25,000 different kinds of fish.

They can be divided into two main groups. The bony fish are the most abundant. They are found in all types of water. For example, the herring lives in the sea, the trout in a river, and the stickleback in a pond. The second group, the cartilaginous fish, have a much softer skeleton and include sharks, rays and skates. All the fish in this group live in the sea.

Fish were the first animals on earth to grow an internal skeleton of backbone and a skull with jaws and teeth. All vertebrates are descended from them.

The coelacanth was thought to have been extinct for some 70 million years when one was found in the sea off the coast of East Africa. The first catch was made in 1939 by some fishermen, and others have been netted since.

Prehistoric survivor

The coelacanth is an interesting fish which has remained virtually unchanged since the Devonian Period, some 300 million years ago. It has curious fins on stalks quite unlike the fins on any other living fish. Another odd kind of fish is the lungfish which can breathe air if the lake water it lives in dries up. Lungfish burrow into the mud to wait until the rains come.

Since fish live in fresh or salt water, and at all depths, they feed differently and vary in shape. A fish like a salmon which has to swim in moving water, often against the current, has a streamlined shape. In a pond the water is still, so a carp or goldfish moves more slowly. Some slow-moving fish with fat and rounded bodies are protected with spines or armour. Long and slender fish like

Below: Some examples of fish with different shapes and habits. The eel can wriggle into holes in search of food, and may even travel overland. The manta ray swims like a huge bat and is harmless. The strange-looking hammerhead shark will follow ships in the hope of finding food. The thresher shark frightens its prey by lashing its tail from side to side and stirring up the water. The dangerous blue shark is a killer, and will even attack humans. Some kinds of shark are hunted by man for their meat and oil.

Common eel

Manta ray

Hammerhead shark

Thresher shark

Blue shark

the eel can wriggle into hiding places to escape from their enemies.

Fish that live near the sea bottom have flatter bodies. Flatfish such as the sole and plaice actually rest on their sides. When a baby plaice hatches it is a tiny but perfectly normal-looking fish. Then it grows thinner and deeper in shape. The skull starts to twist and one eye moves over to meet the other. The adult plaice can lie almost undetected on the sea bed.

Among the cartilaginous fish, shape also varies. A shark swims freely and is streamlined for fast movement when hunting. Skates and rays have flattened bodies with widespread "wings" which are actually the pectoral fins. They live mostly on the sea bed and feed on

Below: Most fish swim away from danger, but this clownfish dives among the tentacles of a sea anemone where it is perfectly safe. For some reason, it is not harmed by the anemone's stings.

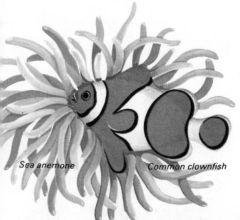

Sea anemone   Common clownfish

shellfish. The largest ray is the giant manta or devil-fish. It is up to seven metres wide, and weighs 1,000 kilograms. Like the whale shark, it is harmless.

Strange kinds of fish live down in the ocean depths where it is dark. Many of them possess organs which can light up. This must help them to find one another, especially for mating. One kind of fish has a tiny male which fixes itself to the female and never lets go. Scientists have learned much about this deep-sea world by going down in special pressurized chambers called bathyspheres.

Finding food

Fish feed in very different ways. A hunting fish like the pike remains hidden among the water plants, then suddenly rushes out to catch its prey. A carp will browse quietly on water plants. A catfish grubs in the mud using its whiskers, or barbels, to pick up food.

Angler fish have a kind of rod with a "bait" on top of their heads. This attracts other fish which are then suddenly snapped up in its huge mouth. The archer fish of tropical Asia comes to the surface and spits a drop of water at an insect to knock it off a branch.

There are some fish which are filter-feeders, like many whales. The giant whale shark takes in water full of tiny sea animals called plankton. The water passes out of the gills and the trapped plankton is swallowed.

Below: Fishermen catch many kinds of sea fish for food, such as the dogfish, the grey mullet and the Norway haddock. Herrings, cod and flatfish are also common varieties seen at the fishmonger's.

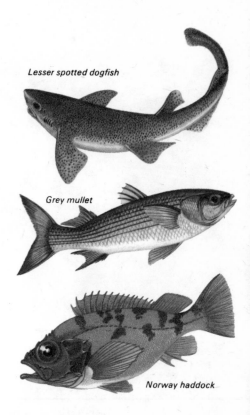

Lesser spotted dogfish

Grey mullet

Norway haddock

Below: These strange fish all live in the deep oceans. Most of them are small with large eyes. Some produce lights in special glands. They are able to stand the enormous pressure of the water at these great depths but die if brought to the surface. Life in the ocean depths is still largely unknown to man. It is difficult to explore in very deep water because of the enormous water pressure.

Angler fish   Opisthoproctus

Ipnops

Structure of a fish

Below: This fish, a perch, shows the various fins on its body. Note that perch have two dorsal fins. The open mouth shows the tongue and gills. Inside are the stomach and intestine, and the sex organs. Both have a common opening, the cloaca.

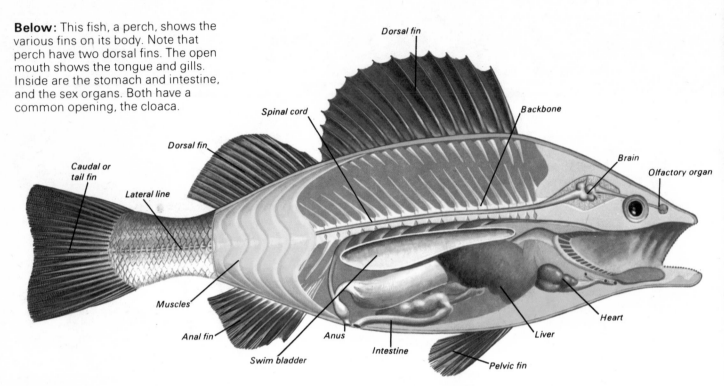

You can recognize a fish in several ways. All fish live in water. A fish also has gills, fins and a covering of scales. There are two pairs of fins – the pectorals in front and the pelvics behind. Normally there is a single dorsal fin on the back, but in the largest group of fish, the perch, there are two. At the base of the tail, near the rear opening, is the anal fin.

How fish eat
Food which passes into the mouth is swallowed whole or in lumps. Hunting fish have sharp teeth for catching and tearing up their food. Others have more flattened teeth

Below: The head of this salmon is cut away to show the gill system. This consists of rows of gill arches lined with blood vessels, which pick up oxygen from the water as it passes through the gill slits. In a bony fish the gills are protected by a covering, the operculum.

for crushing food such as shellfish. Most fish have teeth either on the jaw bones or on bones further down the throat. Food passes into the stomach and intestine and is absorbed into the blood and circulated round the body.

A special sense
A fish's body is supported by a skeleton of backbone, ribs and a skull. The brain has a main nerve cord passing down the back through the backbone. Nerves branch out from the sides of the nerve cord and lead to sensitive "pits" in the body wall. These pits form rows along each side of the body, which appear as a dark line, called the lateral line. A fish can "hear" with this line by picking up vibrations in the water. This explains, for example, why a goldfish does not hit the glass sides of its aquarium. As the fish moves, it sends out pressure waves which

bounce back off the glass like an echo. This warns the fish of an obstacle ahead, even though it cannot see the glass. Fish navigate in this same way when they are in their natural habitat.

Keeping afloat
Bony fish have an air-sac or swim bladder which takes the place of lungs. The bladder contains gas and can change pressure to match the water pressure outside. In effect, this makes the fish weightless so it can "hang" in the water at different depths. In other words, the fish can stop swimming and take a rest when it wants to.

Sharks and rays have no swim bladder and will sink if they stop swimming. It is their body shape that helps to give them lift. The pectoral fins at the front work a bit like an aircraft's wings, while at the back the large upper lobe of the tail tends to give the fish lift.

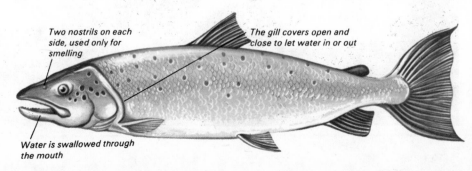

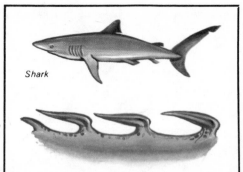

Above: Sharks and rays have no gill covering. The shape of the tail helps in balance, since sharks have no swim bladder.

Bichir

Above: This African fish, a bichir, belongs to an ancient group of bony fish. It is related to the lobe-finned coelacanth on page 96.

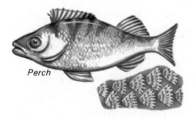

Perch

Above: The perch has scales with spines along its hind edges.

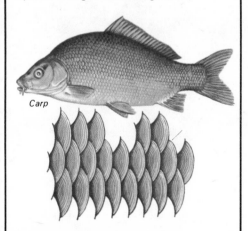

Carp

Above: The carp has scales in regular rows which are rounded. It is a vegetarian whereas the perch is a hunter. Carp are intelligent fish, quick to recognize the danger of the fisherman's bait, so they are often difficult to catch.

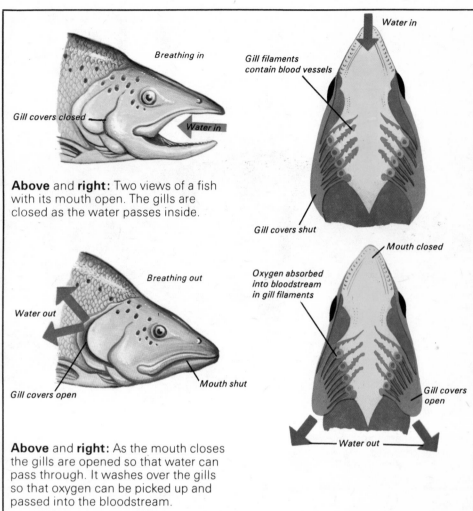

Above and **right:** Two views of a fish with its mouth open. The gills are closed as the water passes inside.

Above and **right:** As the mouth closes the gills are opened so that water can pass through. It washes over the gills so that oxygen can be picked up and passed into the bloodstream.

Gills

Fish breathe the oxygen dissolved in water through their gills. On each gill arch is a lining of delicate skin full of blood vessels. These pick up oxygen as water passes through the gill slits. The oxygen dissolves in the blood and carbon dioxide is given off into the water. In bony fish the gills are covered and protected by a shield which is called an operculum.

Scales

Fish scales vary enormously. Sharks and rays are covered with hard scales resembling minute enamel teeth, making the skin rough and painful to touch. Such skin does have a use for man, however. It is sometimes used as a kind of leather for polishing and is called shagreen.

Most other fish have scales in regular rows. Carp-like fish have round and bony scales. Perch scales have little spines along the hind edge. Catfish are scaleless and covered with a leathery skin. The sturgeon has only a few rows of large, bony scales. The eggs of the female sturgeon are eaten as a delicacy in many parts of the world, and are known as caviare. You can of course eat the eggs of other female fish. At the fishmonger's this is usually called hard roe. Soft roe is the testis of the male fish.

The sense of smell

A fish's nostrils do not breathe in air, except in the case of lungfish, but they are connected to the brain by nerves. They are used for smelling and are of particular help in finding food. Sharks especially are attracted by the smell of blood. They have an extremely acute sense of smell.

How fish swim and see

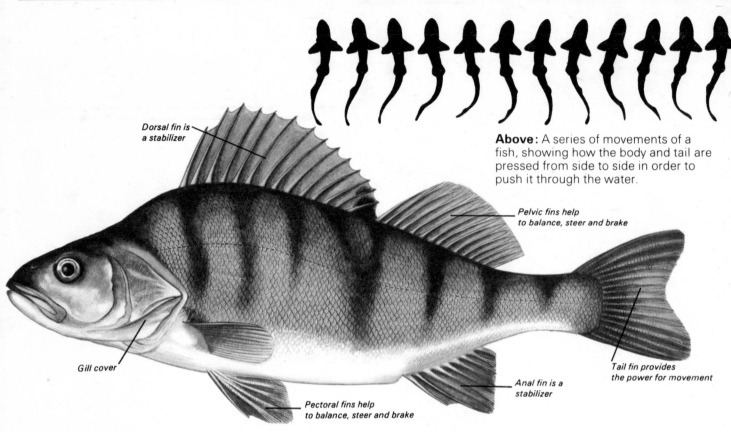

Dorsal fin is a stabilizer

Above: A series of movements of a fish, showing how the body and tail are pressed from side to side in order to push it through the water.

Pelvic fins help to balance, steer and brake

Gill cover

Pectoral fins help to balance, steer and brake

Anal fin is a stabilizer

Tail fin provides the power for movement

Above: The perch, which is a hunting fish, has its body marked with vertical stripes. These match the stems of water plants among which it lives and help to hide it from both its enemies and its prey.

Since fish have no arms or legs they do not swim as we do. Instead, they use the muscles running down their body, to wriggle from side to side. They also lash their upright tail from one side to the other to push against the water and drive themselves forwards. The average fish has a streamlined shape that tapers towards the tail so that the water parts more easily as it moves.

Dolphins and whales, which are sea mammals, swim in a similar fashion, except that their tails are horizontal, and their bodies move up and down.

Fins

In most fish the tail fin is the main propeller driving the fish forwards. The dorsal fin on the back and the anal fin near the tail help to keep the fish balanced. The remaining pairs of fins – the pectorals and the pelvics – are mainly used by the fish for steering.

Flatfish, such as sole or plaice, swim with their flattened bodies sideways, and use their fins in a wave-like action. Skates and rays do the same, but in their case the body is in the upright position.

A flying fish is a good swimmer but it can also glide over the water surface. Moving its tail rapidly from side to side it "taxies" over the surface, then takes off by spreading out its large pectoral fins. It can glide for up to 400 metres, and keep airborne for 20 seconds.

Colour camouflage

Camouflage is a feature of many fish and gives them protection. They also use it to remain hidden when after prey. Unlike land animals, a fish can be seen from all sides. To make it less visible the upper side is dark and the lower side pale. Seen from above, the dark back matches more closely the sea bed or river bottom. From below, the pale underside blends with the sky.

Some fish are camouflaged with spots or stripes. This helps them to match their surroundings. A trout is spotted to imitate the pebbles

over which it rests. A perch or pike will hide among water plants, waiting for something to approach before darting out to catch it. Its body is striped to blend with the stalks of rushes or reeds.

Flatfish are coloured to match the sea bed. As it settles, a flatfish will wriggle its body to stir up the sand, so that it becomes half covered. It will even change its colour to match the sand and stones on which it lies.

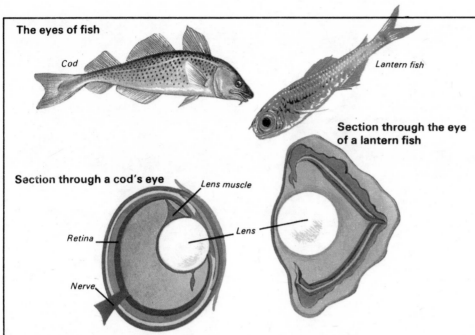

The eyes of fish

Cod

Lantern fish

Section through the eye of a lantern fish

Section through a cod's eye

Lens muscle

Retina

Lens

Nerve

Most bony fish have colour vision and their eye structure is similar to our own. However, in fish the lens moves backwards and forwards to focus,

unlike our eye in which the lens changes shape to focus. Lantern fish have large eyes and organs which luminesce.

Above: Hatchet fish have a formidable array of light organs which cleverly disguise their outlines and protect them from predators.

Some fish have odd shapes. The sea-horse looks totally unlike a fish and could be mistaken for a piece of seaweed. The sea-dragon is even more unrecognizable, since its body is covered with outgrowths looking like leaves.

The razorfish has a very thin body and stands on its tail. In this position it can hide among the spines of a sea-urchin, or among seaweed.

A real danger to skin-divers is the stone-fish. It lies on the sea bottom, looking like a stone covered in seaweed. It has a sharp spine on its back. If the spine is touched or stepped on by accident, it pierces the skin with a deadly poison. Some divers have died or lost a hand or a foot in this way.

Coral fish from the tropics are brilliantly coloured, yet they are well hidden among the bright corals and seaweed. An interesting feature of some coral fish is

the way their eyes are covered with a dark stripe. They also have two conspicuous "eyes" near the tail. This can confuse an enemy into attacking the wrong end.

Eyesight

How well a fish sees depends on what it eats. Vegetarians usually have poor sight and rely on smell and taste. Hunters are more sharp-eyed, in order to catch their prey.

The blind cave fish lives in Mexico. The young have normal eyes, but skin slowly grows over them, so making the adults blind. Eyes would be useless since these fish live in permanent darkness.

Right: Razorfish have very thin bodies. By standing on their tails among the seaweed, or in this case among the spines of a sea-urchin, they can hide from danger.

Left: The sea-dragon has many outgrowths on its body which make it look like a piece of seaweed. Like its cousin the sea-horse, it sucks up food particles through its tube-like mouth. Both the razorfish **(right)** and the sea-dragon **(left)** have very good camouflage.

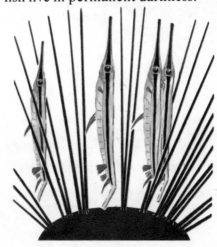

Reproduction and life-cycles

Life history of a salmon

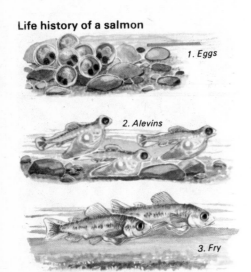

1. Eggs

2. Alevins

3. Fry

4. Parr

6. Male salmon

5. Smolt

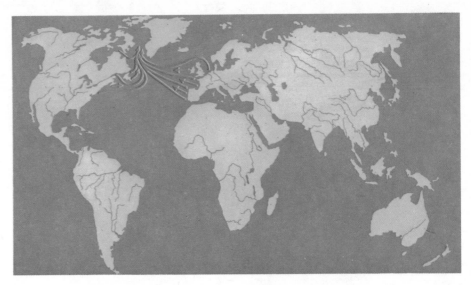

Above: This map shows the journey of the Atlantic salmon to its feeding grounds.

Above: Watching salmon battle against a waterfall is a thrilling sight. Somehow they manage to get through, even though they are often bruised.

Above: These drawings represent the stages in the life cycle of a salmon *1:* the eggs; *2:* baby alevins with yolk sacs; *3:* salmon fry; *4:* young parr; *5:* smolt, and *6:* a male salmon. Males have a hooked lower jaw.

Most fish lay eggs which are then fertilized by the male outside the body. Only in sharks and live-young bearing tooth-carp are the eggs fertilized internally.

Sharks lay their eggs in cases called "mermaid's purses" which can sometimes be found washed up on the beach. The baby shark grows up in the case until the yolk is used up, then swims free.

A number of popular tropical aquarium fish are called tooth-carp. In warmer countries they live wild in shallow streams. In the male the anal fin is specially built for mating. This is very noticeable in the swordtail. Other fish which give birth to live young are the top minnow, the platy, the molly and the guppy.

The breeding season

In the tropics fish breed all year round. In northern countries breeding occurs usually during early summer. This is when fish like the roach, carp, pike and perch are spawning. For the fisherman this is the "close season" when fishing is not allowed.

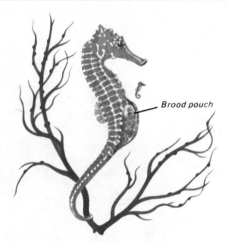

Sea-horses certainly deserve their name, for they look so unlike a fish. They swim in the upright position, using the dorsal fin to move about. The

tail is used for hooking on to plants when resting. These two **(left)** are courting and about to mate. In the centre is a male with his brood pouch

full of young. The long snout is used for sucking up small food particles. Sea-horses have been kept and bred successfully in aquaria.

With sporting fish like the trout and salmon, breeding takes place late in the year. The salmon which enter rivers have been resting and feeding in the northern Atlantic or Pacific. They make their way upstream, and can pass over weirs and waterfalls.

Salmon which get through reach shallow pools near the river's source. The Pacific salmon may travel 1,600 kilometres up the Mackenzie River to spawn. Once at the spawning ground, the female digs a hollow in the gravel by turning sideways and flapping her tail. This scatters the small stones to make her nest, or redd. Then she lays her eggs. The male salmon fertilizes them, and then the female covers the eggs. Here they will remain through the winter.

The eggs hatch into baby fish called alevins which have stomachs swollen with yolk. When the yolk is used up they turn into baby salmon called parr. These remain in the area for about two years, then they change to a more silvery colour and are called smolt. This is the stage when the salmon leaves its birthplace and starts a long, slow journey to the sea, where it will feed and grow up. Meanwhile, after spawning, the thin and weak parents drift back to sea, but many die on the way.

When mature, the young salmon returns to its birthplace to breed. Fish marked with metal discs on their dorsal fins have told us much about salmon movements, but how they find the same river is still a mystery.

Parental care

Some fish take care of their eggs. The well-known stickleback chooses a corner of a pond in which to build a nest. This is made with pieces of plants cemented together with a sticky fluid from his kidneys, and weighed down with tiny stones. He then finds a female, does a kind of dance in front of her, and leads her down to the nest. She lays her eggs inside, and is driven away. The male takes charge, and will chase away any enemy or rival male. His bright red throat warns them to keep away.

Some tropical fish, like the Siamese fighting fish, build a bubble nest at the surface. This is a

mixture of air and a sticky glue from the lining of the mouth which is blown into bubbles. The male collects the eggs from the female and pushes them into the nest which he then guards. Two rival males, if put together, will fight to the death.

Other fish called mouth-breeders, carry the eggs in their mouths until the young hatch. The babies will even go back into the mouth for shelter. This is common among fish of the cichlid and tilapia families, which are often kept in aquaria.

In the case of the strange-looking sea-horse, the male keeps the eggs inside a brood pouch until they are ready to hatch.

Below: This tilapia fish is ready to take her babies into her mouth if there is any danger. This is also where she kept the eggs before they hatched.

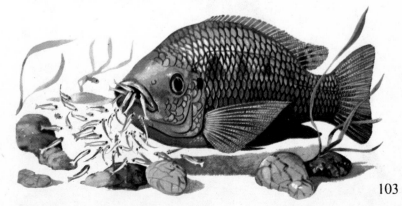

Amphibian groups

Most amphibians are animals that can live in water and on land and the name amphibian means having two ways of life. Amphibians lay eggs without shells and, in order that the eggs do not dry up, they must be laid in water. The young amphibian hatches out and spends its early life in water like a fish. Then its body may change as it grows until it can leave the water for land. There it stays for the rest of its life, except for the breeding period, when it must return to water or to a very damp place.

Most amphibians are born with gills like those of fish so that they can breathe in water. To live on land they often lose the gills and grow lungs to breathe air. Amphibians can also breathe through the skin, as long as it is kept moist. Oxygen in the air dissolves in moisture on the skin, and passes into the amphibian's bloodstream.

Amphibians are mostly found in tropical regions, where it is warm and wet. They do not like dry places, as they easily lose water from their bodies by evaporation through the skin. However, some manage to live in deserts by hiding in damp burrows during the day. Amphibians do not like cold places either, though they can live in winter by hibernating in ponds or damp holes. No amphibians live in the sea, as the salt would draw out water from the amphibian's body.

The three orders
There are three orders of amphibians: frogs and toads, newts and salamanders, and caecilians.

The largest order is that of frogs and toads. They begin life as fish-like tadpoles. They grow short front legs and long back legs which they jump with and they have no tails when fully grown. Newts and salamanders do not lose their tails as they grow, and their limbs are all the same size. Some keep their gills when they are fully grown. Caecilians, the smallest group, have no legs and look rather like worms.

Eating and being eaten
Tadpoles eat plant food and animal remains which float in water, but adult amphibians eat only live animals. Most hunt small creatures such as insects, worms, slugs and snails, but large amphibians can capture mice, fish and birds as well as other amphibians of their own and other species.

In turn, amphibians are hunted by larger animals, including snakes, herons and birds of prey, large fish, and mammals such as raccoons. The amphibians are not strong enough to fight back.

While frogs and toads may be able to jump out of harm's way,

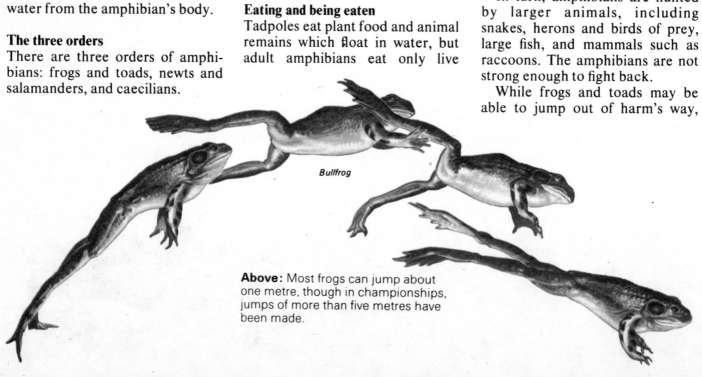

Bullfrog

Above: Most frogs can jump about one metre, though in championships, jumps of more than five metres have been made.

most amphibians cannot flee from danger. Their best defence is camouflage. Many amphibians are coloured green to merge with grass or leaves and some can even change colour. Several have bright colours and do not have to hide because bright colours often indicate to a would-be enemy that an animal is poisonous or unpleasant to eat. In fact, many amphibians have poison glands in their skin. One frog has such a deadly poison that a small cup of it would be enough to kill all the people who live in a city as large as London.

Newts and salamanders

Most newts and salamanders live in the Northern Hemisphere. The giant salamander is the largest of all amphibians, growing to a length of up to 1.5 metres.

Some salamanders never grow up. They stay like new-born salamanders, keeping their gills and small legs. The gills enable them to live in water all the time, and many never emerge to live on dry land.

Caecilians

Caecilians are large amphibians which have no legs and may grow more than a metre long. They live underground in burrows in tropical forests. Many caecilians are blind, and many bear live young.

Above: This scene shows several kinds of amphibians, and different stages of growth. In nature, these creatures would not all be found living together in the same place. They are *1:* common frog; *2:* fire salamander; *3:* marbled newt; *4:* tadpoles; *5:* frog-spawn; *6:* caecilian; *7:* common toad.

The male hairy frog of West Africa appears to have growths of hair on its back legs and on its sides. The growths are not in fact made of hair, but of skin, and they help the frog to breathe. The hairy frog has very small lungs, and it needs extra oxygen when it is very active, particularly during the mating season.

Frogs and toads

Frogs and toads

Frogs and toads are to be found in most parts of the world, from cold polar regions to hot deserts. However, most of them live in the tropics, where it is warm and wet. They vary in size from tiny frogs as short as a centimetre up to the rare Goliath frog of central Africa. This giant frog has a body about 30 centimetres long and, with its legs outstretched, it measures up to 80 centimetres.

Tree frogs

Among the most interesting frogs are tree frogs, which live in tropical forests around the world. These frogs live in trees or on the ground, and many are coloured bright green so that they merge with the leaves. To help them clamber through the branches in search of insects to eat, many tree frogs have suction pads on their

When a pair of frogs mate, the male climbs on the female and clasps her tightly. The male grows a pad of hard, rough skin on his fingers to help grip her slippery body. He then fertilizes the eggs as the female lays them.

Above: Some tree frogs lay their eggs in foam attached to leaves.

Below: The female marsupial frog puts her eggs in a pouch on her back.

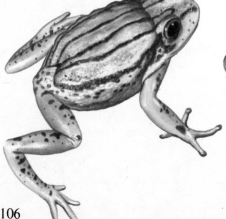

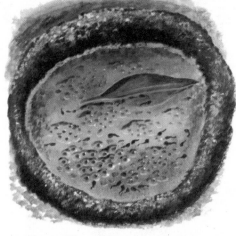

Above: The smith frog lays her eggs in a mud nest containing water.

Below: The male midwife toad carries the eggs laid by the female in strings around his legs. He goes to a pond when the young are ready to hatch.

toes and fingers. Others can use their fingers to grasp twigs.

The most unusual method of travel among amphibians is that used by the flying frog. This tree frog does not fly like a bird but jumps from a branch and glides through the air to another tree. It has large webbed feet that it spreads out like small parachutes and it can make flights up to 30 metres.

Many tree frogs have special ways of breeding. Some lay their eggs in pools of water in hollow trees or in cup-shaped leaves. Others make special nests for their eggs. Some tree frogs produce clumps of foam from the jelly of the eggs, and stick the foam to leaves hanging over some water. The eggs develop inside the foam, which hardens on the outside to protect them. When the tadpoles hatch from the eggs, the foam softens and they fall into the water. Other tree frogs make nests by sticking leaves together with egg jelly. The eggs are laid inside, and when the first tadpole hatches, the nest collapses into the water below.

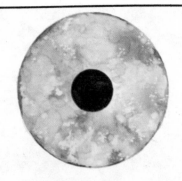

Frogspawn consists of large clumps of frog's eggs. Each egg contains a black egg cell surrounded by jelly.

The egg grows and hatches out as a tadpole. The tadpole swims like a fish and has gills on its head to breathe.

Soon a fold of skin grows over the gills so that they are inside the body. The tadpole eats plant food.

A pair of hind legs begin to grow at the base of the tail. A pair of fore legs are also beginning to form. The tadpole now eats animal remains.

As the hind legs grow larger, the fore legs burst through the skin by the gills. At the same time, the tail begins to get shorter.

Finally, the tadpole loses its tail and turns into a small frog. It has grown a pair of lungs to breathe air, and can leave the water for the land.

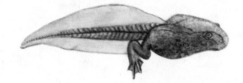

Some frogs lay their eggs in damp soil. The young become tadpoles while still in the egg, and hatch as tiny frogs. In one group of frogs from Chile, the male carries the eggs in his throat. The young hatch there, and do not leave until they have become frogs. Female marsupial frogs of South America carry their eggs in a pouch on their backs. Fully formed frogs hatch from the pouch.

Several toads also have unusual breeding habits. The male midwife toad takes charge of the eggs after the female has laid them, winding them round his back legs. When the eggs are ready to hatch, he takes them to some water. The male Surinam toad takes the female's eggs and places them in pockets on her back. Skin grows over the eggs, and the young go through the tadpole stage there, so that fully formed young toads hatch from the pockets.

The Surinam toad has long fingers to help it find food among the mud of the South American rivers where it lives. Similarly, the clawed toad of South Africa uses its claws to dig for food in ponds. If the pond dries up, the toad survives by burying itself in the mud.

Migration
Most amphibians in the Northern Hemisphere breed in a quiet pond or stream. They may travel long distances over the ground to reach a particular breeding site, using the same place year after year, just as birds migrate to their breeding grounds. Amphibians may use the position of the sun to guide them, or they may use their sense of smell to direct them.

Breeding
As they enter the water, the male frogs and toads begin to croak loudly to attract a female. As a female enters, several males compete for her attention. The "winner" clings to the female's back and she begins to lay eggs. The eggs are fertilized by the male's sperm as they are laid. Frogs produce large clumps of eggs, called spawn, whereas toads lay strings of eggs. Many thousands of eggs may be produced. A bullfrog, for example, may lay as many as 25,000 eggs at one time.

Newts and salamanders reproduce in different ways. The male performs a courting display in which he moves around the female, and he then lays packets of sperm on the bottom of the pond or stream, or sometimes on land. The female picks up the packets, and the sperm fertilizes the eggs inside her body. The female then lays the eggs either in small clumps or separately.

Caecilians mate before laying their eggs, which are usually placed on damp ground near water.

With frogs and toads, a great change takes place as the young develop. This change is called metamorphosis. The egg hatches to produce a tadpole, which swims with a long tail and breathes with gills. Legs begin to grow and the tail gets smaller, while lungs begin to form inside the body. Over several weeks, the tadpole changes into a small frog or toad and can leave the water. The young of newts and salamanders are like tadpoles at first, but soon grow legs so that they begin to look like adults much earlier on.

Crocodiles and turtles

There are three main groups or orders of reptiles: lizards and snakes; turtles and tortoises; and crocodiles and alligators. There is also a fourth order containing only one animal, the tuatara of New Zealand. The tuatara looks like a lizard, but it has a different kind of head. It is an interesting animal because it is the only reptile alive today that is more or less unchanged since prehistoric times.

Reptiles are covered with dry scales, and do not have moist bodies like amphibians. Most reptiles also have four limbs that enable them to move easily over the land, although legless reptiles such as snakes can also get about well. The protective scales and the fact that they can move, allow reptiles to live away from water, and many live in dry places.

Another feature that enables reptiles to live away from water is their method of breeding. Most reptiles lay eggs with a tough leathery shell that protects the young reptile inside. The egg does not have to be surrounded by water or moisture, and can be laid anywhere on land. A few reptiles bear live young instead of laying eggs.

Although they are able to live on land, some reptiles including turtles, crocodiles, alligators and many snakes prefer to live in water. However, those that lay

eggs come on land to breed. Most reptiles live in warm, tropical areas of the world.

Reptiles hunt other animals for food, and sight is their most important sense. They can usually see in colour. Most also have a good sense of smell, and snakes can often track their prey by flicking bits of soil or sand into their mouths to find a particular scent. Hearing is usually not very good in reptiles, though snakes know an animal is approaching by the vibrations it produces in the ground. Snakes can also detect the heat given off by some animals.

Land tortoises and some turtles and lizards eat plant food, but most reptiles eat animal food. Small reptiles hunt insects and other invertebrate creatures, but large reptiles are able to kill almost any animal that comes near.

In turn, reptiles are eaten by other animals – often by other reptiles. Birds of prey are good reptile hunters, and so are mammals like raccoons and foxes. Snakes, with their sharp fangs, can fight back and the cobra can even spit poison at its enemies. Other reptiles may try to bluff their way out of danger. Grass snakes pretend they are dead and the Australian frilled lizard raises a large umbrella-like fold of skin around its head which makes it look much bigger and more fright-

Above: Two crocodiles lie in the sun, idly threatening one another. Reptiles are cold-blooded animals and do not make their own body heat. They often bask in the sun to gain warmth.

ening than it is. Chameleons are particularly good at changing colour to match their surroundings. Another advantage some lizards have is that they can grow a new tail if theirs is bitten off during an attack.

Below: Alligators make nests for their eggs by piling rotten plants over them. The female alligator stands guard, driving away any animal that comes near.

Crocodiles and alligators

Crocodiles and alligators, with their huge jaws full of sharp teeth, are the biggest and most fearsome of all reptiles. The marine crocodile grows to a length of about four metres, though there are reports of some twice this size.

Crocodiles and alligators look very much alike apart from their jaws. The alligator has a broader snout than the crocodile. In both cases, the fourth tooth from the front on each side of the lower jaw is longer than the other teeth. In crocodiles, this tooth fits into a notch in the upper jaw when the mouth is closed and can be seen. In alligators, the fourth tooth fits inside the upper jaw and cannot be seen when the mouth is shut. There are two other kinds of crocodile-like reptiles. Caymans are related to alligators and look like them. Gavials or gharials have very long narrow jaws.

Crocodiles live in rivers, lakes and swamps in the tropical regions of the world. The marine crocodile, which swims out to sea, lives in south-east Asia. Caymans live in the tropical parts of America, and alligators are found only in North America and China. Gavials live in south-east Asia.

Crocodiles and alligators spend much of their time lying quietly in the water, with just their eyes and nostrils poking above the surface. But when a likely victim comes near, they whip into action. Swimming strongly with their powerful tails, they seize their prey and drown it, if necessary, before eating it. They feed mainly on water animals such as fish and turtles, but they will also make a dash from the water and seize an animal that is standing on the shore.

Crocodiles and alligators come ashore to breed. Crocodiles lay their eggs in a pit, while alligators make a nest of rotting plants.

Turtles and tortoises

Turtles and tortoises have large shells that fit almost completely around their bodies. Only the head and legs poke out of the shell, and they can be withdrawn into the shell when danger threatens. The shell is usually hard and rigid.

Some of these reptiles can be called either turtles or tortoises, but usually, a turtle lives in water and a tortoise on land. Turtles are found in the sea and in fresh water, while terrapins, which are like small turtles, live only in fresh water. Turtles and terrapins can swim well, and many of them are fierce underwater hunters, while others eat only plant food. Tortoises walk slowly about on land, feeding on plants and capturing animals such as earthworms.

Although they may seem ill-fitted for a life on land, tortoises are in one sense the most successful of all land animals, for they live longer than any other animal. It is thought that tortoises may live for as long as 200 years.

Sea turtles come ashore to breed, each female burying up to 400 eggs in the sand before returning to the sea. The baby turtles hatch, struggle to the surface and then make a desperate run to the sea, trying to escape the sea birds and other enemies that lie in wait for them, but few survive.

Above: Sea turtles have flippers instead of legs. Their bodies are streamlined so that they can swim quickly.

Left: Tortoises have a heavy "suit" of armour. They have short, thick legs to carry the weight of the shell, and can only move about slowly.

Snakes and lizards

Apart from their legs, lizards are very much like snakes. In fact some lizards do not have legs and can be told apart from snakes only by examining their heads. Lizards have eyelids and ear openings, which snakes do not possess.

Snakes

Among the longest snakes are the reticulated python of south-east Asia, which reaches ten metres and the anaconda of South America, which can grow to eight and a half metres. The shortest snake in the world is the thread snake of the West Indies which grows to only 12 centimetres.

The long body of a snake does include a tail, but it is joined to the main part of the body so that you cannot see where it begins. The skeleton consists of a long row of as many as 400 ribs, inside which the body organs are stretched out.

The mouth can be opened very wide to swallow prey, and is lined with sharp teeth, some of which may be poisonous fangs. Snakes have a long tongue that is forked at the tip. A snake constantly flicks its tongue in and out of its mouth, even when the mouth is closed. There is a notch in the upper jaw through which the tongue moves. Snakes do not strike with their tongues. The tongue in fact takes the place of a nose. It picks up odours and carries them to an organ inside the mouth known as Jacobson's organ, which detects the odours. In this way, a snake can sense food and enemies, as well as females and any rival snakes.

Although they have no legs, snakes can move easily over the ground, clamber through branches, burrow into soil and even swim if necessary. They move mainly by bending their bodies. A snake may bunch up its body and then straighten it out, gripping with its tail to push the rest of the body forward. Or it may continually bend its body, pushing against the ground as it does so to move forward. Snakes move sideways over sand in this way. They can also crawl without bending their bodies, using the scales on the undersides of their bodies to push themselves along.

Snakes live mainly in warm parts of the world, and mostly on land. Sea snakes live in tropical oceans. One species lives in the water all the time and bears live young. Other sea snakes come ashore from time to time.

Snakes hunt animals for their food, though birds' eggs are a favourite with several species. Many snakes simply bite their prey to subdue it, but others have poisonous fangs that inject a deadly venom. Snake venom can be poisonous to humans, and about 40,000 people die from snake bites every year.

Boas and pythons kill their prey by constriction. They grab their victims with their mouths, and then immediately wind their bodies around them. The snakes squeeze as hard as they can, not to crush their prey but to prevent them breathing and stop their hearts beating. Most of these constrictor snakes are large and they often live along river banks where they surprise animals coming to drink. Others live in trees from where they can drop onto their victims.

Above: The chameleon is a lizard with a very long tongue. It keeps completely still, waiting for an insect to come near. When it spots a likely meal, it quickly darts out its sticky-tipped tongue to capture its prey.

Iguana

Having killed their prey, snakes swallow it whole. They open their mouths wide, and slowly gulp the body down. A snake that has just eaten is often swollen with the body of its victim.

Snakes either lay eggs or they bear live young. The baby snakes look like small versions of their parents. As they grow, snakes have to shed their skins because these cannot stretch.

Lizards

Of all the animals that now live upon the earth, lizards look most like the prehistoric monsters that once ruled the world. However, most of them are small creatures and almost all are harmless to man. The largest lizard is the Komodo dragon. This animal may grow to a length of three metres. It lives on a few small islands in Indonesia, the biggest of which is called Komodo.

Most lizards have long tails and four legs, though some have no legs and resemble snakes. Legged lizards can move swiftly and dart for cover if disturbed. The flying lizard can glide through the air by extending folds of skin along the sides of its body so that they act like wings.

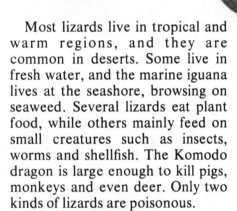

Anaconda

Most lizards live in tropical and warm regions, and they are common in deserts. Some live in fresh water, and the marine iguana lives at the seashore, browsing on seaweed. Several lizards eat plant food, while others mainly feed on small creatures such as insects, worms and shellfish. The Komodo dragon is large enough to kill pigs, monkeys and even deer. Only two kinds of lizards are poisonous.

Lizards either lay eggs or they give birth to live young.

By far the largest number of snakes and lizards live on land in the earth's warmer regions. Only a few species live in water, like the sea snake **(below)**. The anaconda **(above)** is a member of the boa family, and so kills its prey by constriction, while the viper **(right)** is a poisonous snake. The iguana **(top)** and the frilled lizard **(below right)** have typical lizard features — long tails, four legs and moveable eyelids.

Rhinoceros viper

Left: Snakes have to shed their skin as they grow. They peel off the old skin, starting with the head and turning it inside-out. Underneath is a new skin.

Sea snake

Australian frilled lizard

Structure

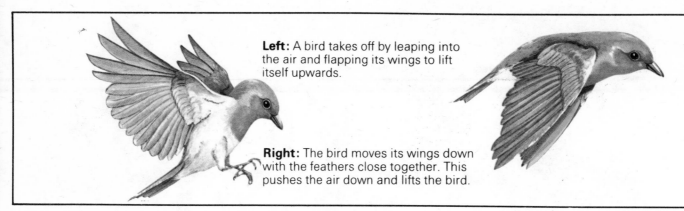

Left: A bird takes off by leaping into the air and flapping its wings to lift itself upwards.

Right: The bird moves its wings down with the feathers close together. This pushes the air down and lifts the bird.

From the outside, birds do not look like other backboned animals such as reptiles and mammals, but on the inside, their bodies have the same basic design. They have the same kinds of bones, although they are very different in size from those of other animals. Compared with a human being, for example, a bird has long jaw bones, which form the beak, and a long neck. The arm and hand bones, which lie inside the wings, are also long, and so are the legs and feet. The thigh bone is hidden beneath the feathers, and what looks like a bird's knee is in fact its ankle. The toes are long and form the bird's claws, or webs may grow between them for swimming. The rib cage is comparatively small, but the breastbone is large because it serves to anchor the big and powerful flight muscles to the skeleton. These muscles drive the wings and give a bird a plump breast.

Although it contains a mass of bones packed tightly together, a bird's body is not heavy, for it has to be lifted easily into the air. The bones are in fact hollow and therefore light. Inside, they are crisscrossed with thin struts to give strength.

A bird has large lungs and hollow spaces called air-sacs inside its body. The lungs and air-sacs not only help to lighten the body, but also provide the bird with large amounts of air for breathing. This is vital during flying when the bird needs plenty of oxygen. Flying produces lots of body heat, and the air inside the body carries the extra heat away.

Birds have one particular feature that no other animal possesses, and that is feathers. Strong feathers called contour feathers cover the body and form the wings and tail. They protect the body from damage, and give the bird the ability to fly. Beneath the contour feathers are fluffy down feathers that keep the body warm when the bird is resting. All feathers are made from keratin, the same substance that is in our hair and nails.

How birds fly

Birds either flap their wings to move through the air, or stretch out their wings to glide or soar. When a bird flaps its wings, it pushes air down to keep itself up, and it pushes air backwards so that it moves forwards. To get into the air to begin its flight, it either jumps from the ground or leaps from a high perch. Some birds like to take a run to get moving, and water birds may splash over the surface to become airborne.

Many birds can stay aloft almost without moving their wings at all. Albatrosses soar over the waves and vultures circle in the sky.

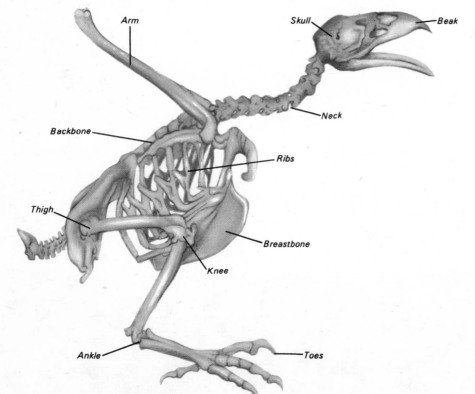

Left: The skeleton of a bird contains the same kinds of bones as a human. In flight, the bird tucks its legs under its body or trails them out behind. The legs are lowered on landing.

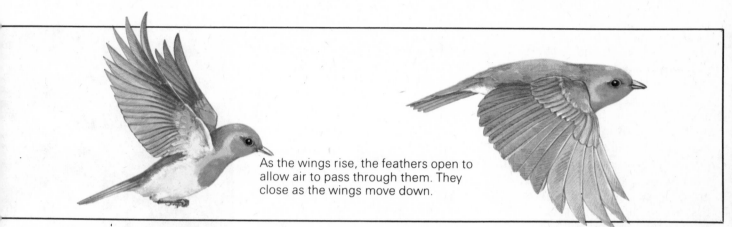

As the wings rise, the feathers open to allow air to pass through them. They close as the wings move down.

These birds glide at a slight downward angle to keep moving. As their wings slice through the air, the movement of air over the curved surfaces of the wings gives lift to the birds and keeps them up in the air. The birds meet rising currents of air that carry them higher.

Some birds can hover in the air. A few, like the kestrel, head into the wind at the same speed as the wind blows them back. In this way, they stay over the same spot.

Below: A feather consists of a central shaft and a vane of barbs with interlocking barbules. The wings are made up of feathers attached to the hand and arm bones. The primary feathers are the main flight control feathers.

Hummingbirds can truly hover, whirling their tiny wings to and fro to stop themselves moving forwards. They can even fly backwards if necessary.

The senses of birds

Birds have the same senses that we have, but some may be better developed than ours and others less so. In general, birds have good sight and hearing, but their sense of smell is poor.

Many birds are brightly coloured and most birds can see in colour. Nocturnal birds do not need colour vision and see in shades of grey. Birds that hunt other animals have very keen sight – as much as ten times sharper than our vision. Owls have their eyes

placed towards the front of the head so that they can easily locate their prey. This prey is often a plant-eating bird or one that feeds on the ground. These birds have eyes at the sides of their heads so that they can see all round and spot an enemy coming towards them.

Birds do not have ears as we do, but they hear through openings that lie beneath the feathers behind the eyes. Birds "talk" with each other by singing and need to hear well. Owls hunt by night, and use their very keen hearing to find their victims by the quiet rustling noises they make as they move.

Birds have nostrils at the base of their beaks, but they use them more for breathing than they do for smelling.

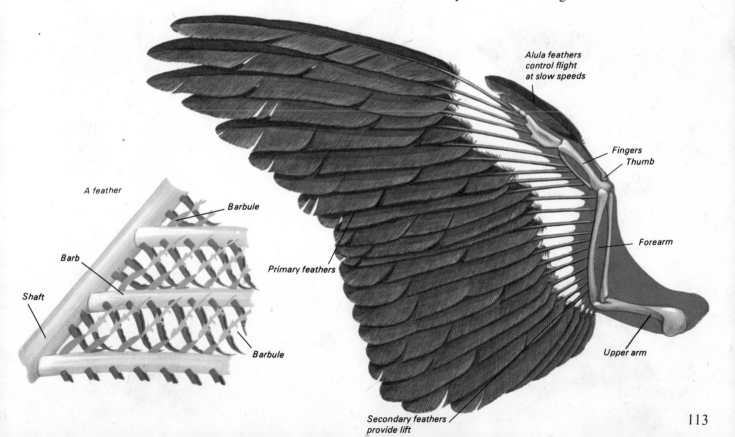

A feather

Barbule

Barb

Shaft

Barbule

Primary feathers

Secondary feathers provide lift

Alula feathers control flight at slow speeds

Fingers
Thumb

Forearm

Upper arm

Classification

There are many different kinds of birds in the world and to show how they are related to one another we place them in groups. The system of classification (grouping) used is based on the kind of body that a bird has. Birds that have similar bodies are placed in the same group. It is the internal structure that matters and not the outside appearance of the bird. This means that some birds which look alike, such as fulmars and gulls, belong to different groups because they are different inside. Also, some birds that look very different may belong to the same group because they are alike internally. Toucans and wood-peckers both belong to the Pici-formes order. The birds share the characteristic of two forward- and two backward-pointing toes.

There are about 8,600 different species of birds. Birds that belong to the same species can breed and produce young that can also breed. The various species do not inter-breed and therefore stay the same. Similar species of birds belong to the same genus, and similar genera to the same family. Related families of birds make up a particular order of birds. In all, there are 27 orders. One contains only a single bird – the ostrich. Other orders may contain many birds, and the order of perching birds contains more species of birds than all the other orders put together.

All birds have English or common names, but different names are sometimes given to birds of the same species. For example, the carrion crow and hooded crow belong to the same species, as do the pied wagtail and white wagtail. Also, the same name may be given to different birds in different places. In America, a blackbird is a completely different bird to the European blackbird. The English or common name of a bird therefore does not always tell you to which particular group a bird belongs. In the scientific system of classification, each species, genus, family and order has a particular Latin name (*see pages 56–7*).

Above: There are more than 80 different kinds of kingfishers, and they make up a single family. Many of them do not in fact fish, but live in forests away from water.

Kiwi

Ostrich

Masked lovebird

Osprey

Rock dove

Great black cockatoo

Great horned owl

Great bustard

Below: These birds belong to 13 different orders. The lovebird and cockatoo are of the same order, as are the tits and the herons. The other birds each belong to a separate order

The Orders of Birds

1. Struthioniformes: the ostrich
2. Rheiformes: rheas
3. Casuariiformes: cassowaries, emu
4. Apterygiformes: kiwis
5. Tinamiformes: tinamous
6. Sphenisciformes: penguins
7. Gaviiformes: divers
8. Podicipediformes: grebes
9. Procellariiformes: albatrosses, shearwaters, fulmars, petrels
10. Pelecaniformes: tropic birds, pelicans, gannets, cormorants, darters, frigate birds
11. Ciconiiformes: herons, bitterns, storks, ibises, spoonbills, flamingoes
12. Anseriformes: swans, geese, ducks
13. Falconiformes: vultures, secretary bird, eagles, buzzards, hawks, kites, osprey, harriers, falcons
14. Galliformes: megapodes, grouse, partridges, pheasants, guinea fowl, turkeys, hoatzin
15. Gruiformes: cranes, rails, moorhens, coots, bustards
16. Charadriiformes: jacanas, oystercatchers, plovers, sandpipers, avocets, stilts, phalaropes, skuas, gulls, terns, skimmers, auks
17. Columbiformes: sandgrouse, pigeons, doves
18. Psittaciformes: parrots, cockatoos, budgerigars, macaws
19. Cuculiformes: turacos, cuckoos
20. Strigiformes: owls
21. Caprimulgiformes: oilbirds, frogmouths, nightjars
22. Apodiformes: swifts, hummingbirds
23. Coliiformes: colies
24. Trogoniformes: trogons
25. Coraciiformes: kingfishers, kookaburras, bee-eaters, rollers, hoopoes, hornbills
26. Piciformes: barbets, honeyguides, toucans, woodpeckers
27. Passeriformes (perching birds): broadbills, ovenbirds, antbirds, pittas, manakins, cotingas, lyrebirds, larks, swallows, martins, pipits, wagtails, shrikes, waxwings, dippers, wrens, mockingbirds, accentors, warblers, flycatchers, thrushes, chats, tits, nuthatches, treecreepers, sunbirds, honey-eaters, buntings, tanagers, honeycreepers, cardinals, finches, weavers, sparrows, starlings, oxpeckers, drongos, bowerbirds, birds of paradise, crows.

Great tit

Varied tit

Blue tit

Mute swan

Wandering albatross

Arctic skua

Lined tiger heron

Cormorant

Agami heron

115

How birds live

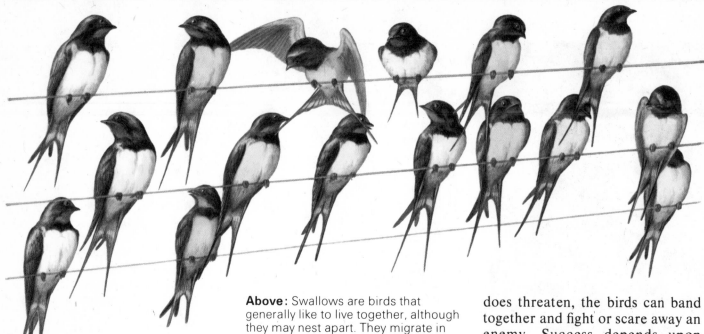

Above: Swallows are birds that generally like to live together, although they may nest apart. They migrate in large flocks, and often gather in long rows on telephone wires before departure.

Birds have several different life-styles. Some always live alone while others are to be seen in groups. Some can be seen only during the day and others emerge at night. There are seasonal changes too. Some birds remain faithful to a particular place all the year round while others stay for only part of the year.

Living alone or together
The one main factor that makes a bird live in a certain way is what it needs to eat. If a food is limited, the birds that eat it will tend to live alone. Birds of prey mostly live in this way. The animals that they require for food are spread out over a wide area, and so the birds spread themselves too. Also, a bird hunting alone is much more likely to take its prey by surprise than a flock of birds hunting together.

Birds that live on plants or on animals that are more numerous will gather in groups. Trees full of berries will attract flocks of thrushes; gulls are seen at harbours seeking fish and scraps of food;

Right: Owls are birds that need to take their prey by surprise and therefore hunt alone. Owls have keen sight and sharp hearing which enable them to hunt successfully at night.

and swifts wheel over towns in search of flying insects.

Availability of food is not the only factor. Birds that live together find safety from their enemies. Although a flock may tend to attract birds of prey and other dangerous animals, the chances of an individual bird being caught are low. Furthermore even if danger

does threaten, the birds can band together and fight or scare away an enemy. Success depends upon some kind of communication between the members of the group. Birds have alarm calls that they give to warn the flock that an enemy is approaching. They may also have markings that show up when they fly. Thus, if one bird takes to the air, the sudden display of markings alerts the others to the danger and they take flight too.

Day and night birds
Most birds like to be active during

the day and to sleep at night. They need the light to find food, and they need the darkness to hide them when they are asleep and helpless. However, some birds like to be up and about at night, when there is no danger from enemies. These birds may not need light to feed. Owls, for example, have such good hearing that they can find their victims in total darkness. Wading birds probe for shellfish and worms and so do not need to be able to see to feed. Dusk brings out flying insects, and insect-eaters such as nightjars prefer to wait until the sun goes down before seeking food.

However, these birds may face a problem when dawn comes. Where are they going to be able to sleep in safety? Owls and large waders do not have much to fear from their enemies, but smaller waders and nightjars have to rely on camouflage to conceal them from predators.

Seasonal changes
Bird life-styles often change in spring. Garden birds such as finches and thrushes, that often spend the winter in flocks searching for food, now split up into pairs to raise their young. Sea birds that roam alone in mid-ocean in winter come ashore to raise their families. Changes in food supply trigger off these changes in life-style. In the winter many birds have to wander in search of food, but as the spring arrives, they can settle in one place because there will be enough food to feed their young. Other birds can stay in the same place all the year round, because they do not need just one type of food and will eat almost anything they find.

Right: Most sea birds spend nearly all their lives at sea, which is where they find their food. They come ashore on islands or cliff faces during the breeding season. These sites are very suitable for rearing a family because the birds are safe from ground predators. Sea bird breeding colonies are often very crowded.

Migration
Many birds do not stay in the same region all the year round. They spend the summer raising their young at their breeding grounds. But as the autumn comes and it gets cold, they find their food harder and harder to find. Instead of wandering to pick up whatever they can find, they make a long journey to another part of the world where food is still plentiful. They remain in these winter quarters until the spring, and then fly back to raise a new batch of young birds. Many birds return to exactly the same place – perhaps even to the same nest – every year. These treks are called migrations.

Many migrating birds are insect-eaters, for insects are scarce in winter. Swallows migrate from Europe to Africa, for example, so that they always live in places with a warm climate where it is neither too hot nor too cold, and insects thrive. Many sea birds make long migrations, often crossing huge oceans. The Arctic tern even flies from the Arctic to the Antarctic and back again every year. Other birds make short migrations. Many waders spend the summer inland on moors and in fields, but as winter comes, they go to the sea-shore where it is easier to dig for food.

Birds somehow know exactly the right direction to take when they migrate. They probably use the positions of the sun, moon or stars in the sky to find their way.

Eating, drinking and cleaning

Birds use a lot of energy flying, and must feed often to stay alive. On the whole, birds can eat anything that nature has to offer, but only a few birds, such as crows, can eat everything. Others prefer to eat only a certain range of food for which their beaks are adapted.

Many birds are plant-eaters. Thrushes like berries, and finches and sparrows go for seeds. Seed-eaters have stout little beaks to crack open the seeds. These birds are usually small, for they have to clamber nimbly over slender twigs to find food. So too are humming-birds. They feed on the nectar in flowers, hovering over a bloom and dipping their long thin beaks into the petals. Larger birds such as parrots and toucans have strong and large beaks to feed on tropical fruits, and swans and geese tear up grass and water plants with their broad bills.

Insects are a common bird food. Warblers seek insects among leaves, picking them up with their little pointed beaks. Treecreepers pull them out of crevices in the bark with their long, curved beaks, while woodpeckers chisel into the bark with their sharp beaks to get insects. Several birds, such as swifts and nightjars, chase flying insects through the air with wide open mouths.

Shellfish and worms are the food of wading birds that live at the seashore and in damp places. These birds have long beaks that they use to probe the sand, mud or soil for food. Many birds hunt larger and more active animals. Several are fish-eaters, but face problems in gripping their slippery catch. Some diving ducks and sea birds have beaks with sawtooth edges to grip fish. Birds of prey such as eagles and falcons, and owls and shrikes, are meat-eaters. They mostly hunt small animals such as mice and birds. They have strong hooked beaks that can tear their prey to pieces.

A few birds use objects to help them get food. A thrush will break open a snail on a stone to get at the meat inside, while gulls drop shellfish onto rocks to smash them. The Egyptian vulture breaks open tough ostrich eggs by dropping a stone on them. The woodpecker finch of the Galapagos Islands gets insects out of crevices in bark by probing for them with a cactus spine or a thorn held in the beak.

Drinking

Birds have to drink as well as eat. Some desert birds can exist on the juices of the food they eat, but most birds have to drink water. They drink by lowering their beaks into some water, and then tipping their heads back to make the water flow down their throats. Pigeons can suck up water and do not have

Above: Anting is a strange action performed by several birds, such as this jay. The bird allows ants to clamber over its body, probably to help clean it.

Left: Birds can often be seen preening—running their beaks over their plumage to attend to the feathers. They remove dirt and pests, and tidy the feathers that are in the wrong position.

Left: Vultures are well known for their habit of feeding on dead animals or carrion. They clean the flesh from the bones of a carcass. The birds perform a useful service in cleaning up remains.

Below: Beaks can be all kinds of shapes and sizes, depending on the type of food a bird eats. The flamingo **(left)** has a very unusual beak. It eats minute water creatures found in muddy lakes. It lowers its huge bill into the lake and takes some water. Inside the bill are comb-like plates that strain the creatures from the water. The crossbill **(below)** cuts open the cones of conifer trees with its scissor-shaped beak to get at the seeds inside. Birds of prey, like the crowned hawk eagle **(bottom),** have powerful hooked beaks to tear their prey apart.

to tip their heads back to drink.

Keeping clean

A bird has to care for its plumage. Otherwise, pests will invade the feathers and they become untidy, making it difficult to fly. Birds spend a lot of their time cleaning themselves, for they are covered with thousands of feathers.

A bird has four main cleaning actions. It has to bathe to clean the feathers, and get rid of pests. Most birds take a dip in a puddle of water and ruffle their feathers. Some bathe in the rain, and others may use some dry dust to rub through their plumage. Preening often follows bathing, but may take place at any time. The bird runs its beak through its feathers to get rid of dirt and pests. It cannot attend to its head feathers in this way, and so scratches its head with its claws or allows another bird to preen its plumage instead.

To help keep the plumage healthy, birds oil their feathers with a waxy substance from a special gland near the tail called the preen gland. They smear the wax over the plumage with their beaks. This makes the plumage waterproof.

Attack and defence

A bird's life is not an easy one. It must always be on the look-out – either for prey if it is a hunting bird, or for hunters if it is likely to be a victim. It must have good methods of attack and defence if it is to survive.

A bird's keen sight enables it to spot a possible meal – or probable danger – a long way off. Birds can make out things way in the distance where we would need binoculars to spot anything. They can immediately take offensive or defensive action and often gain an advantage. Sharp hearing helps birds too. Experts believe that owls, for example, hear as much as 100 times better than we do.

Hunters

Many birds are hunters and need to capture other animals in order to survive. The birds of prey are the most savage hunters, particularly some of the small falcons. They will dart through the air at great speed, twisting and turning as they pursue their victim, or dive earthwards at great speed. Like eagles and most other birds of prey, they are fearsome hunters, killing their victims with a slash of their sharp talons.

Most hunters are solitary birds, but in the tropics, "armies" of birds often forage. They rampage through the trees, disturbing insects which they then eat. A few birds make other animals do this work for them. Antbirds follow ants to snap up the insects that are fleeing away from the ants. Cattle egrets live with cattle to pick up the animals disturbed by them.

Some birds are very cunning when hunting. Owls generally search for their food under cover of darkness. The snowy owl has to hunt by day for part of the year, for it lives in the Arctic, where the summer nights are short or even non-existent. To compensate, the snowy owl has white plumage, which is hard to spot in a land of ice and snow.

Many birds hunt fish. Of course, living in both air and water does present problems for most fishing birds. They have to be as light as possible to be able to fly, yet must force their bodies underwater

Right: The ostrich lives on the grassy plains of Africa. It is the world's largest bird, growing to a height of almost three metres. Ostriches deal with danger by running or by kicking out at their predators.

Below: The snowy owl lives in the cold Arctic wastes. Its feet are feathered to keep them warm. Its white plumage also serves to hide it from its prey, mainly lemmings and Arctic hares.

The robin is an aggressive little bird, particularly towards other robins. When it is about to attack, it points its bill at the sky and shows off its red breast as a threatening signal.

when catching fish. Large fishing birds, such as ospreys and gannets, simply splash into the water and rely on their fall to carry them down. Others, like auks, divers and grebes, dive into the water and swim in pursuit of a fish. They are well equipped for swimming, with legs set well back and webbed feet to act as propellers. The best swimmers of all are penguins, which can reach 36 kilometres an hour underwater. Penguins cannot fly, but they use their flipper-like wings to "fly" underwater whilst steering with their feet.

Several birds do not bother to do their own hunting, but rob other birds of their catch. One of the most persistent robbers is the frigate bird of tropical oceans. The frigate bird cannot easily dive for food and so it chases other sea birds, such as boobies and pelicans, that have made a catch and forces them to drop it. The frigate bird then swoops down and snatches its meal from the air before it strikes the water.

Defence methods

Birds simply take to the air to escape from enemies on the ground. However, this tactic is not much use against birds of prey, which are among the swiftest of birds. In this case, it is better for the bird to hide and hope that it will not be noticed.

Flightless birds cannot of course fly to escape danger, and their main defence is to run. These birds are mostly tall and have long necks and long, powerful legs, like the ostrich and emu. They live on grassy plains, and their height enables them to spot danger a long way off. In fact, herds of animals may look to the ostrich to warn them of approaching danger, such as a lion out hunting. The plains present no obstacles and the birds can run rapidly away, reaching speeds of 60 kilometres an hour in the case of the ostrich.

These large flightless birds can also fight back if they are cornered, and will defend themselves with a powerful kick. Several other birds will fight back when threatened and people who watch birds will know that they are likely to be attacked by sea birds if they get too near their nests. Smaller birds are unable to mount such a defence on their own, but they will gather together and "mob" an enemy to drive it away. Owls trying to get some sleep in a tree during the day often find themselves being disturbed by angry woodland birds intent on making them move on somewhere else.

Many birds use camouflage as a defence. They resemble their surroundings so much that a hunter will not spot them. The ptarmigan even changes colour every year from brown to white in order to match both the summer plants and the winter snows.

A clever defence is used by some plovers. They decoy enemies away from their nests by pretending to be injured. When they have lured the enemy to a safe distance, the birds then give up their pretence and fly off.

Here, the ptarmigan is in its winter clothing. The colour of its plumage has changed from brown to white, to match its snowy surroundings. This makes the bird very difficult to see.

Below: A peregrine falcon swoops on a game bird, killing it with its sharp talons. Peregrines are now rare.

Peregrine falcon

Courtship and breeding

Every bird has an instinctive urge to produce young, and sets aside a large portion of its life for breeding. Almost every bird has a breeding season once a year. In warm and cool climates, breeding takes place in the spring and summer. In the tropics, many birds breed either during the wet season or dry season. The season is chosen so that food will be plentiful when the young are born.

Before the female bird can lay eggs, it first has to mate with a male bird. The two birds will form a pair, and the pair will often stay together for the whole of the breeding season to raise their young. In some cases the male may leave after mating and the female will have to raise the young alone. A few birds, such as eagles and swans, form pairs that stay together for life. Birds must change their behaviour greatly as the breeding season approaches. This special behaviour is called courtship.

Attracting a mate
Birds court each other for several reasons. The male has to attract a female bird to be its mate, and the birds have then to get to trust one another if they are to live together. The courtship behaviour also warns off rival male birds.

Many birds sing to find a mate. They often use a songpost, such as an exposed branch, to show themselves off. Other male birds will hear the song, but they will interpret it as a warning to stay away. Some birds make special noises instead of singing. Woodpeckers rattle their beaks on a hollow branch or tree trunk to produce a loud drumming sound, and snipe dive through the air with their tail feathers held out to make a buzzing or bleating noise.

Many male birds put on a special appearance at courting time. They change colour or show off colourful parts of their plumage. In the male chaffinch, the crown of the head changes from brown to blue-grey. The black-headed gull only lives up to its name during the breeding season, for its head is white otherwise. Ruffs are so-called because of their bright collars of plumage that they put on to court their mates. The peacock (male peafowl) raises a gorgeous fan of blue-green tail feathers, and the birds of paradise have marvellous displays in which they show off sprays of lacy plumes.

Birds have special courting actions too. Many parade before their mates with special postures, raising their heads or wings in odd ways. These poses may also be taken up by the female birds. By these actions each bird reassures the other that it intends no harm. In some cases, the birds dance with each other. The dances of the great crested grebe are the most interesting. The pair rush to and fro over the surface of a lake, shaking their heads and raising their wings at each other. At the climax of the dance, they both dive and then rear up out of the water, facing one another with pieces of weed in their beaks. Actions like this, which resemble feeding, help the two birds to trust one another and stay together. Courtship activities may go on throughout the breeding season to keep the pair together.

Going it alone
Many birds court one another but do not form pairs that stay together. They mate, and then the female goes off to lay the eggs and raise the young alone. This behaviour may help the birds to raise their young, for it often occurs with birds in which the male has bright colours but the female is drab. If the male stayed with his family, his gaudy plumage would attract enemies. These birds include showy birds, such as birds of paradise and hummingbirds, and also such birds as ruffs and grouse, which gather at courting grounds as the breeding season opens.

Territories
Birds take on territories as the breeding season begins. This is a piece of land on which they will raise their young. With many birds, the territory has to supply the family with food. It will be large

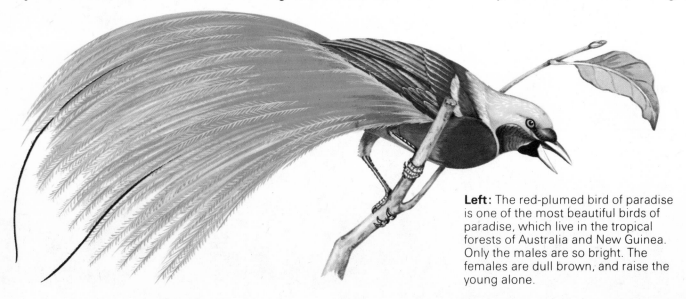

Left: The red-plumed bird of paradise is one of the most beautiful birds of paradise, which live in the tropical forests of Australia and New Guinea. Only the males are so bright. The females are dull brown, and raise the young alone.

Above: The peacock (male peafowl) raises its magnificent tail feathers to attract a peahen (female peafowl) to be its mate. This is one of the most spectacular courting displays of the bird world.

and also strongly defended against other birds of the same species. A robin will attack a rival robin that enters its territory. It becomes enraged at the sight of anything red, which it takes to be another robin, though it will be afraid to go into another robin's territory.

Many birds, especially sea birds, breed in large colonies. Within the colony, each family has a small territory on which it nests, but the territory is not used to provide food. Instead, the birds feed in the sea nearby.

Above: A pair of chaffinches mate. The male bird mounts the female so that openings at the ends of their bodies touch. The male sends a fluid containing sperms into the female. One of the sperms meets an egg-cell containing yolk from the female's

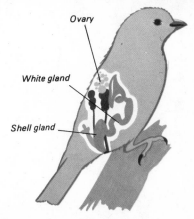

ovary, and fertilizes the cell. The white, and then a shell, form around the egg-cell as it moves through the female's body, producing an egg. The female then lays the egg and the chick develops inside the egg until it is ready to hatch.

123

Nests

Eggs have to be kept warm if the baby birds are to grow inside and hatch out. Most birds lay their eggs in a nest and then sit on the eggs to warm them. The nest has to be strong, and it must be in a safe place, where other animals cannot get at the eggs or young.

Nest materials

Many birds weave their nests with blades of dry grass or with twigs or sticks. They fashion a deep cup to hold the eggs, or they may even build a chamber with an entrance hole just big enough to allow the parent bird to enter. Weaver birds build chambers with long funnel-shaped entrances to prevent snakes and other enemies getting into the nest. The nest is lined with soft materials such as moss or feathers.

Although birds are good at weaving, they may have to stick the nest together as well. Mud is often used. Swallows make their nests of mud and grass or straw. Swifts glue their nests together with their sticky saliva, and the cave swiftlets of south-east Asia make their nests of dried saliva only. Spiders' webs are sometimes used.

Building the nest

A pair of birds must choose a site for their nest before the female can lay her eggs. She will often choose where the nest is to be. Many birds hide their nests in the foliage of a tree, where the nest cannot be seen and it is difficult for a ground animal to reach. Either the male or the female or both birds do the building. It may involve hundreds or even thousands of trips to gather materials, but the job usually takes only a few days.

Several birds do not make new nests each year, but return to an old nest. Swallows do this, and repair the old nest if necessary. Eagles return to their nests of sticks, making them bigger and bigger each year until they may measure as much as three metres across.

Hole nesters

Many birds prefer to use a hole of some kind in which to nest. They may burrow into the ground or a bank, use a burrow abandoned by an animal, make or use a hollow in a tree, or nest in the crevices of a rock face or a wall. In these cases the bird often does not even build a nest inside the cavity but simply lays its eggs on the bare surface.

Using a hole for a nest is a good way of keeping the eggs and young out of danger. Many birds are hole

Left: The baya weaver **(top)** builds a chamber nest with a hanging entrance tunnel. The tailor bird **(bottom)** makes a cup between two leaves that it sews together first. Both birds are from south-east Asia.

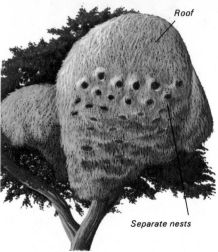

Roof

Separate nests

Top: The woodpigeon builds an untidy nest of sticks and twigs, usually in trees and bushes.

Above: The social weavers of Africa build nests like blocks of flats. The birds make a roof, and then each builds a nesting chamber with its own entrance beneath.

Below: An owl nests in a tree hollow.

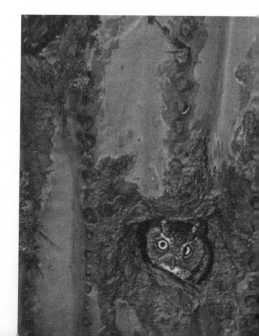

nesters. Puffins and kingfishers burrow into soil to nest, and woodpeckers carve nesting chambers in tree trunks. Many garden birds, such as tits, wrens and sparrows use natural holes. Nuthatches improve on nature by plastering the entrance with mud until it is just big enough to admit the parent bird. One of the most unusual hole nesters is the hornbill, a large tropical bird. The female hornbill enters a hole in a tree and then the male plasters up the opening, leaving only a tiny hole for the female's beak. She remains here to raise the young, while the male feeds her through the opening.

Several birds take advantage of buildings to nest. Swallows, swifts and house martins make their nests on walls and under the eaves of roofs, and owls often nest in ruins. Some garden birds, such as robins and blackbirds, sometimes nest in objects such as old kettles and abandoned cars and tractors. City-dwellers such as pigeons make use of ledges on buildings, and tits may nest inside lamp-posts.

Ground nesters
Many birds survive, even nesting on the ground, either because they hide their nests or place them out of harm's way.

Plovers and larks like to nest in fields, hiding their nests in the grass. Several birds, including terns, lay their eggs directly on sand and pebbles. However, the eggs are mottled and look just like stones, so that they are hard to spot. Some other sea birds, including guillemots, lay their eggs on the bare ledges of cliffs. There the eggs are safe from raiders such as foxes, though not from aerial robbers, such as gulls, so they are mottled for camouflage. Guillemot eggs are also pear-shaped, so that they roll in a circle if disturbed and not over the edge of the ledge.

Most penguins are also ground nesters. The adelie penguin uses a heap of pebbles for a nest, while the king penguin and the emperor penguin both use their feet as a nest. Because it is so cold where these birds live, the birds hold the egg on their feet and lower a warm fold of skin over it.

The fairy tern lays its egg on a branch of a tree and sits precariously over it. The megapodes, large fowl-like birds of Australia and nearby regions, bury their eggs in mounds of rotting vegetation or in warm sand. The heat incubates the eggs, and the chicks scramble out when they hatch. The parents tend the mounds so that the eggs do not get too hot or too cool, but they do not care for the chicks once they are born.

Below: Flamingoes live in large colonies at shallow lakes and at the coast in warm parts of the world. They build mud nests, laying their single eggs on the top of a heap of dry mud.

Rearing the young

Above: A bird has to keep its eggs warm after laying them, so that baby birds can grow inside the eggs. The eggs must be kept at a temperature of 34° Centigrade, nearly as warm as the human body.

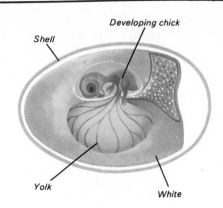

Shell
Developing chick
Yolk
White

Above: The growing chick uses up the yellow yolk inside the egg for food. Air passes through the egg shell so that the chick can breathe. The white helps to support the little bird as its body forms inside the egg.

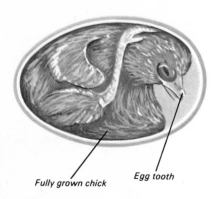

Fully grown chick
Egg tooth

Above: The chick grows until it fills the shell. It is then ready to hatch out. Its body is folded up inside the shell, and it has a tiny tooth on the end of its beak, called the egg tooth.

Above: The chick uses its egg tooth to break open the shell when it hatches. It taps the shell with its beak and the tooth cracks it. Poking with its beak, it widens the crack.

Above: The shell breaks open, and the chick is born. However, it is so tired from the effort of hatching that it rests. The egg tooth drops off, its work done.

Above: The young chick is still wet from the white in the egg, but soon dries out. Then it can stand and walk about. It begins to peck for food.

Most birds work hard to raise their young, tending the eggs with great care and devoting most of their time to feeding and protecting the young once they are born. The birds look after the young by instinct. It is instinct that drives a pair of blue tits to make as many as 500 trips every day to gather food for the young; or makes an emperor penguin go without food for two months so that it can keep its egg warm in the bitter Antarctic weather.

How many eggs?
Several birds lay only one egg during the breeding season. They include many birds that raise their young side-by-side in colonies, such as gannets and auks. Others lay many eggs—partridges may lay 16. Obviously, most of these eggs do not hatch into young birds that survive and grow, otherwise the world would soon be overrun with them. It is only the strong chicks that live. This helps the species to remain healthy overall and therefore survive.

Most common garden birds lay about four or five eggs, as do robins, finches, swallows and thrushes. The ostrich, the world's largest bird, lays the largest eggs—as many as 12 at a time, each as big as 24 hen's eggs. The smallest egg is that of the bee hummingbird, the smallest bird. The egg measures just over one centimetre in length, and the bird lays two. However, a huge bird such as the wandering albatross, which has the longest wingspan of any bird, lays only one egg, while tits, which are small garden and woodland birds, usually lay between seven and eleven eggs.

The exact number of eggs that a bird lays often depends on the availability of food. Tawny owls will only lay at all if there are enough mice and voles about to feed their young. Many birds raise one brood and then another if there is enough food for them. In a good year they may raise three broods.

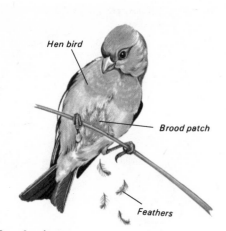

Hen bird

Brood patch

Feathers

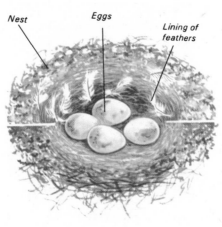

Nest

Eggs

Lining of feathers

Nest

Brood patch

Feathers

Incubation

Most birds sit on their eggs to warm them so that the baby birds develop inside. Some have other ways of incubating their eggs. Several sea birds, for example, use their warm feet whilst the megapodes bury their eggs in mounds of warm plants or in warm soil or sand. Incubation takes from as little as ten days in the case of some woodland birds to as long as 80 days for albatrosses and kiwis. The wandering albatross takes so long to rear its young that it can breed only once every two years.

A cuckoo in the nest

Several birds do not raise their own young at all, but get other birds to do the job for them. In Europe, the best-known of these parasite birds

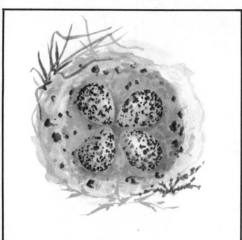

Birds of the plover family, which includes the lapwing, nest on the open ground. They scoop a shallow hollow in the ground and sometimes line it. Although they are exposed, the eggs are mottled and difficult to spot.

Left: Some of the breast feathers fall out, leaving warm brood patches.

Centre: The nest is lined with feathers or other soft materials.

Right: The soft lining and the brood patches keep the eggs warm.

is the cuckoo. Cowbirds in America, and honey-guides and weavers in Africa behave in the same way.

At breeding time, a female cuckoo selects a nesting female bird of another species and watches it. As soon as it leaves the nest, the cuckoo flies down and immediately lays an egg in the nest, heaving out the other eggs if it has time before the other bird returns.

The cuckoo then leaves its egg, never to see it or its young again. The foster bird incubates the egg and feeds the young cuckoo when it hatches, driven by instinct to place food in its hungry mouth even though the young cuckoo may grow larger than its foster parent. The young invader soon hatches and, in its urge to survive, pushes the foster bird's own eggs and young out of the nest. It grows quickly and in only two weeks is ready to leave, already equipped by instinct with all it needs to know for survival.

The first days of life

Some birds hatch from their eggs already well prepared for life. The young are covered with downy feathers, and can move about on their own. Ducklings and hen chicks begin life like this. Their parents need only guard them as they find their own food.

However, most birds are born totally helpless. They are naked and blind, and cannot leave the nest. Their parents must bring them food as they grow. However, they grow very quickly, and may be ready to leave their parents before young birds that are born with the ability to feed themselves. Young larks are born helpless, in nests on the ground, but within a week they can get out of the nest and hide in the surrounding grass if danger threatens. They are able to leave the nest only two to 12 days after hatching. The whole process of rearing the young takes as little as three weeks.

Below: Most birds have to bring food to their young, which sit in the nest, their mouths open to eat anything they are given. Here, the mother bird has returned with several worms.

What is a mammal?

Mammals are warm-blooded animals with backbones whose young are fed on the mother's milk. They grow hair, and the young are usually born alive.

The platypus and echidna are the only two egg-laying mammals. Both live in Australia. This is also the home of the majority of pouched mammals, or marsupials, although a few marsupials are scattered through South America.

These two more primitive groups of mammals have been largely replaced by the modern placental mammals which are world-wide. Their young are fed inside the mother's body by the mother's blood through a filter, or placenta. The babies are therefore born at a more advanced age than in other kinds of mammals.

Mammals range in size from the minute shrews to the giant blue whale. Different species lead very different kinds of lives, and are found below and on the ground, in trees, in water and in the air.

Being well adapted for a particular life-style is very important when it comes to searching for food. Usually, the main differences are seen in the limbs and the teeth. In some mammals the legs are best suited for running, in others for hopping, yet others for burrowing, climbing, swimming and flying.

Teeth are used for nibbling, chewing or for tearing flesh. Whether a mammal eats mainly plant or animal matter shows in the kind of teeth it has.

Because mammals are warm-blooded and covered in hair, they

Right: Bats are the only mammals capable of true flight. They can find their way through darkness by picking up echoes of high-pitched sounds, called sonar. The photograph shows a vampire bat.

Left: This clumsy-looking walrus is a sea mammal. It uses its limbs, or flippers, for swimming. A walrus finds its tusks useful for hauling itself out of the water and for digging up food on the sea bed.

can live in cold as well as hot countries. To avoid freezing or overheating they behave differently. They keep more active in polar regions, since exercise increases body heat. Polar animals are also more thickly furred. On the other hand, in the tropics, large mammals like the elephant and hippo have naked bodies so as to lose heat more rapidly. Some mammals lose heat by perspiring, as we do. Dogs pant in order to lose heat.

Choice of food

Mammals can be carnivorous, herbivorous or omnivorous. A few types are scavengers, feeding on dead remains. However, with the exception of some specialized feeders, such as the Australian koala and the South American three-toed sloth which eat only certain leaves, most mammals will eat what is available if they have to.

The food canal in herbivores is usually much longer than in carnivores since plant food is more difficult to digest. Some mammals have stomachs with several compartments which break down the plant food more easily. Others, like rabbits, are helped with bacteria and other organisms which break down the food in their intestines.

Types of mammal

The largest group of mammals are the rodents, or gnawing mammals. Their incisor teeth are curved and chisel-shaped for nibbling. They have no canine teeth. Squirrels, rats and mice, and porcupines are all rodents.

Rabbits and hares, although they also gnaw food, belong to a quite separate group of mammals. They have an extra pair of incisors in the upper jaw, long ears and long hind legs.

Carnivores include dogs and cats, weasels, hyaenas, mongooses, bears, raccoons and pandas. Most eat only meat, but some, like bears and badgers, are omnivorous, and pandas are mainly

vegetarian, eating bamboo shoots.

Some mammals, like seals, walruses and manatees, are specially built for swimming. The whale family and its smaller cousin, the dolphin, are even more expert swimmers. They are not able to live on land.

Mammals called edentates include anteaters, sloths and armadillos in their numbers. They are only found in South America, and

Right: The dormouse is one of the mammals which spend the winter in hibernation. Here, a mother is suckling her babies.

Above: The African elephant is the largest of all land mammals. African elephants are easily distinguished from Indian elephants by their large ears. This female is feeding her calf.

feed mainly on insects and grubs.

There are two groups of ungulates, or hooved mammals. One group has an odd number of toes, like horses, zebras and rhinoceroses. The other group is even-toed and includes the large deer and antelope families, pigs and hippos, various cattle, sheep and goats, as well as camels and giraffes. Some ungulates are ruminants and can chew the cud.

Ungulates usually live in herds and are plant-eaters with strong molar teeth for chewing. The canine teeth are small or totally absent.

Bats are mammals which rival a bird's skill at flying. Their forelimbs have long fingers to provide a

framework for the wings. Mostly they fly at night, hunting insects.

Primates

The last group of mammals are the primates. They consist of lemurs and bush-babies, monkeys, apes and man. All of them have grasping hands for holding and climbing. Although some are strict vegetarians, others eat more varied food and are omnivorous. Primate teeth are less specialized than those of other mammals.

Monotremes

There are four things which mammals have in common. They are warm-blooded, they grow hair, their young are born alive and then fed on mother's milk. It therefore came as a great surprise when a strange animal was discovered which grew hair, yet laid eggs like a bird. This animal was found living in Australia.

Duck-billed platypus

The first specimen was sent to England in 1798. It had been caught beside a river in eastern Australia. Scientists who examined it found that it had a furry coat like that of an otter, a duck-like beak, and a beaver's tail. It was such a strange-looking animal that some people thought it must be a hoax. It looked just as if a joker had sewn a duck's bill to a mammal's skin.

Further examination showed that, unlike mammals, the specimen had a single rear opening, or cloaca, such as occurs in birds and reptiles. Also, when further captives were studied, it was found that the body temperature was much lower than is normal for mammals, only about 25° centigrade. A soft-shelled, whitish egg was found in one animal.

This curious mixture of mammalian and reptilian characteristics was confirmed when a female was found in her burrow suckling her young on milk. The creature was given the name of the duck-billed platypus. Many scientists believe it forms an evolutionary link between the first reptiles and modern mammals.

How a platypus lives

The platypus is found along the

A baby echidna is only about one centimetre long at birth. It feeds and grows inside a temporary pouch of skin on its mother's belly. The mother shown below is lying on her back, and the minute baby can be seen in her pouch. Below the pouch is the single rear opening typical of a monotreme. The powerful claws are used for digging, and the long snout with its sticky tongue picks up the ants and termites on which it feeds.

banks of streams and lakes on the eastern side of Australia and Tasmania. It has a unique life-style. At dawn and dusk, and on cloudy days, it enters the water in search of food such as shrimps and insect larvae. Under water its eyes and ears are closed by folds of skin. It propels itself through the water with its front feet, and steers with its hind feet and flat tail. The feet have broad webs (platypus means "flat feet") which are good for swimming. The webs can be folded back to uncover the claws for digging.

The flat beak is fleshy and very sensitive, and can detect small water animals such as snails, crustaceans, small fish and frogs, as well as worms.

Rearing the young
The platypus digs its burrow in the river bank. Some burrows can be as long as ten metres. A pair usually live together. After mating during the Australian springtime, the female leaves the burrow and digs her own tunnel with an oval nest-chamber at the end. She lays two or three eggs there, which take about ten days to hatch.

The babies lick the milk which oozes from the milk glands on the mother's stomach. There are no teats. Each time the mother leaves the nest to feed she blocks the entrance with earth to keep out enemies, and to hold in the warmth. The young leave the nest after about four months.

The female platypus will mate and conceive again after the birth of her young. However, the fertilized egg will not start to develop until after the babies are past the suckling stage.

Because of the single rear opening the platypus is called a monotreme, meaning "single opening". Monotremes are the most primitive mammals alive today. The platypus is the only mammal to have a poisonous weapon. The male has a sharp spur on each hind leg which can cause a very painful injury.

The platypus is quite rare and is a protected species. One of the chief dangers it has to face is being caught by accident in fishermen's traps, so that it drowns.

Spiny anteaters
The only other monotreme alive today is the spiny anteater, or echidna. There are five different kinds distributed through Australia and New Guinea. All five look similar, and resemble a large hedgehog, with their upper parts covered in long, sharp spines.

Echidnas prefer wooded country with plenty of undergrowth. Like hedgehogs they roam about at night, searching for insects and other small prey by smell, since their eyesight is poor. The echidna uses its strong forelegs and sharp claws to dig its way into the soil. It captures its prey with its long, sticky tongue which it flicks out from its mouth, located at the end of its snout. Its food consists mainly of ants and termites. The echidna is powerful enough to tear open termite hills, and can burrow at a surprising speed. When alarmed, it rolls into a ball. The spines easily ward off any enemies.

Reproduction
The echidna produces a single egg in late summer, but does not build a nest. Instead the egg is passed into a temporary pouch which consists of a fold of skin on the mother's belly. It is not known how the egg enters the pouch. It may fall in by itself, or it may be placed there with the help of the mother's feet or beak. The egg hatches in about ten days.

The newly hatched baby licks milk from its mother and stays in the pouch for about ten weeks. By that time the sharp spines have begun to harden. The baby echidna is then left in a safe hiding place which the mother visits regularly in order to feed it. After about a year the youngster will have developed into a fully grown adult.

Living in captivity
Echidnas can live to a great age – up to 50 years. They are also easy to keep in zoos. In contrast, the platypus is not easily kept in captivity, and usually dies. However, one Australian naturalist was successful in breeding. He built a tunnel and nest-chamber attached to a swimming pool. The platypuses mated and the female produced two young. One died but the other survived and grew into a healthy adult.

Like most expert swimmers, the platypus has broad, webbed feet. In the water, a platypus looks very streamlined.

Left: This drawing shows a nesting burrow in the bank of a river with a mother platypus and her baby.

Below: A platypus can remain under water for up to five minutes.

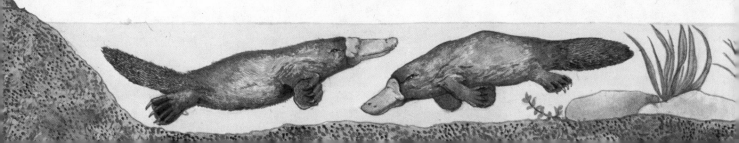

Kangaroos and wallabies

A marsupial is a mammal that has a pouch in which it carries its babies. The chief home of marsupials is Australia, and of all the different kinds, the kangaroos are the best known. They were hunted for centuries by the Aborigines, who included them in their ritual dances and paintings. Today the kangaroo is the national emblem of Australia.

In all, there are some 90 different kinds of kangaroos. The larger ones are commonly called kangaroos, and the smaller ones wallabies. The smallest are the rat kangaroos.

One of the largest and tallest is the red kangaroo. It is two metres high and lives in the more open grasslands of the interior, in groups or mobs. The mob usually feeds at night and rests in the shade by day.

When it is moving slowly, or feeding, the red kangaroo goes on all fours, placing its tail on the ground and swinging its hind legs forward. The tail is important for balancing when the kangaroo is bounding, which is the way it moves fast. An adult can make leaps up to ten metres long, and jump a fence two and a half metres high. The powerful hind legs and claws are used for defence, for example when two males are fighting or when the animal is attacked by farm dogs, and can do quite serious damage. Kangaroos are good swimmers and good diggers. They will dig holes in search of drinking water.

Among the smaller wallabies, the brush-tailed wallaby prefers dense undergrowth. The rock wallaby lives in stony places. Bennett's wallaby, which is often kept in zoos, prefers grassland.

There are about eight kinds of small rat kangaroos, and the rufous rat kangaroo is the smallest of all. It measures only 30 centimetres from the tip of its nose to the tip of its tail. Rat kangaroos are not the same as kangaroo rats, which are rodents.

It might seem strange to see a kangaroo in a tree, but these do exist. The tree kangaroo climbs along branches rather clumsily, using its long claws to grip.

Birth

After its parents have mated, the unborn baby kangaroo develops inside its mother for about 30–40 days. Sometimes there may be a long delay before birth. This is because the fertilized egg-cell remains dormant in the mother's womb for some time before it starts to grow. This is called "delayed implantation", and also occurs in badgers and some deer.

A day or two before giving birth the mother lies on her back, licks her stomach and cleans her pouch. The new-born kangaroo is tiny, two and a half centimetres long. It barely weighs one gram, and its legs are only short stumps. It clings on to the mother's fur, and in about three minutes struggles out of its mother's birth passage, along her stomach, and into her pouch without any help.

Once inside it finds a milk teat, and grips it so tightly that it is difficult to remove it. The baby, called a joey, feeds and sleeps inside the pouch for about 190 days before it leaves it for the first time. By then it has grown a coat of fur.

The joey will leave the pouch for longer periods as it grows, but will go back there if it is in any danger.

Right: Rival male kangaroos sometimes have vicious fights. They "box" each other with their fore limbs. A fighting kangaroo will often lean back on its tail and lash out at its opponent with its powerful hind legs.

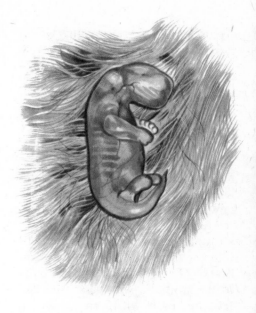

Above: This mother kangaroo is busily cleaning out her pouch, ready for the baby, which will be born soon. The little joey is less than 2.5 centimetres long. Without any help from its mother, the new-born baby finds its way into the pouch.

Below left: At 50 days old, the baby kangaroo is still blind and hairless, and feeds from its mother's nipple. When it is well grown and covered with hair it will leave the pouch for short periods to eat grass.

Above right: A baby kangaroo is blind at birth and has useless stumps for hind legs. As soon as it reaches the mother's pouch, it takes her nipple into its mouth and remains attached like this for a full six months.

Below: The young kangaroo in this picture is several months old, and no longer a baby. It hangs out of the pouch to feed along with its mother.

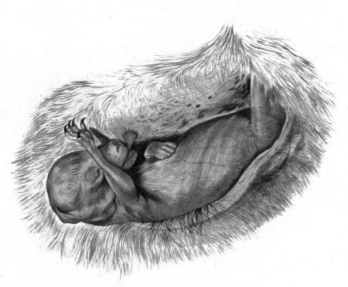

It enters head first, does a somersault, and ends curled up with head and hind feet sticking out. In about seven months, it can hop around and feed itself.

Hunters

If hunted, a mother may push her baby out and abandon it, to almost certain death. She does this to make herself lighter, so she can move faster.

Before the white man arrived in Australia, kangaroos had very few enemies, apart from dingos and eagles which preyed on the young.

Then, as farming increased, grassland was needed for sheep and cattle, and it was fenced off to keep the kangaroos from eating it. The rabbit was introduced, and it also needed grass. The result was a war by men against both kangaroos and rabbits.

Where marsupials live

Apart from a few opossums which live in North and South America, nearly all marsupials live in Australia. Australians call these marsupials possums because they are different from the American opossums.

Fossils show that marsupials were once found all over the world and have existed for some 70 million years. During this time, some new mammals appeared, which were like most of the mammals we know today. These have a sort of filter, called a placenta, in their bodies. This joins the unborn baby to its mother's womb, so she can feed her baby with her own blood until it is born. By then it is well developed. We call these mammals placental mammals.

Many placental mammals protect their young by hiding them in a nest. A helpless baby marsupial on the other hand is born far too soon for this and must be carried and fed by its mother in the pouch.

It is possible that the placentals had an advantage over the marsupials in rearing their young, and so gradually drove the marsupials out of the rest of the world into Australia, which was then joined to Asia. Then the sea broke through, cutting Australia off, and leaving the marsupials to develop in their own way.

Possums
The large family of possums, or phalangers, are squirrel-like, and eat leaves and fruit. Some can swing by their tails. They are mostly nocturnal. The smallest is the honey possum which has a long tongue and sips nectar from flowers. The largest is the slow-moving cuscus.

The American opossums are different, as they hunt small animals and insects. The Virginian opossum, widespread in the U.S.A., produces a large family which it carries on its back after it leaves the pouch. When the opossum is alarmed it may collapse limply, as if it is dead. This is described as "playing possum".

Burrowing marsupials
The wombat is the best known burrowing marsupial. Like a badger it sleeps underground by day, coming out at night to shuffle along like a small bear. Its pouch points backwards so as not to pick up any dirt as it burrows. People often keep wombats as pets.

The only other real burrower is the marsupial mole. This has no eyes or outer ears, and behaves like a true mole. Little is known about its habits and breeding, but like the wombat, its pouch points backwards.

Hunters
The native "cats" or dasyures are hunters, and look and behave like weasels. There is another larger hunter, called the Tasmanian devil which, in spite of its name, makes a gentle pet. It has been exterminated from the mainland, and only lives in Tasmania.

Koalas
The koala is not often kept in zoos because it is hard to feed. It only eats the leaves of the eucalyptus or gum tree, and then only the tender tips of certain kinds, since some leaves are poisonous even to a koala. Today koalas are only found along the eastern side of Australia.

The koala lives in trees and has paws rather like human hands. It has sharp claws to give it a firm grip on branches and bark.

It has one baby at a time. At first the baby lives in its mother's pouch, feeding on her milk. Then the mother passes green half-digested food out of her body and the baby licks this up. The mother's pouch points backwards so that the baby can reach the food.

Koalas get all the moisture they need from their food. The word "koala" is aboriginal, and means "no water".

Right: The koala bear is not really a bear at all. It is a tree-climbing marsupial.

Below: The cuscus lives in the forests of northern Australia and New Guinea.

Koala bear

Spotted cuscus

Below: Most of the marsupials on this page are Australian, except for the two American opossums (*left* and *bottom*). Most American opossums are expert climbers and can grip branches with their prehensile tails.

Marsupial mole

Virginian opossum

Bandicoot

Bennett's wallaby

Tasmanian devil

South American opossum

Insect-eaters

Many mammals feed on insects and other small animals. The mammals come from different groups, and most are small and unable to tackle larger prey. This is true of the scientific group called the Insectivora, which includes shrews, moles and hedgehogs.

Small animals

The smallest of the Insectivora are the shrews, which are sometimes mistaken for mice. But mice are rodents (*page 150*) which nibble their food with strong incisor teeth, while insectivores have sharp, pointed teeth like needles. The world's smallest mammal is the Etruscan shrew of the Mediterranean, which is less than five centimetres long.

Shrews have pointed snouts, which they constantly twitch as they search restlessly for food, night and day. They are constantly burning up energy, and some live little more than one year. Shrews have strong scent glands which make them taste unpleasant, so they are usually left alone by other hunters, apart from some owls. They are the most primitive of all mammals, and are very similar to the tiny mammals which existed in the age of the dinosaurs.

The elephant shrews of Africa have the most pointed snouts of all the shrews. Like the others, they hunt insects.

Shrews run about in the undergrowth, whereas moles are built for burrowing. They dig their way

Above: The tiny mouse possum of Australia is about to tackle a locust as big as itself.

Right and **below right:** A tree-climbing pangolin has a heavy "armour" with large scales. When disturbed it can curl up into a tight ball. The scales are a specialized form of hardened hair.

through the soil with their strong shovel-shaped front feet, pushing up mole hillocks above the ground, along the line of their tunnels.

Moles hunt worms and insects. They are very sensitive to vibrations and can detect the movement of worms in the soil.

The golden moles live in Africa. They have attractive, shiny golden fur unlike the black coats of most other moles.

Hedgehogs come out at night and snuffle around, rooting among the leaves and soil for insects and other small animals. They move about noisily, and rely on a coat of sharp prickles for defence. The prickles are specialized hairs which harden with growth. A hedgehog curls up when disturbed, so few enemies will tackle it. However, it faces danger from traffic on the roads at night, and many get run over. The European hedgehog is one of the few mammals that hibernates.

There are hedgehogs of a different kind in south-east Asia, covered in hair instead of prickles.

Tenrecs are only found in Madagascar (Malagasy Republic), and resemble hedgehogs as they have

Pangolins

New Guinea anteater

spiny coats.

There are some midgets among the marsupials of Australia. These include the mouse possum which hunts insects larger than itself.

Eating ants
Among the large insect-eaters are the South American anteaters. The giant anteater, nearly two metres long, lives in open forest country and grassland. It has no teeth but uses its very long snout and sticky tongue to lick up termites. It uses its strong claws to tear open the ant-hills. Some dwarf anteaters live in trees and can hang on with their tails. Anteaters have only one baby at a time.

Another animal which tears open termite nests is the armadillo. It has thickened skin on its back which forms a strong, horny armour, giving it a scaly, reptilian appearance. Its few teeth are small and peg-like. Armadillos vary in size, like the anteaters. The giant armadillo measures about one and a half metres, whereas the tiny hairy armadillo is about ten centimetres long. It has a fringe of thick hair along its sides. Armadillos, like hedgehogs, curl up tightly when alarmed.

Below: The aardvark, New Guinea anteater and the numbat are all anteaters. The aardvark has no close living relatives, but the New Guinea anteater is an egg-laying relation of the platypus. Numbats are marsupials.

All the members of the armadillo family live in South America, and only the nine-banded armadillo extends its range north into the southern part of North America.

Pangolins live in the Old World, and are like armadillos. They are covered with a remarkable layer of scales on their heads, backs and sides, even the tail. Normal hair grows between the scales. The mouth is small and it has no teeth. Like birds, pangolins swallow stones, which help to grind up the food. The acid in the ants they eat also helps with digestion.

Some pangolins live on the ground, others in trees. The giant pangolin grows to more than two and a half metres. All are nocturnal and solitary animals.

Earth pigs
The aardvark lives in Africa — its name is Afrikaans for "earth pig". It lives in bush country south of the Sahara. It has strong claws for digging, and is an active burrower. It uses its long snout and tongue to catch and feed on termites and locusts. The aardvark is nocturnal, and its one or two young are born in a burrow.

Primate insect-eaters
A number of lower primates, or lemurs, are insect-eaters. The bushbabies of Africa come out after dark to go insect-hunting. By then

many insects have gone to rest in hidden places, so the bush-baby searches by dipping its hand into cracks and holes to find a meal. In the Far East their cousins, the slow-moving lorises, are expert stalkers of insects. Both bushbabies and lorises have big eyes to see in the dark.

Among the higher primates the chimpanzee has been seen to use a stick to catch insects. It pokes the stick into an ants' nest. The ants cling to this and are pulled out and eaten.

Although classed as carnivores, the badger and some bears will also eat insects. Using their powerful claws they can tear open tree stumps and fallen logs, or dig into the ground in search of grubs. Anything sweet is particularly well liked and they will break open bees' and wasps' nests for the grubs and honey.

Many bats are nocturnal insect-hunters, and take over from the swallows and swifts which hunt them by day.

Since insects are so common and widespread most mammals will eat them at some time or another, especially if their normal food is in short supply. Mice, squirrels, as well as many birds, lizards, frogs and toads, are all insect-eaters.

Below: The three-banded armadillo has the perfect form of defence—it curls up into a very tight ball, and is almost impossible to prise apart.

Three-banded armadillo

Aardvark

Numbat

Even-toed ungulates

Even-toed ungulates are plant-eating mammals which have hooves divided into two or four parts. Many are large and live in groups or herds. The limbs between the "wrist" and "ankle" joints are elongated, and the legs, especially in deer and antelopes, are often long and slender and built for speed. Pigs, however, are short-legged and stockily built.

Pigs

Pigs eat plants, roots and even carrion. The biggest, the barbirussa, lives on the island of Celebes. Like other pigs it has large canine teeth curved into tusks, which are used as weapons and for rooting in the soil. The African pig, the warthog, is said to be the ugliest animal in the world.

The wild boar lives in Europe, Asia and India, and has become rare. For centuries it has been hunted for sport. It is now protected in game reserves in some places.

Domestic pigs are descended from the wild boar. Like some other farm animals, a sow may occasionally attack a human in defence of her litter. Although pigs are sometimes considered dirty animals they are in fact very clean.

Peccaries live in South America. They are small pigs that can be dangerous. Wild pigs are nervous, and may attack without warning.

Submerged

Hippopotamus means "river horse". Hippos live in Africa and can grow to four metres, and weigh three tonnes. They live in groups on the banks of rivers and lakes, or in the water, almost submerged, with their eyes, ears and nostrils showing. Hippos can dive and walk along the river bottom. They have a web between their toes which helps them to swim. Hippos feed on water plants, and at night graze on the waterside vegetation.

The pig-sized pygmy hippo, a small cousin, lives in the tropical forests of the Congo and spends much of the time in water. Its oily skin protects it from the heat.

Above: Pigs are animals which root around the ground, looking for food. They have large litters of young.
Below: The hippopotamus lives mainly in the water, feeding on water plants. Hippos give birth to only one baby at a time.

Camels

There are two kinds of camel. The one-humped Arabian dromedary is now only a domestic animal. For centuries camels have provided the only means of crossing a desert, and even today, the camel is as valuable to an Arab as the horse is to a cowboy. It is called the "ship of the desert", and can travel for miles without food and water.

The two-toed feet of a camel are well padded to support its weight on loose sand, and the slit-like nostrils can be closed to protect it from sand storms. Camels have been used and trained for warfare, and can run swiftly.

Two humps

The Bactrian camel, which has two humps, lives in Asia, and is more at home in rocky country. A few truly wild ones still exist in the Gobi desert. Most of them are valuable beasts of burden, and were used along the old caravan routes before there were cars and trains. The Bactrian camel has a thick coat and can withstand cold weather.

In America, where camels ori-

Right: This camel, the one-humped dromedary, is the "ship of the desert" of the Sahara and Arabia. It has made travel possible across the deserts where man could not travel alone.

ginated, there are smaller versions. The vicuña and guanaco still live as wild animals in the Andean mountains of South America. The llama and alpaca are the domestic forms, used by the South American Indians. The llama is used to carry burdens and the alpaca's hair is woven into cloth.

Camels have complicated stomachs for digesting their harsh and prickly food. Their soft and flexible lips help them to feed.

Below: Wildebeeste, or gnu, graze on the open grasslands of Africa. They are usually found in herds of up to 50 animals, although in times of drought, when they travel long distances in search of water, these groups can be very much larger.

Santa Claus

Another beast of burden is the reindeer, a member of the deer family. Unlike its North American relative, the caribou, it is no longer wild. Reindeer live in herds, and are kept by the Lapps and other northern peoples, providing them with milk, food and clothing. Like the African antelopes, reindeer migrate during the winter, travelling south to warmer parts. The wide hooves make a clicking sound when the reindeer moves, and help to give support over the snow. Reindeer feed on the "reindeer moss" of the tundra, which is really a lichen.

Cattle and other grazing animals

Giraffes and okapis

Giraffes are another family of even-toed ungulates. They live in Africa, south of the Sahara. They have a neck which like a human neck has only seven joints. At six metres, the giraffe is the world's tallest animal. The blood vessels in the neck have valves to help pump the blood up to the brain. They have short horns on the head, covered with hairy skin.

The giraffe lives in herds, browsing on trees. The pattern on its coat makes it hard to see. It is so tall that it has to spread its legs out sideways in order to reach down to drink water. Although it looks clumsy it can run as fast as a race horse.

Its relative, the shy okapi, lives in the dense forests of the Congo and was only discovered in the 1900s. Its neck is shorter than the giraffe's, and it has a dark coat which helps camouflage it. It often stands in water and has white stripes around its legs.

Cattle

The largest family of even-toed ungulates is the cattle family, which includes domestic cattle, sheep, goats, deer and antelopes.

The farm cattle we know are mostly descended from the auroch, a large animal, two metres tall, which roamed the forests of Europe and northern Asia. The last one was killed in Poland in 1827.

Water buffalo are common in the Far East and are used for ploughing. They are not the same as the Cape buffalo, of Africa, which is wild.

Other kinds of cattle are the Arctic musk ox and the shaggy yak, which the people of the Himalayas use as a beast of burden.

The massive European bison was once common in forests, but was almost wiped out by man. Today it is found in some zoos, and in a Polish game park.

Millions of American bison or buffalo once roamed the plains, hunted by the North American Indians who used the flesh for food

and the hide to make clothing and tepees. With the arrival of fire-arms, farming and railways, the buffalo was almost exterminated. A few were saved, and are kept in game parks.

Cattle have four-chambered stomachs. Plant food is swallowed and is stored in the first chamber, the paunch or rumen. Then it passes to the reticulam, where minute bacteria and protozoa break down the cellulose in the plants. While the animal is resting it coughs up lumps of food and chews them thoroughly. The food then goes to the third chamber the omasum, and then to the fourth, the abomasum, where it is fully digested.

This complicated process is called ruminating or chewing the cud. It helps protect the animals, as they are able to eat quickly at dawn and dusk, and then hide away to digest the food. The domestic cow, which has no natural enemies, will lie down in the middle of a field to ruminate.

Goats and sheep

Goats and sheep are also ruminants. The wild bezoar goat of the mountains of south-west Asia is probably the ancestor of the farm goat. Another wild goat, the ibex, lives on mountains in Europe. The Rocky Mountain goat lives in the American Rockies.

The ancestor of the domestic sheep, the mouflon, lives on the islands of Corsica and Sardinia.

Deer

Deer are the most northerly ruminants. The males carry branched horns called antlers, which they shed and regrow every year. The only female deer to have antlers is the reindeer, the most northerly deer.

Above: Both male and female giraffes have a pair of "false horns". They are short, stubby growths.

Below: Cows are among the most common hoofed animals.

Below: Gnus are among the last large antelopes that can still be found in vast numbers. The Serengeti Park in Tanzania is a particularly important feeding ground for them.

In the Middle Ages hunting deer was the sport of kings, especially hunting the stag, the male red deer. There is a similar deer, the wapiti, in North America.

The moose, called the elk in Europe, is the largest deer. It often goes into swamps to eat water plants.

The attractive spotted fallow deer came from Asia, but has been introduced to many countries. The roe deer lives in conifer woods and is very shy.

Antelopes

Antelopes live in Africa and Asia. They look like deer, but both sexes have unbranched horns which spiral or curve, and which are not shed. The biggest antelope is the eland, nearly two metres tall, and the smallest is the royal antelope, only 25 centimetres high.

The pronghorn buck

The pronghorn buck lives on the North American plains. Like antelopes, both sexes have permanent horns; an outer layer of these is shed each year. But the horns are branched, more like a deer than an antelope. It is neither an antelope nor a deer, but a separate animal.

Warning signals

When a springbok **(left)** is startled it leaps high into the air. The white hairs along its back are raised and the stripes on its side seem to flash, warning other springboks of danger.

The pronghorn antelope has a patch of white hair around its tail. When alarmed this hair stands up on end **(below right).** This tells other pronghorns that there is some kind of danger. It is a good way of warning others because the pronghorn can do it silently, without attracting the attention of its enemies.

Odd-toed ungulates

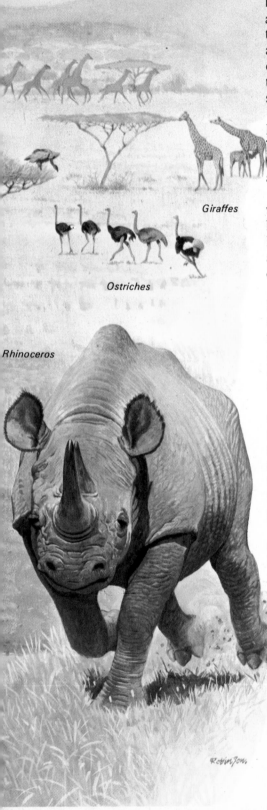

Giraffes

Ostriches

Rhinoceros

Above: A charging black rhino is rather like a tank and can be very dangerous. It may attack without warning, and has been known to hit cars. It can be four metres long and weigh up to two tonnes.

There are two groups of ungulates, or hoofed mammals. There is an even-toed group, in which the two middle toes are the largest, and an odd-toed group, where the central toe is the largest, though there may be smaller toes on either side.

Horses

The horse family consists of the wild and domestic horses, zebras and asses.

Seventy million years ago there was a terrier-sized animal, a "dawn horse" with four toes on its front legs and three on its hind. Gradually, horses increased in size, reducing the number of toes.

Horses have long slender legs to help them run fast over open country. There is little cover in this, their natural home and they need speed to escape. All members of the horse family have good sight.

Only one kind of wild horse still exists. Przewalski's horse, named after a Polish explorer, survives in small numbers on the Mongolian steppes. It is a close relative of the tarpan, the extinct true ancestor of the horse which early man hunted and drew in his cave paintings.

Horses have since been bred in many forms, as riding and work horses.

The Mongolian wild horse is stockily built and has a short, stiff mane. Similar horses, such as the British Exmoor pony, now roam half-wild in several countries.

In America, where horses were introduced, those that escaped and lived wild are called mustangs. They were adopted by the American Indians who had never seen horses before the white man arrived.

Asses

There are two kinds of wild asses, one which lives in south-west Asia and one in Africa. They are lightly built and have longer ears than horses. They live in dry desert country. The donkey is a domesticated ass.

Zebras

Zebras are striped horses which live on the plains of East Africa. There are three kinds, all with different patterns of stripes. The stripes make the zebras hard to see at dusk and dawn when the lion is hunting.

Rhinos

There are five kinds of rhinoceros, two in Africa, and one each in India, Sumatra and Java. The "horn" is made of compressed hair and is valued in the East as a love potion.

The African and Sumatran rhinos have two horns, the others have only one. Rhinos are solitary and usually peaceful, but the black rhino is bad tempered and may attack unexpectedly.

The black rhino browses on bushes, the white rhino, which is actually grey, grazes on grass. Its name comes from a wrong translation of the Afrikaans word for "wide"; it has a broad mouth.

Tapirs

Tapirs are heavily built, with long snouts. They are shy and nocturnal, living in tropical forests, close to water. They are about one metre tall. South American tapirs are grey, but Malay tapirs are boldly marked in black and white. All young tapirs are striped. Tapirs hide in the thick undergrowth, feeding on leaves and fruits.

Elephants

Elephants are very large, with ivory tusks and a long trunk. The trunk is an elongated nose, used to reach up for leaves, pick up objects, suck up drinking water, take a dust bath and to smell danger. This last is particularly useful as elephants are very short sighted. The trunk can also be used as a weapon. The tusks are the upper incisor teeth, used for digging, fighting and picking up heavy objects.

The African elephant lives in herds in the bush country of East Africa. It has large ears, a rounded forehead and a hollow back. The tip of the trunk has two lips. A large bull can be nearly three and a half metres tall, and weigh up to six tonnes.

They are seldom tamed, but there is a smaller kind which lives in the forests of the Congo basin and has been trained to work for man. These elephants once lived as far north as the Atlas mountains, close to Carthage, and may have been the kind that Hannibal used to cross the Alps to invade Rome.

Indian elephants

The Indian or Asiatic elephant lives in India, Malaysia and the East Indies. The cows have only very small tusks, which are hidden behind the trunk. These elephants have been used by man for centuries, helping to move timber.

Elephants seldom live for more than 70 years. They become mature at about 15 years. A single calf is born about 21 months after mating.

These two horses clearly have very different builds. The Arab horse **(above)** has a sleek appearance and it can run very fast. The Italian heavy draught horse **(left)** has a stocky build which makes it slow-moving.

Right: Baby zebras can stand up as soon as they are born. They soon learn to run to keep up with the rest of the herd.

Below: Elephant herds are usually led by old females as they trek across the African plains. There is usually at least one mature bull elephant to each herd.

The cat family

Cats, big and small, are easily recognized as hunting mammals. They have a rather flat face and short jaws, and their eyes are placed in the front of the head. Apart from the cheetah, a cat's sharp claws can be withdrawn when it is not using them. Cats move on the tips of their toes, like dogs. The fifth toe, or dew-claw, stays above the ground.

Hunting
They usually hunt by lying in ambush, or by stalking prey quietly, creeping up on it and then pouncing at the last moment. Unlike dogs, cats are not long-distance runners. Even the cheetah, the world's fastest animal, which can reach a speed of 100 kilometres an hour, can only sprint a short distance. Its hunting behaviour is more like that of a dog than that of any other cat.

Cats and dogs have powerful jaws which work in an up and down movement, unlike the sideways chewing action of plant-eaters. The strong canines tear off pieces of meat, and the cutting molars slice it up into small pieces for swallowing.

Lions
Most cats are solitary hunters, but lions stay in groups called prides. Two or three lionesses with their grown-up young team up to catch big animals, such as antelopes and zebras. Some will drive their prey towards the others, which are waiting in ambush. There is usually only one adult male with them.

Lions are common in the open game country of East Africa. They also live in the Gir Forest, a game park in north-west India. Its large size and maned head makes the lion a majestic animal, and it is sometimes called "King of the beasts". Yet, on occasions, a lion seems to be a coward, and will retreat from an antelope mother protecting her young. Lionesses even desert their cubs on occasions.

Lions spend much of the time in a lazy way, resting in the shade.

Yet, when aroused, they can be both agile and swift.

Tigers
The tiger lives in India and the Far East, and even ranges as far north as Siberia, where it can survive the bitter winters. Unlike lions, this big cat does not object to water, and will frequently bathe. This is especially true of the tigers in the warmer south. Its striped body makes excellent camouflage in the tall grass of jungle undergrowth and bamboos.

Leopards and jaguars
The spotted leopard is also well camouflaged. It lives in many places, both in Africa and Asia. It is an expert climber, and is considered to be one of the most dangerous cats. It usually carries its prey up a tree. Occasionally a cub is born black. A black leopard is called a panther.

The jaguar is similar to the leopard and lives in South America. It is more heavily built and its spots are more open.

Pumas
The fawn coloured puma or mountain lion, also called the cougar, lives in North America.

It often appears in Western films as a dangerous animal, but is really shy and timid, and avoids man. It has a very wide distribution in all kinds of country, from mountains and forests to deserts. It has been driven away from intensively cultivated farming land.

The lynx
The lynx is an average sized cat of more northerly countries, and lives in the mountains and forests. It has tufted ears and a short tail.

Some cats have now become rare, because of their beautiful fur which is in great demand for fur coats. Most attractive of these is the clouded leopard, a tree-dweller of south-east Asia. The serval is a small spotted cat which lives on the African plains. It is also hunted for its fur.

Domestic cats
Domestic cats are descended from the wild cat of North Africa. The first farmers who settled around the Mediterranean and Near East needed a way to protect their stores of food from rats and mice, and found the cat useful. The domestic cat slowly spread across the world, and like dogs has been bred in many different ways. But they still behave like wild cats.

Above: The puma is an American member of the cat family. It is found in very different surroundings, from hot deserts to mountains and forests. Pumas can be nearly as long as lionesses, but most are not much bigger than a great dane.

Below: The stripes on an Indian tiger camouflage it in long grass. There are very few tigers left in the world. They are not quite as large as lions, but they sometimes kill animals as big as buffaloes.

Below: Lions are tawny brown in colour to blend with the parched grass of the African savannah lands. They are unusual cats because they hunt in groups. (Most cats hunt alone.) Like other predators, lions are not always successful at catching their prey. They probably catch less than 50 per cent of the animals they chase. Hunting usually takes place at dawn and dusk or during the night. Well-fed lions sleep or rest for much of the time.

Dogs and bears

Below: Dogs and wolves may have a common ancestor. Some scientists believe the dog is descended from a small wolf which is now extinct.

Bat-eared fox

Dhole

Bush dog

Cape hunting dog

Dogs, like cats, are meat-eaters. They have long legs and run on their toes. But whereas cats usually hunt alone, catching prey by surprising it, dogs wear it down by chasing it over long distances.

Apart from the fox, dogs do not hunt alone. They have a keen sense of smell, and good hearing. They are highly social animals and live in groups called packs. Each pack has a leader.

Wolves

This is well illustrated in the wolf. Wolves hunt in small packs or family groups of about six animals. They are still widely distributed in North America, Europe and Asia, though they have been driven out of the areas which are farmed. In spite of their reputation, they rarely attack humans.

The smaller coyotes of North America, and the jackals of Africa are scavengers rather than hunters.

Below: Two spotted hyaenas grooming one another. This is a sign of affection.

There are several other kinds of dogs, including the dhole of India and the hunting dog of Africa. The dingo was probably introduced to Australia by the Aborigines, who arrived there long before the Europeans. Its ancestor is unknown, but it may have been bred from the jackal as a tame dog, which then went wild again.

Domestic dogs

Most of the northern breeds of dogs such as huskies and the chow-chow are almost certainly descended from the wolf. They behave in similar ways. Dogs like these tend to look on their master as a sort of pack leader, and depend on him much more.

A dog will gulp its food, just as a wolf does. Cats have better table manners. This is because a wild cat can feed at leisure, but wolves and dogs live in a group, and the fastest eaters get the most.

Both puppies and kittens are playful. Play is preparation for the serious business of hunting as an adult.

Domestic dogs have been bred for many tasks. These include hunting, retrieving, use as guide and guard dogs, and for pulling sledges and as house pets.

The fox

A fox tends to live and hunt alone, stalking its prey in a cat-like way. Foxes are hunted and face other dangers from man, so they have become shy, hunting mainly at night. But the European fox is still common, and will even enter towns to look for food.

The smaller Arctic fox lives in the far north. It turns white in winter. The silver fox is bred on fur farms.

Hyaenas

Hyaenas look like dogs, but belong to a different family. They are less powerful runners, and have a weak-looking sloping back. There are four kinds of hyaenas. The spotted and brown ones live on the plains of Africa, the striped hyaena is north African and the aardwolf lives in southern Africa. The aardwolf lives mainly on insects and has weak jaws. The others are scavengers, with powerful jaws that can crack large bones.

People used to think that hyaenas were cowardly animals who would wait around a lion's kill for the left-overs. But now we know that they catch their own

Below: Relatives of the dog are spread over a wide area of the world. Some look and behave very differently from one another.

Fox

Wolf

Jackal

Wild dog

Domestic dog

prey and will even drive off a lion. The laughing cry of a hyaena is a familiar sound in the African bush.

Bears

Bears are the heaviest of all the meat-eaters. They walk on all fours, on the flats of their feet, so that all five toes leave tracks. Some are good climbers. Although they have the large canine teeth and strong jaws of carnivores, they are omnivorous, and will eat anything from grubs and berries to large prey.

Most bears are northern animals. They have thick coats to withstand the cold winters. The most widespread bear is the brown bear, which has a range extending from North America, across Europe, into Asia and India. It varies greatly in size, the largest being the grizzly of the American Rockies and the giant Kodiak bear of Alaska.

Black bears also live in North America, while sloth bears live in India.

The most northerly bear, the Polar bear, lives among the ice and snow of the Arctic. It wanders about alone most of the time, and hunts seals.

Tiny cubs

Bears eat a lot in the summer, and grow fat. When winter comes, they hide away in a safe warm place. This is when the cubs are born. They are tiny, and are among the smallest babies in relation to their parents. A female grizzly can weigh up to 220 kilograms, but her cubs weigh no more than a few ounces each at birth. They feed on their mother's milk, and first go outside the den in spring. They stay with their mother for up to three years.

Bear cubs have been reared and even trained as circus animals.

Bears are large and powerful animals that include a large amount of plant food as well as meat in their diet. They walk on the flats of their feet, like humans, and can also stand upright.

In winter, bears rest and sleep. Their cubs are born at this time, and only come out into the open in spring.

The largest of all bears is the Kodiak bear of Alaska, a brown bear related to the grizzly. Polar bears stand over two metres tall, and live in the Arctic. There are five kinds of black bear, all of which are quite scarce.

Polar bear

Black bear

Brown bear

Otters, badgers and raccoons

Most members of the weasel family have long slender bodies and short legs. They run in a loping fashion. Most of them are fierce hunters, but some will eat plants and insects.

Weasels and stoats

The European weasel is one of the smallest members of the family. The male is only about 22 centimetres long, and the female is even smaller. It is usually solitary, though sometimes a family stays together to hunt as a pack. Weasels eat small mammals such as mice and voles.

The larger stoat hunts rabbits and ground birds. Its tail has a black tip. In northern places the stoat will turn white in winter and is then called ermine. Like weasels, stoats will sometimes hunt in packs. Both weasels and stoats will go into other animals' holes in order to hunt them.

Members of the weasel family have scent glands which they use to keep in touch with each other and also to defend themselves. The scent of the polecat and the skunk is so unpleasant that it will drive enemies away. The old name for a polecat is "foumart", which means "foul marten".

Martens and mink

The pine marten and its relatives are tree climbers, and can even catch squirrels. Like the mink and the sable, the pine marten is hunted for its fur, and so has become rare in places.

The mink, originally from North America, is bred for its fur and some have escaped from fur farms to live in the wild in parts of Europe. They threaten water birds, as they are good swimmers and hunters.

The wolverine and badgers

The wolverine, one of the largest members of the weasel family, lives in northern Europe, Asia and America. It looks like a large badger.

Badgers are ground dwellers.

They are powerful diggers, and live in a family home called a sett, made up of a number of holes. They keep this clean, regularly clearing the entrances and removing old bedding from the nesting chambers. They dig small pits nearby, which they use as latrines.

Badgers are omnivorous, eating plants, roots, small mammals and birds, grubs and earthworms. They have powerful feet, strong claws and like all weasels they walk on the soles of their feet, leaving a flat-footed impression.

The European badger usually lives in woodland, while the American badger lives on open prairies. Like skunks, badgers are strongly marked in black and white as a warning to enemies. They can bite hard.

The honey badger of Africa will dig out wild bees' nests.

Otters

Otters are graceful water weasels. They are expert swimmers, with a streamlined shape, a tapered tail for steering and webbed toes. They are nocturnal and shy, so are rarely seen. They are great wanderers. In some places the otter has become rare, partly due to hunting, but also

Below: Otters are about one metre long and have webbed hind feet. They have waterproof fur and hunt in water for fish, mussels and frogs.

Below: Weasels are the smallest meat-eaters. They are fierce hunters and eat rats, mice, moles and even rabbits.

Above: The lesser or red panda is a relative of the raccoon. It is a tree climber and lives in the Himalayan mountains. It eats fruit, leaves and small animals.

Above: This raccoon has caught a crayfish, and is about to give it a wash before eating it. The Germans call the raccoon the "washing-bear"

Raccoons eat fish, birds and eggs as well as crayfish. Sometimes they eat plant food also, such as vegetables and grain.

because the rivers where they would normally catch fish have become polluted. Young otters are very playful and delightful creatures to watch.

The sea otter lives off the west coast of America, spending much of its time floating on its back. It has the unusual habit of bringing up stones and shellfish from the sea bed, and laying the shellfish on its stomach while it uses the stone to crack open the shell. Sea otters were nearly exterminated by fur hunters, but are now protected.

Mongooses
Mongooses look like weasels, but are more closely related to dogs and cats. They belong in the Old World, but have been introduced to New Zealand and the West Indies in order to keep down snakes and rats.

The Indian mongoose has a reputation for killing snakes, particularly the cobra, but it will kill

all kinds of prey, including farm stock, such as chickens.

The mongoose has a relative, the genet. This is like a spotted cat with a ringed tail. It climbs well.

Raccoons and pandas
Raccoons live in America. They have pointed faces and are flat-footed like badgers. They climb well and usually live in forests close to water.

A raccoon will search under stones for fish and crayfish. It is often kept as a pet, but at one time trappers used to wear its fur and tail as a hat.

The pandas, which some scientists think are probably related to the raccoons, are found in Asia. The large, bear-like giant panda lives in central Asia. The much smaller red panda, or cat-bear, lives in the south-eastern parts of the Himalayas. It climbs trees and feeds mainly on leaves, fruit, small animals and birds' eggs.

Above: Honey badgers live in Africa and India. They eat small reptiles, but also love honey. Here a honey badger is tearing open a bees' nest.
Below: Badgers leap-frogging during courtship.

Gnawing mammals

Above: Squirrels are active climbers, gripping with their claws as they run up and down vertical tree trunks.

Below: The coypu, like the chinchilla, is farmed for its soft fur. It belongs to one of the three major groups of rodents.

Rodents or gnawing animals are the largest, and in many ways the most successful group of animals. This could result from their high birth-rate, small size and, in most cases, nocturnal habits. The large incisor teeth work like curved chisels for nibbling their food.

Their varied diet consists of seeds, fruit, buds, bark, leaves, grasses and people's food.

Squirrels

Rodents are adapted to all kinds of surroundings, on or below ground, in trees, in snow and in deserts.

Squirrels are adapted to tree life. They leap among the branches, using their sharp claws for climbing and their long tails for balancing. They eat cone seeds, acorns, beech nuts, buds, bark and occasionally young birds.

Some tree squirrels have folds of skin between their legs, which help them to glide as they leap from branch to branch. There are also ground squirrels, such as chipmunks.

Marmots and lemmings

The marmot and the gopher, or prairie dog, are burrowers which live in colonies. Gophers live on open plains and marmots live in mountains.

The Norway lemming also lives in mountains. It is well known for its remarkable migration. Occa-

sionally, the population builds up and hordes of lemmings move down from the mountains, sometimes even falling into rivers or the sea on their way, and drowning.

This is one of nature's ways of controlling the numbers. Such rises and falls in the population also occur among other rodents, such as voles. Birds of prey also help to control numbers.

Voles, rats and mice

Voles have small ears, blunt faces and short tails. The family includes the American muskrat, which is bred for its fur.

Rats and mice have large ears, pointed faces and long tails. They have been closely associated with humans since people first began to farm. Since then, rats and mice have lived with man, causing enormous damage to crops and property, and have spread diseases such as typhus and the bubonic plague.

They live in houses, farm buildings and anywhere else that is convenient for them. They have spread all over the world, travelling with man in his ships and caravans.

One of the smallest mice is the little harvest mouse, which builds nests among the cornstalks and tall grasses. It uses its tail for support as it climbs.

Gerbils and jerboas are desert mice. A jerboa hops about like a tiny kangaroo.

The chinchilla

The chinchilla is a rodent which is valuable for its fur. It lives in the Andes mountains of South America, where it is rare but protected.

The coypu, another animal valued for its fur, also comes from South America, but is kept on fur farms in many other countries. Like the mink, many coypu have escaped and now live wild.

Porcupines

Porcupines, like hedgehogs, are protected by sharp quills, which are a kind of hardened hair. The

Old World porcupines are ground burrowers, but those of the New World climb trees.

Cavies are the wild relations of the guinea pigs. People used to eat them, but now they are often kept as pets.

Dormice climb trees and build nests above the ground. They are well known for their habit of hibernating in winter. Their name comes from the French *dormir*, meaning "to sleep".

Beavers

Beavers are waterside rodents. They have webbed feet and flat tails to help them to swim.

They build their home, or lodge, by using their strong teeth to cut down trees. They build a dam across a stream, forming a lake in which the lodge is built of branches and mud. It has an underwater entrance for safety.

Rabbits

Although not members of the rodent family, rabbits and hares are also gnawing mammals. The rabbit originated in southern Europe, and has spread far and wide, to Britain and Australia, where it was introduced by man.

At first it was carefully protected, in areas called warrens, as a valuable fur and food animal. But it is adaptable, and eventually spread to become a serious pest. A virus disease, called myxomatosis, was released in Europe and Australia. It spread rapidly and nearly wiped the rabbits out. But they are now recovering, and may return to their former numbers.

Rabbits live in colonies below ground. Their babies are born there, blind and naked.

Hares, which are larger, live above ground and are usually solitary. They rely on speed to escape from danger. The babies, or leverets, can run about soon after they are born. Unlike rabbits, which live close to the cover of hedgerows and woodlands, hares prefer open country, even mountainsides.

Above right: The tiny harvest mouse builds its nest among corn stalks. In this drawing you can see how its tail is used for support.

Below: Gophers are a kind of rodent that live in colonies on the American prairies. They dig burrows, which makes them unpopular with farmers, as farm animals fall into the holes and injure themselves.

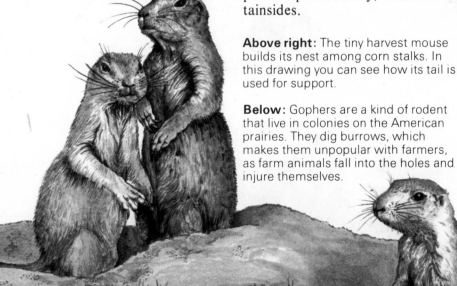

Seals, walruses and dugongs

There are three groups of seals, the true seals, the eared seals and the walrus.

True seals

True seals have no outer ears, rather short flippers and swim mainly with their hind limbs. They use their fore limbs when they move on land, pulling themselves along in a wriggling movement.

Sizes range from the three-tonne elephant seal to the small freshwater Baikal seal, which weighs about 80 kilograms.

Most seals hunt fishes and squids, but the crab-eating seal of the southern ocean eats other sea creatures as well. The leopard seal hunts sea birds and other seals. It can strip the skin off a captured penguin with one shake of its powerful head.

In the Antarctic penguins stay with the pack ice, making a blow hole in it to breathe through. Eskimo hunters will wait by a blow hole to spear the seal. Weddell's seal of the Antarctic will bite holes in the ice.

The harp seal is a migrant, spending much of its year in the mid-north Atlantic, and breeding on the Norwegian coast and on a small mid-ocean island. It has large black spots and a dark band over its neck and down the sides of its body. It can dive to 270 metres, and can stay under water for 30 minutes.

Two seals that are becoming rare are the bearded seals, which live in small herds around the coast of the north Atlantic, and the soli-

The seals shown on this page have streamlined bodies, with the hind flippers pointing backwards. The Californian sea-lion's flippers are placed under the body. The manatee **(bottom right)** is a sea-cow.

Bearded seal

Elephant seal

Californian sea lion

Common seal

Hooded seal

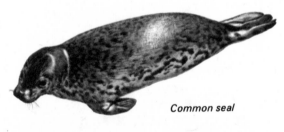
Manatee

Harp seal

tary monk seal of the Mediterranean.

The common seal likes flat coastlines with sandy beaches and mud banks. It lives around the coasts of Norway, Denmark and parts of Britain and the Baltic. It has a greyish-white and greyish-yellow spotted coat and a round head.

The grey, or Atlantic, seal has a curved face. It prefers rocky coasts. It lives on the Atlantic coast of Britain and in the Baltic.

Seals come on shore to bask. Some can sleep in the water. Their main enemy, apart from man, is the killer whale.

Eared seals

Sea lions, or eared seals, have outer ears and long webbed feet which they use to swim very fast. On land, they can turn their hind flippers under their body and move at a clumsy gallop.

They occur throughout the world except in the Indian Ocean and the north Atlantic.

Sea lions include the so-called

Right: Walruses have two tusks up to one metre long. They use the tusks to dig up shellfish on which they feed. The soft parts of a shellfish are sucked out and swallowed whole.

Below: Dugongs are also called sea-cows. They are slow-moving, placid grazers.

fur seals which are hunted for their skins.

The Californian sea lion, one of the best known members of the family, is often kept in zoos and does balancing acts in circuses.

The walrus

Walruses are massive and ungainly seals. They belong to a different family from other seals. They live in the north Atlantic and Pacific in large herds. The bulls use the downward pointing tusks for fighting, and to help to climb out of water.

The sea cows

Sea cows are a different family from seals. They have no fur and their front limbs are webbed. They have flat tails and heavily whiskered faces. They eat water plants. A single young is born in winter.

Two members of the family are the dugong and the manatee. The dugong lives in the Red Sea, and along the east coast of Africa. It is about two and a half metres long.

There are three kinds of manatees. One kind lives along the coast of West Africa and the other two are American.

Breeding in sea mammals

Seals come ashore to breed, unlike whales and sea cows which produce their young at sea. For most of the year seals live at sea, occasionally coming on to land to bask and rest. Then, as the breeding season approaches they form into herds, and make for certain beaches, called rookeries, in order to produce their young. Some seals migrate long distances to reach the shore.

Males first

The males or bulls arrive first, to establish their territories. The smaller cows arrive later. Within days each female gives birth to a single pup from a previous mating. Shortly after giving birth, they mate again, to produce another baby the next year.

The pup is suckled by its mother, who keeps going back into the sea in order to feed, and so keep up her strength. The bulls stay on shore guarding their territories.

There may be serious fighting at the rookery. The bulls rear up, roaring and slashing with their large canine teeth, sometimes inflicting severe injuries. The bull

elephant seal looks very fierce, blowing up his huge snout and using it as a sound-box.

This is a general description of the way seals breed. In some kinds of seal the mother may produce her pup not in a rookery, but on her own. The ringed seal, for example, which lives in polar regions, gives birth in a cave in an ice-floe. In other cases the seals gather in large colonies. The cows are herded into "harems", each with one bull in charge. When the pups are strong enough they are gathered into a separate nursery. The mothers are able to find their own young among the hundreds of others. They can probably do this by recognizing the particular scent of their baby.

Grey seals and common seals

Grey seals breed in late autumn along the rocky shores and islands of the north Atlantic and the Baltic Sea. Many of the pups are drowned in the wintery gales.

The common seal, on the other hand, chooses flat, sandy shores. As soon as a pup is born the mother deserts and swims out to a

Above: This roaring elephant seal has blown up its balloon-like nose to produce a loud roar. It is preparing to fight for its territory and to attack any rival males.

sandy bank. The hungry pup soons follows to a safe place offshore.

Whales

Whales and dolphins give birth at sea. Mating between two large whales is spectacular. They rear up out of the water, and fall back. Apart from tremendous splashes, they make no sound. However, whales do communicate. One whale can signal to another many kilometres away, by giving off very high-pitched notes. When these sounds were first recorded on ships' instruments during the World War Two they were thought to be signals from submarines. Since then, further recordings have been made of whales "talking", but as yet, scientists do not understand the meaning of the sounds.

The blue whale travels to the Antarctic every year to mate and feed on the small animals called krill which it can find there in spring. Later in the year, blue whales travel north to warmer seas to have their young. The calf is born up to 18 months later. It can be eight metres long, and weigh well over a tonne. No mother on land could carry such a huge weight inside her. But the sea can

Below: The bull sea-lion is far bigger than the cow. Notice how in sea-lions the hind flippers can be tucked under the body. In the true, earless seals these can only be dragged behind.

Below: A colony of grey seals at their rookery, with a larger bull in charge.

support the weight of the whale, just as it can support a ship.

The whale calf's first problem is to find air, because it is born under water. Sometimes, the calves can find enough energy to swim up to the surface by themselves, but usually, the adults have to help them by nudging them upwards. At the surface, the calves take their first breaths through their nostrils.

When it is strong enough to travel for longer distances the calf accompanies its mother back to the Antarctic, to feed and grow.

Many whales make similar journeys between feeding areas and a place to have their young.

Below: A solitary ringed seal with her pup on an Antarctic ice-floe. A blow-hole is nearby. She uses this to breathe, and to go in and out of the cave in search of food.

Whales and dolphins

Whales, dolphins and porpoises belong to a group of mammals called Cetacea. They are built for a life entirely in water. If they are stranded on land they are crushed by their own weight.

Sizes vary from the small porpoises, less than 1.5 metres long to the world's largest animal, the 35-metre blue whale, which can weigh up to 120 tonnes.

Streamlined

A whale's body is streamlined and hairless, apart from a few whiskers. It has a thick layer of fat called blubber to keep it warm. The front limbs, or flippers, act as paddles, as does the tail. There are no back limbs apart from two small bones inside the body, the last traces of the legs the whale's ancestor had.

All cetaceans must surface to breathe. The nostril, or blow hole, is on the top of the head. When the whale breathes out the breath condenses in the air, making a cloud of oisture or a spout. Toothed whales have a single spout, but baleen whales have two nostrils and make a double spout.

Toothed whales

Toothed whales have rows of curved teeth used to grasp prey such as fishes and squids. Most are small, apart from the sperm whale, which can be 30 metres long. It has a square head, with teeth in the lower jaw. There is a waxy substance called spermaceti in its head. This is used to make soap.

Sperm whales travel in schools, hunting squids and cuttlefish. They can dive to 3,000 metres and stay below for more than an hour. Their undigested food, called ambergris, is used to make perfume.

The pygmy sperm whale is only three metres long.

Dolphins

Among the smaller whales are a number of dolphins and por-poises. Dolphins have sleek bodies, beak-like jaws and a large fin on their back. The common dolphin, the best known, is about two metres long. It goes about in schools, and often follows ships. It can swim up to 32 km/h and can leap out of the water.

Dolphins have been studied in captivity. They are very intelligent, and can learn tricks and play with their keeper. Like bats, they find their way using echo location or sonar (*See also page 158*).

The pilot whale owes its name to the fact that the members of a school will all follow the leader. If the leader gets stranded on the beach the others will follow it there and may all die.

The largest member of the dolphin family is the killer whale. It can grow to nine metres. Packs of killer whales hunt seals and penguins. They hunt mainly in cold polar seas, and will sometimes attack a larger whale. In captivity the killer whale is quite docile.

Porpoises are more thick set than dolphins and have blunt noses. They travel in schools, hunt-

Above: Killer whales have about twelve conical teeth on each side of the upper and lower jaws. The teeth fit closely together when the whale's mouth is closed.

ing fish such as herrings. The common porpoise tends to keep to northern seas, and even rivers.

The narwhal

The narwhal is unusual. The female has no teeth, but the male has two. One of these, on the left side, grows into a long spiral tusk. Whalers used to sell this tusk as the horn of the legendary unicorn.

Baleen whales

The baleen whales are usually gigantic. They have no teeth, but a row of "baleen" or "whalebone" plates hanging from the upper jaw. These work as a strainer, for catching food such as krill.

A school of dolphins with their calves. A baby dolphin is born tail first. The mother guides it to the surface to take its first breath. After this, the young dolphin can swim and breathe without any help. Dolphins are very intelligent animals and devoted parents. Dolphins have been bred successfully in captivity.

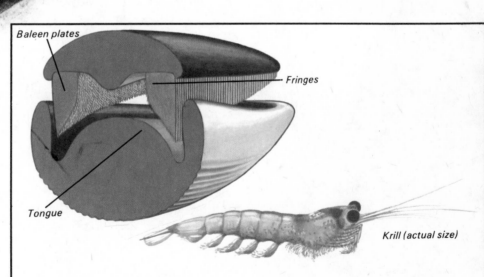

Baleen plates

Fringes

Tongue

Krill (actual size)

Above: This humpback whale is leaping out of the water probably in play. The furrows along its body, typical of baleen whales, are clearly shown.

This section of the head of a baleen whale shows the whalebone or "baleen" hanging in plates from the upper jaw. A mouthful of water is squirted out through the baleen to catch the krill (the whale's main food). Masses of krill appear every year in the Antarctic Ocean.

Bats

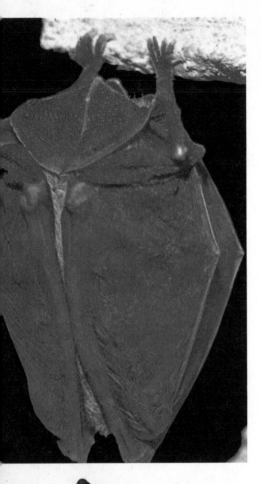

Of all the mammals the bats are the only true flyers. Their wings are made of skin extending from the sides of the body. This is stretched over greatly elongated fingers, and reaches to the hind legs, and even to the tail in some bats. The hind legs are twisted outwards and backwards so as to give the wings support. This means that bats move very clumsily when not flying. Their hook-like thumbs are used for holding food and for climbing.

In flight bats rival the birds, but do not compete with them since they are mostly night hunters. Their group name of Chiroptera means "handwing".

Because of their secretive habits, dark colouring and evil-looking faces, bats have been treated with fear and superstition down through the ages. This is particularly the case with the vampire bat whose diet is exclusively blood.

Sonar

The mystery of how bats can fly in total darkness has now been solved. It is not true that bats are blind, but they have small eyes. Instead, the bat sends out a high-pitched note which bounces off an object in its path, and is picked up as an echo. This system is very similar to radar, but involves much shorter distances – about a metre.

Bats would appear to be able to distinguish shapes by the echoes that are received. They will thus head towards an insect that is moving yet avoid a stationary object. Whales and dolphins also use this method, called sonar, under water (*see page 156*).

A bat usually has only one baby

Top: The horse-shoe bat is asleep, hanging from the roof of a cave by its hind feet.

Left: The sword-nosed bat has a nose shaped like a sword.

Right: The vampire bat lives on blood. The long-eared bat hunts insects. On the far right is a leaf-nosed bat which hunts other bats as well as insects.

at a time, and will carry it whilst it is still young, even when out hunting. The young bat clings tightly to the mother's body. In countries with cold winters bats hibernate in hidden places, such as buildings, caves, mineshafts and hollow trees. Even while they are resting, their bodies are quite cold. When evening comes they have to flap their wings to raise their body temperature enough for flight. Some bats travel long distances, up to 2,000 kilometres, to reach their winter quarters.

Main groups

There are two main groups of bats – the large fruit bats or flying foxes, and the small insect-eating bats and vampire bats. Fruit bats are Australasian and Old World inhabitants and some have a wingspan as wide as two metres. There are probably as many as 2,000 species of bats in existence.

By day fruit bats spend their time hanging from trees and cave roofs, coming out to feed at dusk. Sometimes they do great harm to fruit crops. They have good eyesight and a keen sense of smell.

The smaller bats are split into many different families. The majority hunt insects such as

Vampire bat

moths, but others feed on nectar and pollen from flowers. The insects are caught in flight. Others catch fish, either as the fish leap or by trailing their hind legs in the water, and some feed on blood. There are several species of carnivorous bat.

One of the largest families is well represented in Britain and Europe. The commonest and smallest is the little pipistrelle. Its body is only 40 millimetres long and has a wingspan of about 200 millimetres. It lives up to eight years. Somewhat larger is the noctule. Although bats are not easy to identify when flying, the long-eared bat should not prove too difficult. These bats are expert flyers, and make full use of their echo-locating ability.

Somewhat different in appearance are the leaf-nosed bats. These species have grotesque faces. The skin around the nose bulges into an odd shape, called a leaf-nose. It may help the bat to beam onto its high-pitched sounds.

Because of the shape of their noses some bats are called horse-shoe bats. The greater horse-shoe bat of Europe normally sleeps and hibernates in caves, hanging from the roof by its hind-feet. Bats that hibernate in such places can be studied by scientists, who mark them with metal discs fixed to their wings. This helps in the study of their movements.

For centuries people have believed in human vampires – the evil spirits which emerged from their graves in the form of bats, and fed on the blood of their victims. When the Europeans arrived in America they discovered bats which actually fed on blood, and called them vampire bats. They prey on other animals at night. A vampire will strip off a piece of skin and suck up the blood from the wound using its grooved tongue. The vampire bat is a known carrier of diseases, such as rabies.

Right: Fruit bats are also called flying foxes because of the shape of their heads. They are among the larger bats and only occur in the tropics where they do great damage to fruit crops.

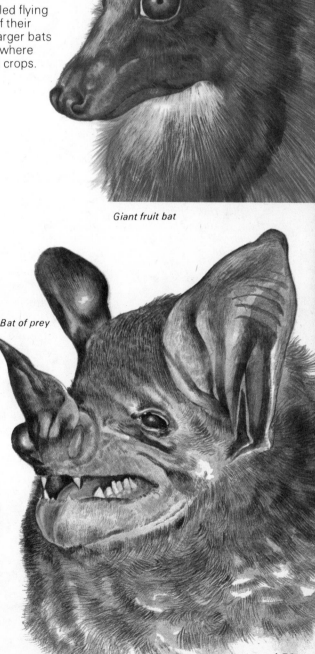

Giant fruit bat

Bat of prey

Grey long-eared bat

Lesser primates

Potto

Bush-baby

Above: The potto of Africa is a slow-moving loris which clings tightly to branches, whereas the bush-baby is a very active little primate and uses its long tail for balance.

Below: The ruffled lemur and the aye-aye live on the island of Madagascar. The slender loris lives in the forests of southern Asia.

Primates include such mammals as lemurs, bush-babies, monkeys, apes and man. Except for man, they are mainly adapted for life in the trees. Touch and sight are the most important senses for life in the trees. Hence these are highly developed whilst the sense of smell is reduced. The tree climbers, or lower primates, have changed little in the last 70 million years. Each hand and foot has the full number of five digits. The thumb is separate and opposite to the fingers, so that the hand can be used for grasping objects, as well as holding onto branches. Many primates can also use their feet in a similar fashion. Primates have two-eyed, or binocular, sight and can judge distances. This is important when leaping from branch to branch. The eyes are usually set at the front of the head. Their teeth are simple and the food they eat is very varied, a mixture of plant and animal material, and this may include insects and their larvae. Most primates have nails instead of claws. Social grooming binds together the primate family troop.

Ancestors

The tupaias or tree shrews compare closely with the first ancestors of the primates. However, there is some discussion as to whether they are primates or should be placed in a separate order of their own. Small and squirrel-like, they live in South-East Asia, and are mainly active tree dwellers. Their resemblance to primates lies in their large brains, tree-dwelling habitats and their lack of specialization.

Lemurs

Somewhat larger and definitely primates are the lemurs. Once widespread, they are now confined to the island of Madagascar which has been separated from Africa for millions of years. This isolation means that they have flourished and filled ecological roles occupied by other mammals elsewhere. Lemurs use their tails for spreading scent and thus marking out their territory. They also raise their tails erect as a signalling device. Dwarf lemurs are the only primates that aestivate (store fat in their tails for the dry season).

The indris is the largest lemur, about one metre long. It has virtually no tail and long hind legs. It is usually solitary and comes out only at night. The sifakas, or monkey lemurs, have very long tails and hind legs. They have whitish, silky fur with chocolate markings.

A close relative of the lemurs is the curious aye-aye, one of the most specialized and rarest of primates. It is the size of a small cat with a long tail and has dark, silky fur. It comes out at night to search for fruit, nuts and insects. The middle finger of each hand is remarkably long and thin, and is used for pulling out beetle grubs from between the tree and its bark.

Ruffled lemur

Slender loris

Aye-aye

Lorises

Although most small primates are very active, some members of the loris family are very slow climbers. The three kinds live in India and South-East Asia. The potto is a very similar African species. Lorises only move fast at the last moment to catch live prey. They are solitary and come out at night. They have large eyes for seeing in the dark and no tails. A loris rarely descends to the ground.

In contrast to lorises the bush-babies, or galagos, are African and very lively. They have very large eyes, long hind legs and long tails. On the ground they hop about like miniature kangaroos. Bush-babies talk to each other by means of scent markings, or loud calls through the forest that are repeated and therefore echo. The

Right: Bush-babies cry like babies when alarmed, and have very appealing faces. Even so they are very nervous creatures and will bite if disturbed.

one or two babies that are carried by the mother cling tightly to her fur.

Tarsiers

Tarsiers live in the islands of the Far East. They are almost identical to the fossil tarsioids which existed some 60 million years ago. Because a tarsier's eyes are fixed in their sockets the neck is very movable and can turn a full circle. The tarsier is only about 15 centimetres long but can make a jump of two metres. The tips of its fingers and toes are expanded into sucker-like discs that grip any surface. Its tail acts as a brake. Using its suction power, the tarsier can sleep on a vertical branch.

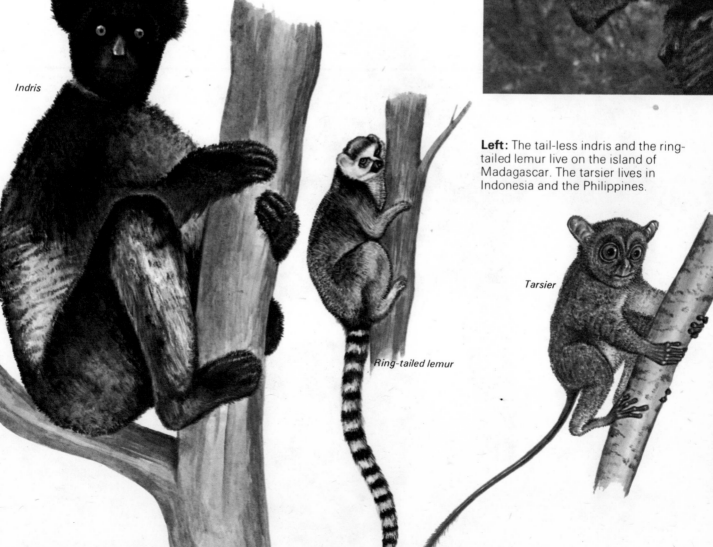

Indris

Ring-tailed lemur

Left: The tail-less indris and the ring-tailed lemur live on the island of Madagascar. The tarsier lives in Indonesia and the Philippines.

Tarsier

Old and New World monkeys

Titi

Saki

Capuchin

Monkeys are mainly tree-dwellers living in tropical forests, both in the New and Old Worlds. Although the two groups may look similar in build and habits they are not closely related, and have been physically separated for millions of years. Both groups have simply adapted to the tropical forest environment in similar ways.

On the ground they move on all fours using the flats of their hands and feet. The marmosets and tamarins have hands which have nails instead of claws, and a thumb-like big toe.

Family groups

All of them are very sociable creatures and live in family groups or troops. The monkeys in a troop all have their own rank. The struggles between the dominant males often upset the order of ranks. Most monkeys are omnivorous and have cheek pouches in which they can store food for a short while.

Like man, monkeys and apes can see in colour. Other mammals only see in shades of black and white. Monkeys usually give birth to one baby at a time. It stays with its mother until it is about five months old.

New World species

New World monkeys are the more primitive. They have flat noses and slit-like nostrils that face sideways. Some can use their long tails for gripping branches and for holding objects. Their tails are very important and aid them to move through the trees at high speed. There are about 40 species of which only one, the douroucouli or night ape, is nocturnal (active at night). The howler monkeys are

Left: The two titi monkeys have long tails which can be used for gripping branches and holding objects, a habit which is only found among New World monkeys. The saki monkey has a fine long-haired fur for which it is hunted. The capuchin monkey is so-named because of its resemblance to a monk wearing a hood.

Red colobus

Golden langur

the commonest species. They defend their territory and scare off neighbours with loud cries which can be heard up to five kilometres away. The capuchin monkey is so-called because its head of hair looks similar to the hood worn by a monk. The odd-looking uakari has a bare face and skull and a short tail. The active little squirrel monkeys are commonly seen in zoos but live in the wild in troops of up to 500. The spider monkeys have wiry fur. They can walk upright on the ground, on all fours along branches, or swing through the trees using their tails as an extra limb. They are the largest of the American monkeys.

The tiny marmosets are close relatives also living in South America. All their fingers and toes apart from the big toe are claw-like, and are an aid in climbing and clinging to trees. The golden lion tamarin of Brazil is one of the rarest monkeys.

African species

Old World monkeys are confined to tropical Africa and Asia, apart from the Barbary apes which live on the Rock of Gibraltar.

These monkeys have more pointed noses, even quite dog-like snouts, especially the baboons. Baboons live together in troops, and will band together to defend their young, even against a lion. There are four main types of African monkeys. The colobus monkeys are leaf-eaters and thus do not need cheek pouches. The guenons and mangabeys are very good climbers. Mandrills look like baboons and the males have very bright facial colours. The beautiful colobus and vervet monkeys are unfortunately hunted for their fur.

Asian species

In Asia the macaque monkeys replace the baboons as ground dwellers. Here, too, live the langurs, especially in India. They are considered sacred and are allowed to live around the temples and villages, acting as scavengers.

Macaques are highly intelligent, and are often kept as pets. They can be amusing and mischievous but are also noisy and aggressive. They are quick to steal things which they hide in their cheek pouches. In some places they are trained to climb palm trees and throw down the coconuts.

A valuable Indian monkey is the rhesus. It has been used in research to help in the study of medicine and our understanding of the different blood groups.

The oddest-looking monkey is the proboscis. It lives in the forests of Borneo and the male has a long and drooping nose.

Above: The colobus monkey of Africa is a leaf-eater and good tree climber. The golden langur is considered sacred in India and allowed to wander where it pleases. Some of these langurs live in high mountains and can withstand the cold climate found there.

Above: Monkeys have small noses and thus do not have a highly-developed sense of smell. The nostrils of this Old World monkey point forwards whereas nostrils of New World monkeys point to the side.

163

Monkey troops

In the animal kingdom, death other than through old age can occur in several ways. One major cause is disease. Another is being preyed on for food by larger carnivores or insectivores. Young animals with little experience of life are particularly open to these dangers. Should the young die in too high numbers then the future of that species is endangered. This is avoided in two ways.

Among most of the lower animals it is done by "safety in numbers". Large numbers of eggs or young are produced, and although there is a heavy death rate, some will escape to grow up and reproduce.

Among higher animals, such as birds and mammals, the families are very much smaller, but the young are given some means of protection. The parents provide some kind of shelter, such as a bird's nest or a mammal's burrow. Also they protect their young from danger, and feed them.

Social organization

With primates, the highest animals, this is commonplace, and families may even join up to form groups or societies. The size of a baboon troop varies from 20 in a dry area to 80 where food is plentiful. The young thus stay much longer in their parent's care. A young monkey clings to its mother's belly for the first five weeks of life. After that it rides on her back. This social organization is typical of monkeys and apes.

Within a monkey tribe there are many families all living together. Since baboons live mostly on the ground they have been studied in some detail. In charge is a dominant male whose word of law must be obeyed or there will be trouble. He usually lives apart from the rest of the troop. If threatened by another male, he will immediately take up the challenge. Fighting does not always result, as some movement or gesture on the part of the dominant male is usually sufficient to stop any attack. The males are usually much larger than the females. Where several males live in the same troop they are ranked in strength from the strongest downwards. Males that are driven from the troop often form small bachelor groups on their own.

Grooming

Monkeys clean one another's fur to remove any loose particles of

Gnu

skin and dirt. Monkeys and apes do not have fleas, only humans do. Once a flea has fed on blood it leaves its host in order to lay eggs. Since monkeys and apes are always on the move, newly-hatched fleas would not have a chance to find a new host. Humans on the other hand live in one place, and fleas are thus able to find a new home.

This "grooming" behaviour is very important to primates. It is a pleasant sensation to be touched or stroked, and it helps to keep up friendly relations within the troop.

Pecking order

Each baboon knows exactly its position or rank in the troop, from the leader downwards. This is called the "pecking order" because it was first studied among farmyard hens. The rank of a particular monkey is shown by the way it behaves when it meets other monkeys. If its head and tail are upright and erect, it considers itself superior. Females with a young baby acquire a temporary rank but there appears to be no strict order among female baboons in a troop.

In every tribe there are look-outs ready to warn about any danger. Should a lion or leopard be spotted then the baboons close

ranks. The males face up to the enemy, and with threats and barks try to drive it away.

Communication

The way in which monkeys and apes communicate or keep in touch varies. For example, the cry may be in anger, pleasure, pain or as a warning. Animals who have no voice tend to rely on colour and signals, such as the raising of a tail. Monkeys use both methods. The expression on a monkey's face could mean "keep away" or "this is my branch" and so on. Making faces is as important to apes as it is to us. Monkeys of Africa and Asia make a repetitive sound by smacking their lips together. This is equivalent to smiling. The easiest primate signals for us to understand are the threatening gestures, such as a gorilla beating his chest. The colouring of parts of their bodies helps to emphasize the signals.

The young in particular rely on sound and touch. A young bird recognizes its mother's call, and a lamb knows its mother by smell. With monkeys, touch is important. A baby monkey will cling to its mother's hairy body. If removed and placed on a bare model it becomes unhappy. If the model is covered with some fur it will appear content.

Above: Unlike other primates, South American marmosets often have twins. Unusually, the young are carried around by the father.

Below: A scene of a troop of baboons on the African plain. Some are feeding, on the far left a baby follows its mother and in the centre a pair are grooming. All looks peaceful but the animals are constantly on the alert.

Zebra

Impala

The ape family

The apes are our nearest relatives. The common characteristics we share are the ability to walk upright, a highly-developed brain, and the absence of a tail. Like us apes have hands for grasping objects, but they can also do this with their feet. Climbing is done by swinging from bough to bough using their long arms and hook-like hands. Their legs are much shorter, and they walk in a clumsy, rolling fashion.

There are four kinds of ape. The gorilla and chimpanzee are African, and the orang-utan and the gibbon live in South-East Asia. They are all good climbers, although the gorilla and chimp spend much of the time on the ground.

Gorillas

The gorilla is divided into two races. The lowland gorilla lives in the Congo rain forest and the mountain gorilla on the higher ground in a very isolated area of Central Africa. The latter species is in grave danger of extinction.

Gorillas breed only once every three or four years, and this must lessen their chances of survival.

When first discovered, this splendid animal was thought to be a kind of wild and hairy man, and very dangerous. When disturbed it stands upright, roars, and beats its chest. This looks terrifying but actually the gorilla rarely attacks. It is a shy and retiring creature, and wanders about in family groups ruled by a dominant male. It is a strict vegetarian.

At night the gorilla family retires into a tree where platforms are built of branches and leaves to make beds. The male in charge sometimes stays at the foot of the tree on guard.

A full-sized male can weigh up to 200 kilograms. The coat on his back becomes silver grey in maturity. He stands up to two metres high when erect. Although tremendously powerful, a gorilla is delicate in captivity and needs protection from human diseases.

Gorillas are less affectionate towards each other than other monkeys and apes. There are no great displays of social grooming. However, infant gorillas and their mothers remain very close up to the age of three or four. This is possibly because the baby is more helpless at birth than other apes.

Chimpanzees

Chimpanzees also live in groups, spending much of the time on the ground. Their high level of intelligence makes them very popular in zoos and circuses, and they readily learn and pick up tricks.

They are the best tool users in the animal world. Although mainly vegetarian, chimps will sometimes catch and eat small mammals, including other monkeys, and birds.

Chimpanzees like company but do not live in permanent troops. They are individuals and tend to avoid quarrels within a group by simply moving to another group. Their society is much more loosely organized than the baboons.

Above: When angry, the gorilla stands up and beats its chest. This is a warning and is usually enough to scare another animal away. Other displays include hurling vegetables, charging and ground thumping.

Above: When an enemy such as a leopard tries to attack a group, the male chimpanzees face up to it with loud cries and will even use sticks to drive it away. Meanwhile the mothers carry their young to safety in the trees.

Our knowledge of these two African apes has been greatly increased by scientists who have lived with them in the jungle and befriended them, even to the extent of being part of the troop.

Orang-utans and gibbons

The orang-utan of Borneo and Sumatra is a large ape with long, reddish hair. Unlike the lively chimp, it is a solemn-looking ape whose movements are slow and deliberate. It also is the most human in appearance. A male weighs up to 100 kilograms and has a heavy pouch under its chin. The name orang-utan is Malayan for "man of the woods".

Much time is spent in the trees, feeding on leaves and fruit, especially the durian fruit. The orang-utan is now in danger of extinction. Hunters kill the mother and thereby catch the young ape which stays with her up until the age of two. It is then sold to zoos. This trade has now been largely stopped. But a greater danger now facing the species is the loss of its forest home. More and more forest is being cut down and turned into farmland.

Gibbons are the most agile of apes, and also the smallest. They weigh only six kilograms when fully grown. They are marvellous acrobats, swinging rapidly through the tree-tops, and even running along branches that are little more than a tight-rope. They can also walk and run along the ground in an upright position, holding out their arms for balance. They and the orang-utans are the best adapted of all the apes for life in the trees.

Gibbons are faithful to their mates, and live in solitary families. They can be very noisy when alarmed, and will hoot and howl loudly. The calls are mainly used in defending their territory. The siamangs of Sumatra have vocal sacs to deepen the sound that they can produce.

Above: The face of an ape can tell us the mood it is in. As with humans, facial expressions can indicate fear or pleasure, pain or anger. A keeper or trainer knows this from experience. When pleased, a chimpanzee will purse its lips. When annoyed, it will bare its teeth in what may look like a smile.

Threatened animals

Extinction has always been a part of the pattern of nature. When new animals evolved, more successful at some particular way of life, their more old-fashioned competitors became extinct. But the evolution of man brought a new type of extinction into the world. For many millions of years, man was not particularly important or widespread. But he has now become so successful that his activities have a great effect on all other forms of life. Other animals are crowded out of existence by his need for space to live and grow crops, or are killed for his food or his pleasure.

Man, the killer

When man was merely a hunter with primitive weapons, he did not wipe out a vast number of herbivores. But the weapons became more and more deadly. The arrows of the American Indians could not kill very many bison. But the guns they bought from the white men soon killed nearly all the millions of bison that had once thundered across the Great Plains. Man was also greedy for space for his own domestic animals, so he killed the wild grazing animals, or fenced them off his land. In the end, that was even more deadly to them than his guns.

The wild carnivores were even more of a threat to man, for they killed his herds. So man hunted the tiger and the leopard, the cheetah and the wolf, till they too became rare and close to extinction.

Above: Only a few years ago, there were a few hundred Arabian oryx left. Now a small herd is being protected from extinction in an American zoo.

Above: Man eats the eggs and also the meat of sea turtles. Handbags are made from the skin of the flippers. Some sea turtles are therefore becoming rare.

Crop spraying

Other animals were a threat to man, because they ate the seeds that he sowed in his fields, or ate the growing plants. So man added chemicals to the seeds, or sprayed chemicals on his crops to kill the insects. But not only the birds and insects that fed on his crops were poisoned, for their deadly flesh killed the falcons and other birds of prey that hunted them.

The chemicals and the fertilizers that man had sprayed onto the fields were washed into the streams and rivers, and into the lakes and seas. There they poisoned the water, and killed the fish. Even the sea birds died from eating the

Above: The peregrine falcon is becoming rare because it lays eggs with thin, weak shells that may not hatch. This is because the falcon has fed on other birds that have eaten seeds containing chemicals frequently used by farmers to protect their crops.

poisoned bodies of the fish. In the seas themselves, man hunted the great whales for the oily blubber in their skins.

There was at least some excuse for man's hunting as long as he killed to eat or to protect his domestic animals and plants. But he has not stopped there. He takes pleasure in killing for its own sake.

Sometimes the excuse is that the animals he hunts are so dangerous that he is risking his own life in hunting them, as when he hunts lions or tigers. Other animals bear beautiful horns or antlers. They are killed so that man can mount their dead heads in his home as trophies. Some, like the rhino, are killed because their horns are used for a medicine that is supposed to make men strong and virile.

Animals with glossy or patterned coats are killed so that men can make them into fashion fur coats. Many animals, such as gibbons and monkeys, are captured to be flown around the world to be kept as pets.

A late awakening

In all these ways, man has been gradually reducing the numbers of many types of wild animals. Many have already become extinct and a great many others have become so scarce that they will soon disappear, unless we take speedy action to save them. Each year, at least one animal becomes extinct.

In many parts of the world, game reserves have been set up, in which hunting is not allowed. But illegal poachers, who kill rhino and elephants for their horns or tusks, are still a danger. The great hunting cats have always been rare and they may hunt over wide areas. So it is difficult to protect them from poachers and several types of leopard and tiger are close to extinction.

Why kill?

Many animals are in danger from man's individual greed. Some of the great whales are in danger from the greed of nations that will not stop hunting them because of the valuable oil that they contain.

At first, man killed to survive. Now he must stop some of the killing, before he clears the earth of some of its most beautiful creatures. Man has a right to life. So have they.

Above: No one knows for sure if the Tasmanian wolf is extinct or not.

Right: Lemurs come from Madagascar. Their natural habitat is forest, but man has cleared most of the trees to plant his crops.

Above: Tigers are found in Siberia, China, India and the larger islands around their coasts. They have long been hunted, both for the danger of the hunt and for the beauty of their coats. Now, some of the types of tiger on the islands such as Java and Sumatra are close to extinction.

Plant features

When the earth is photographed from a spacecraft, it looks many-coloured. Soil, rocks, water and clouds all add different colours to the picture. Some or all of these colours could also be photographed on other planets, but one thing that makes earth look different from its fellow planets is the plentiful green colour—the colour of its living plants.

This green area includes the forests and grasslands which cover many parts of the earth's land surface. These plants are vital to all land animals, including man. The most important reason is that they provide food. Animals have very different eating habits. Some eat only plants, others eat only animals, and yet others eat both plants and animals. Yet all animals ultimately depend on plants for their lives.

Plants, the self-feeders

What, then, do plants feed on? The answer is that green plants make their own food, so building up their own bodies. All that they need to do this is sunlight, carbon dioxide gas from the air, and mineral salts from the soil.

When a gardener grows plants in a greenhouse, he is making the best possible use of the sunlight that his plants need. He may even add extra carbon dioxide to the air in his greenhouse to help his plants grow. Farmers and gardeners also provide their plants with extra mineral salts in the form of fertilizers.

Simple plants

We think of plants most readily as trees, bushes, flowers and grasses. Rather surprisingly, by far the greatest numbers of plants live not on the land but in the sea. These are the marine, or sea-living, algae. Even more surprisingly, most of these algae are so small that they

The palm tree **(far left)** and the honeysuckle bush **(top)** are both examples of flowering plants which make their own food, using the energy of sunlight. The yew tree berry **(left)** is highly poisonous.

cannot be seen with the naked eye. They exist, in vast numbers, as a sort of soup floating beneath the sea's surface. This soup is called the plankton.

Some types of algae are more familiar to us than the plankton types because they are larger and more often seen. These are the seaweeds, some of which are very large indeed. But all algae, large or small, are rather simple plants when compared with higher plants such as trees.

Fungi are also rather simple plants. Unlike the algae, most kinds of fungi live on land. These include the best-known kinds, mushrooms and toadstools. However, many much smaller fungi, like many algae, live in ponds, rivers and lakes. These and the smaller land fungi are often called moulds.

Fungi are not green plants and cannot make their own food. Some live on the remains of dead animals and plants. Others live in or on the living bodies of animals and plants, often causing disease.

Higher plants

These are the best-known plants, the ones we notice most when taking country walks. Some, however, such as the mosses and liverworts, are small enough to be easily overlooked. Others, like ferns and horsetails, are somewhat larger. All these green plants reproduce themselves by means of spores.

Highest of all plants are those that reproduce themselves by means of seeds. These include all trees, flowers and grasses.

What else do plants do?

Besides providing food for man and animals, green plants also help to refresh the air of our planet. They take in the carbon dioxide breathed out by animals and made by man's fires, factories and motor vehicles. They give off oxygen which is vital for animals and man to breathe. Whatever would we do without plants!

171

Making and storing food

Chlorophyll and growth

Plants are given their green colour by the pigment chlorophyll. This special substance enables a green plant to make its own food and so to grow. A plant's chlorophyll is found inside some of the cells of its body, particularly in its leaves but also in other green parts. Inside the cells, chlorophyll is contained in tiny packets called chloroplasts.

How does chlorophyll work? To answer this question, we must first ask another: what are plants made of?

Like other living organisms, a plant consists mostly of carbon substances and water. The carbon substances are what scientists call organic chemical compounds. These compounds are mostly made of carbon but also contain smaller amounts of other chemical elements, particularly nitrogen, oxygen, sulphur and phosphorus.

A green plant gets its carbon from carbon dioxide in the air and most of its other chemical elements from mineral salts in the soil. It gets the water it needs both from the soil and from moisture in the air. From the air plants take in gases through their leaves and stems and they take minerals from the soil through their roots.

Inside its green cells a plant builds up the simple compound carbon dioxide into more complicated compounds. This process is called photosynthesis. "Synthesis" means building-up, and "photo" refers to light energy, which is also needed. Normally, this light energy is provided by the sun, although plants can be made to grow in artificial light.

The first of the complicated carbon compounds to be formed inside the plant are sugars. These give the sweet taste to the sap of a plant. These sugars may be further built up to make larger compounds of two main kinds.

Starch is a food compound that the plant stores inside its cells, and which nourishes us when we eat bread and other starchy foods. Cellulose is a large compound also formed from sugars, but this is found mostly in the stiff, hard walls surrounding plant cells. We cannot digest cellulose as food, but we often wear it as clothes—cotton is nearly pure cellulose.

Above: The sword-shaped leaves of this iris spring from an underground stem called a rhizome, which is swollen with stored food. Iris rhizomes lie either on top of the ground or just below the surface.

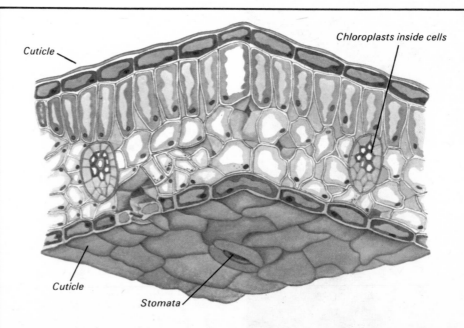

Above: Chlorophyll is the green pigment with which plants make their own food. This cross-section of a leaf shows the cells which contain the chlorophyll. Inside these cells, the pigment is held in many tiny packets called chloroplasts. Leaves have tiny pores called stomata.

Other plant substances

Sugars, starch and cellulose are all examples of chemical compounds called carbohydrates. Besides carbohydrates, the bodies of plants contain many other chemical compounds, large and small. Important among the large ones are fats and plant proteins.

Fats, like carbohydrates, contain only the chemical elements carbon, oxygen and hydrogen. Unlike carbohydrates, however, fats are not built up inside plant cells from sugars, but from other small chemical compounds. They include liquid fats, or oils, which are often stored as food inside plant cells. The delicate membranes of these cells are partly made up of solid fats. We often use plant fats in the form of margarine.

Plant proteins are very large chemical compounds which contain nitrogen and sulphur as well as carbon, oxygen and hydrogen. They are of two main kinds. One

Below: A few kinds of flowering plants have lost their chlorophyll. Like a mushroom, this flowering plant takes its nourishment from organic matter in the soil.

kind is found in the structural parts of plants. For example, plant proteins occur, together with fats, in the cell membranes.

Most other proteins in a plant are the ones called enzymes. These are found in the liquid part of the cells. They are absolutely vital to the life of the plant because they enable most of the chemical reactions to take place in its cells. Taken all together, these reactions are called the plant's metabolism.

Storing food

A plant uses the food it makes in two ways. First, it uses some right away for energy. Like an animal, a plant needs energy to grow and make movements, although plant movements are usually much slower than those of animals.

Second, a plant needs to store food for times when food becomes difficult to make. For example, a plant needs to store food over cold, dark winter months so that it can grow quickly when spring comes. Also, the seeds of a plant usually contain a small store of food. This gives the young plant a start in life before it begins to make its own food by photosynthesis.

Plants store food in various parts of their bodies which often become swollen as a result. Onions and tulips store it in bulbs which are swollen leaves clustered around a short stem. Crocuses store food in a corm, a short, swollen stem with a bud. Both bulbs and corms "overwinter" underground before putting out new shoots in the spring.

Rhizomes are underground stems that can also store food, but they are longer than corms and grow horizontally through the soil. Some types of rhizomes are called tubers, a good example being the potato. Many plant roots become swollen with stored food and carrots, parsnips, and turnips are just some examples of roots we eat. Whenever we eat beans, we are consuming foods stored by plants in their seeds.

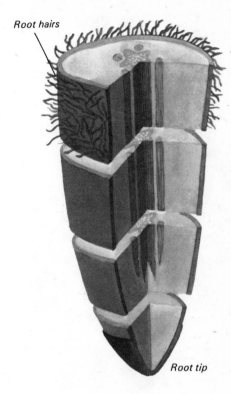

Root hairs

Root tip

Above: To grow, plants need mineral salts, dissolved in water. These salt solutions are absorbed by the root hairs.

Below: Plant bulbs store food over winter in their swollen leaves.

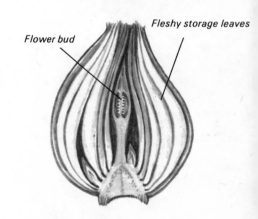

Flower bud

Fleshy storage leaves

Below: The swollen stem of this cactus stores water and mineral salts.

Plant distribution

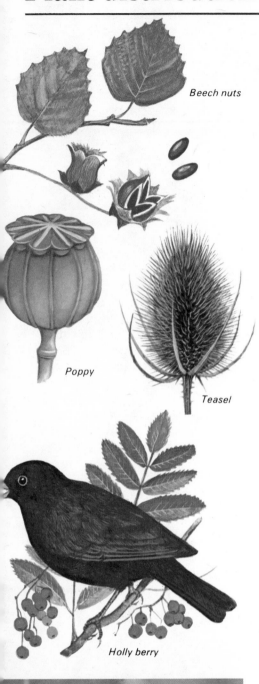

Beech nuts

Poppy

Teasel

Holly berry

Not only animals but also plants like to spread from one place to another. They will make full use of any new habitat if this is suitable for their growth and multiplication.

Plants spread, or distribute, themselves in many different ways. New generations may grow from seeds or spores that have come from the parent plants. This is rather like the way animals multiply, by having offspring.

But often, unlike an animal, a single plant can spread itself over a wide area. The banyan tree of tropical countries can spread over several hectares by putting down roots from its branches into the soil. The roots then give rise to more trunks and branches.

Floating plants, such as the water hyacinth and the tiny algae of the plankton, are carried about by water currents and so spread in this way. Many plants will grow from bits broken off them. The rather simple plants called liverworts spread naturally in this way, from bits that break off and float away. In the sea, bits broken off seaweeds by the waves help to spread these plants over wide areas. Many of the microscopic single-celled algae of the plankton are able to swim about, so spreading themselves within much smaller areas. Climbing plants, such as vines, will spread over the ground and other vegetation, sometimes for very long distances.

Spores, seeds and fruits

Most plants that are not seed plants reproduce by means of spores. These consist of only one or two cells and so are very tiny. The spores of algae and water fungi often swim away from the

Left: Plant seeds are distributed in many different ways. Some float away on parachutes. Others are carried away by birds. The seed-head of the teasel catches in the fur of animals. That of the poppy shakes out its tiny seeds like a pepperpot.

Above left: Birds eat holly berries, so helping to distribute their seeds. The seeds pass out of the bird's body unharmed, along with its waste.

Above: Water lilies have large leaves with air spaces, which help them float.

Left: Mangrove trees live in airless swamps. Their specially adapted roots, called pneumatophores, poke up from the water to take in air.

parents before giving rise to the next generation. In land plants, spores are usually carried far away from the parents by the wind. Huge numbers of spores can be made by a single plant. A giant puffball fungus contains as many as seven thousand million spores!

Seeds are larger than spores and are spread in other ways. Some have hairy parachutes, or wings, that help them float away from their parents on the wind. Others drift away on water, and some are scattered from seed pods which split open, sometimes so violently that the seeds are flung far and wide.

Many seeds are spread by animals which eat the fruits containing them. Other fruits have sharp spines or prickles which catch in animals' fur and are carried away.

Most seeds and spores never grow up into new plants. It is for this reason that plants make so many of them and are adapted in so many ways for spreading them.

The new generation

What makes a seed grow where it falls? First, it needs the right kind of soil. Depending on the plant, the soil must not be too hard, too loose, too acid or too alkaline. It must contain enough mineral salts of the right kind to nourish the plant.

Looked at another way, the plant must be properly adapted to grow well in the soil. But even if the soil is suitable, the plant may not grow well if, above ground, there is too little sunlight or too much chilling wind. Plants are adapted in various ways to put up with such conditions as these.

Its particular adaptations give to a plant its typical appearance. This is most obvious in the shape, size and number of its leaves.

Plants that live in very dry con-

Left: Palms are adapted in many ways to live in warm climates, even in deserts.

Right: These plants adapted for creeping all live in temperate climates.

ditions are adapted to hold water for a very long time. For this purpose they may have thick, fleshy leaves with a waterproof surface. Or, like the spiny cactuses, they may have few or no recognizable leaves.

Water-living plants may have two very different types of leaf. Those always covered by water are long and thin, whereas those growing above the water surface are broader and look more normal. Water lilies have large leaves which float by means of many air spaces.

Most plants live neither in deserts nor in water, but in rather less extreme surroundings. All the same, they have many special adaptations to suit them to their ways of life, as you will see in the following pages. The life-styles of plants, like those of animals, vary greatly with their environments.

Clematis

Honeysuckle

Ivy

Bindweed

Virginia creeper

175

Defence and adaptation

Many of the adaptations shown by plants help them to survive severe living conditions and damage by animals and man. We have already seen that plants living in or near deserts have swollen bodies in which to conserve water.

Above: The prickly heads and leaves of thistles deter all but those animals with the toughest mouths, such as goats and donkeys.

Many other plants have special coatings on their leaves or bodies which reduce water loss. These include evergreen shrubs and trees which keep their leaves in winter. The leaves of pines are tightly coiled and so lose very little water by evaporation.

Plants which live in salt marshes, such as the strange-looking glassworts, have waterproof bodies and very small leaves. Their protective outer coating prevents both the loss of body water to the outside and the inward flow of salt water. If either of these things happened, it would harm the plant.

Delicate, living tissues in woody stems and tree trunks are surrounded by a protective layer of corky bark. This acts like an insulating blanket, protecting the deeper tissues from the cold.

Insects damage trees by boring into their leaves and bark. Fungi worsen this damage by rotting away larger parts of the tree. Some trees have developed special cells which make gums or resins that discourage insects and fungi.

Below: Black nightshade belongs to a family in which many plants contain very poisonous substances called alkaloids.

Almost any tree, when wounded, produces a callus or protective overgrowth, which soon seals up the wound.

Avoiding being eaten

Spines, thorns and prickles may protect a plant against being eaten—but some animals, such as goats, have very tough mouths! Also, the prickles on seed parts usually do more to spread the seeds by clinging to animals, rather than to protect them.

Some plants are better protected against being eaten by the poisonous substances they contain. Deadly nightshade, hemlock and datura are among many plants that contain very poisonous substances called alkaloids. The leaves of laurel bushes, the roots of the cassava plant and American arrow grass all contain the deadly poison hydrocyanic acid.

The upas tree of Asia and the manchineel tree of central America are so poisonous that local people avoid touching them or sleeping under them. More familiarly, we avoid touching poison ivy or the stinging hairs of nettles.

Some plant poisons, such as alkaloids, seem to be waste

Below: Nettles defend themselves with sharp hairs which inject an irritating substance called formic acid.

materials rather than special adaptations, but they protect just the same!

The parasitic life

Parasites live in or on other organisms; some are very harmful to their hosts, others less so. All plants harbour parasites and many plants are themselves parasites.

Among plants, fungi include the greatest number of parasites. Fungi are also frequently parasites of other plants, and therefore among the farmer's worst enemies. Moulds, mildews and fungal rots attack leaves, buds and fruits. Rusts and smuts darken and ruin the ears of cereal crops.

In woods and forests, toadstools, such as the honey fungus, attack and often kill trees. Some fungi are parasites of animals and man, causing serious diseases such as aspergillosis, and relatively minor complaints such as athlete's foot and ringworm.

Higher plants include fewer complete parasites. Dodder is a small, twining plant that uses suckers to absorb food from its hosts. It has flowers but no leaves or any other green parts. Most astonishing among higher plant parasites is *Rafflesia*. This is a jungle plant with the largest of all flowers but a fungus-like body that is a parasite of vines.

Right: A pitcher plant is carnivorous. Visiting insects fall into its slippery pitcher. They are unable to get out and are eventually digested as food.

Other higher plants include partial parasites. These have green leaves and so can make some of their food, but they get the remainder by parasitic means. A familiar example is mistletoe, which puts down suckers into the bark of a tree to reach the living tissue underneath. Broomrape and toothwort are two common root parasites.

Insect-eaters

Insect-eating plants have very special adaptations for catching and digesting small animals. They live in marshes and jungle soils which contain little of the nitrogen that the plants need. Instead, they get nitrogen from their prey.

Best known are the sundews, which catch their prey with leaves which have sticky tentacles, and the Venus flytrap, which has hinged leaves which spring together, trapping the prey.

Bladderworts are water plants which trap very small forms of swimming life in almost equally small underwater bladders. Even lowly soil fungi can be animal trappers—one type catches worms with a sort of lasso!

Below: Mistletoe is a partial parasite. It gets some of its food from the living cells of trees. *Rafflesia* is a total parasite. It takes all its food from tropical vines, and has no green parts to make its own food.

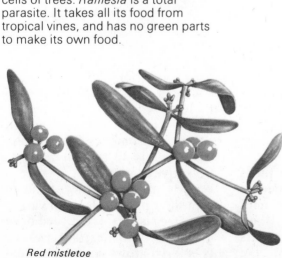

Red mistletoe

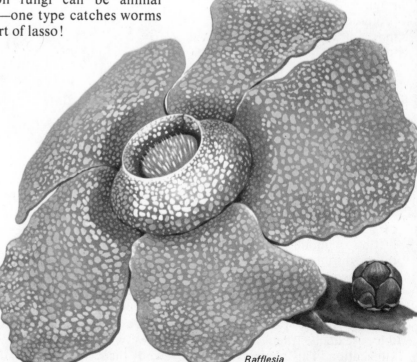

Rafflesia

Reproduction and growth

Sexual and asexual reproduction

Plants reproduce and multiply in two very different ways. These are called, respectively, sexual and asexual reproduction.

Sexual reproduction happens when the nucleus of a male cell combines with the nucleus of a female cell. Male reproductive, or sex, cells include sperms and pollen grains. Female reproductive cells are called eggs or ova. Fertilization is the word used to describe the combining of male and female nuclei inside the egg cell. The fertilized egg cell then divides and multiplies to grow into the new plant.

In asexual reproduction there is no combining of male and female nuclei. Plants reproduce asexually in a number of ways. One way that we have seen already is for a bit to break off a plant, and then to grow into a whole new plant. Another is for a plant to put out runners overground, or rhizomes underground, which give rise to new plants. These ways of asexual reproduction are called vegetative propagation.

Reproduction in simple plants

Many algae and fungi reproduce asexually. Algae which consist of a single cell, or only a few cells, reproduce asexually when one or more of their cells simply divide into two.

The simplest fungi—types of water moulds—reproduce asexually by dividing up into many tiny swimming cells called zoospores. A zoospore swims off, settles down and grows up into an adult water mould.

But even very simple plants also often reproduce sexually. For example, water moulds and algae may make not one, but two types of tiny swimming cells, which are rather different from one another. These swim off and combine with one another in an act of fertilization.

Very often a plant will reproduce sexually, then asexually, in alternation. This happens not only

Below: Some tropical flowers are fertilized by hummingbirds.

Right and **below:** Pollen grains contain the male nucleus for fertilization of the plant egg. They are very small and sometimes have highly decorative surfaces.

Lime pollen

Scots pine pollen

in very simple plants, but also quite distinctly in higher plants such as mosses and ferns. It is called alternation of generations.

Reproduction of seed plants

Plants which reproduce by seeds are the most advanced members of the plant kingdom, and the ones made most familiar to us by their beauty. They include pines, firs and their relatives, and all the

many and various flowering plants.

A seed can be compared with the fertilized egg of a bird or reptile. It contains an embryo, together with some food for the embryo. This is all surrounded by a protective coat or shell.

Seeds are spread, or distributed, from their parent plants in various ways (*see page 175*). If a seed develops, or germinates, successfully, its embryo grows up into the adult plant. Thus the cycle continues.

In all seed plants, fertilization of the egg takes place on a parent plant. In most cases, pollen is carried by the wind or by flying insects from one plant to another. Pollen grains, each containing a male nucleus, stick to a projecting, outer part of the ovary. Inside the ovary are one or more egg cells.

A tube then grows from the pollen grain down into the ovary. A male nucleus travels down this tube to fertilize an egg cell. The fertilized egg then divides and multiplies to form the embryo.

Fruits

The embryos of flowering plants, inside their seeds, are further protected inside fruits. Fruits are the ripened ovaries of flowers and they contain one or more seeds. They include not only those succulent foods we usually call fruits, but also nuts, pods and other kinds of seed containers.

Pine or fir seeds, however, are not contained in fruits. For this reason they are called naked seeds. They are shed from the female cones of the parent plant—the familiar woody cones.

From seed to adult

When a seed begins to develop, or germinate, its embryo at first grows with the aid of food surrounding it. Food is sometimes also supplied by small cotyledons or seed-leaves, which are part of the embryo itself.

After a while the embryo, or seedling as it is now called, puts out its first small root and shoot. You have probably seen a bean seedling, growing on blotting paper, doing this.

The shoot rises above the ground and puts out its first true leaves which begin to make the seedling's food by photosynthesis (see page 172). Meanwhile, the rootlet enlarges and branches in the soil, drawing from it the mineral salts the plant needs for growth. Energized by the sun's rays, the plant continues to grow.

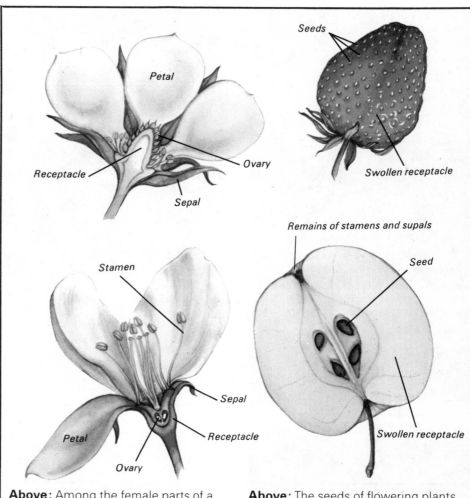

Above: Among the female parts of a flower is the ovary, which contains the plant eggs or ova. Stamens are male parts which contain pollen.

Above: The seeds of flowering plants contain the plant embryo. Seeds are contained inside fruits. Apples and strawberries are succulent fruits.

Below: Plant growth is fastest in the spring, when leaves extend and begin to make food by photosynthesis. Stems lengthen and new wood is laid down in twigs.

Movement and life-cycles

Above left and **below left**: The leaves of this sensitive plant, a species of mimosa, can make very sudden movements. Under normal conditions, the leaves of this tropical tree are held erect during the day but hang downwards in the evening in a "sleep position". However, if the tree is given a sharp blow, its leaves will flop and fold together quickly even in the daytime. This is caused by a sudden loss of water from cells at the base of each leaf stalk and also at the junction of the leaflets. As these cells absorb moisture, they regain their pressure and the leaves rise again.

The plants all around us are usually active. We do not often see their movements because, compared with those of animals, these are so slow.

These slow movements are generally caused by growth. If you have watched a speeded-up film of grasses or other plants growing, you will have seen that their stems move in an upward spiral. Cells first on one side of the stems grow faster, then on the other, to cause this spiralling.

Stimuli

Sometimes this growth movement is linked to a definite stimulus. The tendril of a creeping plant, when it touches a branch or a post, will curl around it. The stimulus of touch causes cells to grow more slowly on one side, so causing the curling movement.

In a similar way the stimulus of light or warmth will cause the petals of a flower to rise and open.

Other stimulated growth movements are in particular directions. The stalk, or petiole, of a leaf may grow so that the leaf is set at a right angle to the light.

A young stem generally grows and bends towards the light. Even earlier in its life, as the shoot grows upwards through the soil from the seed, it grows *away* from the force of gravity which pulls downwards. A rootlet, on the other hand, is stimulated by gravity to grow downwards.

All these growth movements are slow but from time to time, plants will also make fast movements. Sometimes these are quite dramatic, like the leaf movements of some mimosa plants. Fast movements of plants are most often caused by changes in pressure within cells.

The leaves of a plant will droop quite quickly if their cells become short of water and so lose their inner pressure. More sudden pressure changes in cells can cause seed cases to split open violently, flinging seeds well away from the plant. Spores of fungi, liverworts, mosses and ferns are also often dispersed by such pressure changes.

Like animals, but unlike higher plants, microscopic algae can often move about from one place to another. They do this in various ways. For example, many single-celled algae move by beating their hair-like flagella, which propel them through the water in which they live.

Other single-celled algae, the diatoms, move steadily along surfaces of leaves and stones by means of a flowing movement of their liquid, inner parts. This flow makes contact with the surface through holes in the diatom's hard shell, so pushing the diatom along.

Life-cycles

On page 178 we saw that many plants reproduce both asexually by means of spores, and sexually by means of sperms and eggs. These two kinds of reproduction play a part in the life-cycles of algae, fungi, liverworts, mosses and ferns.

Below: The life-cycle of a fern. The adult fern plant (**1**) produces many asexual spores. These are contained in sporangia situated on the underside of leaflets (**2**). A sporangium (**3**) releases spores which are scattered by the wind (**4**). Any spore that is lucky enough to germinate in the soil grows to be a tiny, heart-shaped plant called a prothallus (**5**). On the underside of the prothallus, male and female sex organs are formed which give rise, respectively, to sperms (**6**) and eggs (**7**). Sperms swim over in a surface film of moisture to fertilize eggs in the female sex organs (**8**). The first fertilized egg to divide and multiply successfully grows up to become a fern plant. At first this is very small (**9**) but eventually it will dwarf the prothallus.

Above left and **above:** The opening and closing movements of flowers are much slower. Buds do not open and close because of changes in pressure within cells, but because the growth of the cells speeds up or slows down.

The diagram on the right shows details of the life-cycle of a fern. From this, you can see that the asexual stage of the life-cycle is represented by the production of spores by the fern plant.

A spore does not, however, give rise to a fern plant but to a much smaller plant called a prothallus. The prothallus represents the sexual stage of the life-cycle. It gives rise to sperms and egg cells, and the fertilization of an egg by a sperm leads to the growth of the familiar fern plant.

The adult fern plant and the prothallus can both be considered as generations in this life-cycle. Ferns therefore offer a good example of alternation of generations.

In the life-cycles of the most advanced plants, such as flowers and trees, this alternation of generations is not so clear. Both egg cells and male sex cells are formed on the adult plant and not on a separate plant as with the fern. The prothallus stage can only be compared with small parts of the ovary of a flower, which produce the egg cells, and small parts of the pollen grain, which produce the male nucleus.

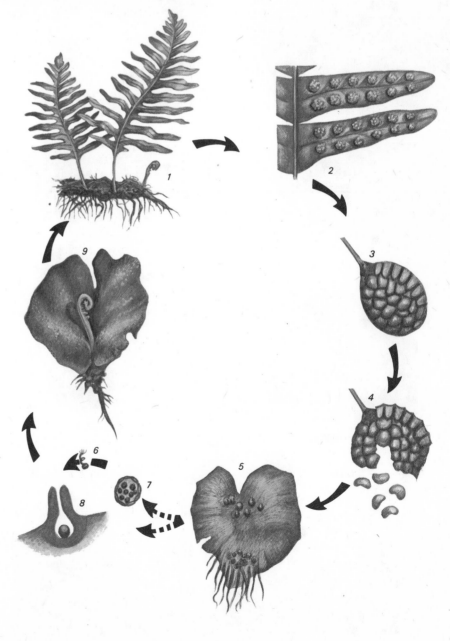

Plant families

On a country walk you will see many different plants. More than 350,000 types have been described by botanists and more are still being discovered. But just what is meant by a particular type of plant?

Generally this is a particular species of plant. For example, in local woods you may see the green spathe and red berries of the plant commonly known as cuckoo pint, lords-and-ladies or Jack-in-the-pulpit. The botanical name of this plant is *Arum maculatum*. It can be recognized by this species name by botanists everywhere, speaking any language.

Gardeners are generally even

Left: Karl von Linné (1707-78), better known by his Latin name of Linnaeus, was a Swedish botanist. He classified many plants into their species, and is sometimes called the father of modern botany.

choosier than botanists in specifying plants. When a gardener buys seed to grow a particular type of flower, vegetable, shrub or tree, he makes sure that the seed belongs not only to the required species, but also to the particular variety of that species that he wants. The same will apply when he buys whole plants or cuttings.

For example, if he is growing camellias, he may specify *Camellia japonicà Abundance,* where japonica is the species name and Abundance the name of the particular variety.

Genus, family and order
We now know what is meant by a particular type of plant. In classifying plants further, botanists put them together in groups of increasing size, according to their relationships.

In the above example, the name camellia itself is that of the plant group known as a genus. This genus contains other camellia species as well as *Camellia japonica.*

Now, camellias are very closely related to the tea plant, so these two types of plant are classified together in the same family. This family is closely related to the holly family, so camellias, tea bushes and holly trees are all classified together in the same order of plants.

A plant order is usually a large group containing many different types of plant. To non-botanists, some of the species in an order may not look at all closely related.

For example, the plant order described above also contains a tropical fruit plant, the mangosteen, and the common wild flower known as St John's wort.

Obviously, camellias, mangosteens and the rest could only be classified together by an expert

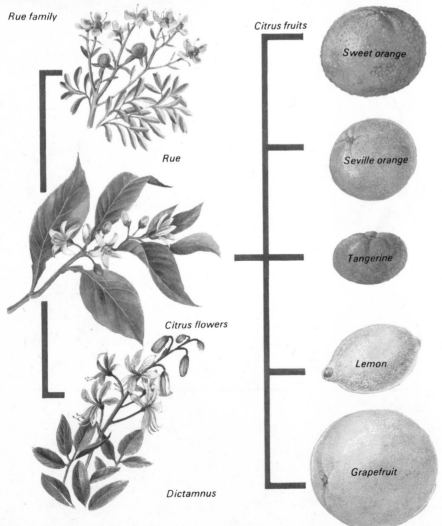

Rue family

Rue

Citrus flowers

Dictamnus

Citrus fruits

Sweet orange

Seville orange

Tangerine

Lemon

Grapefruit

Left: Family relations. The rue family contains many different genera including rue itself, *Citrus* and *Dictamnus.* But these genera each contain several or many species, represented here by the various kinds of citrus fruits.

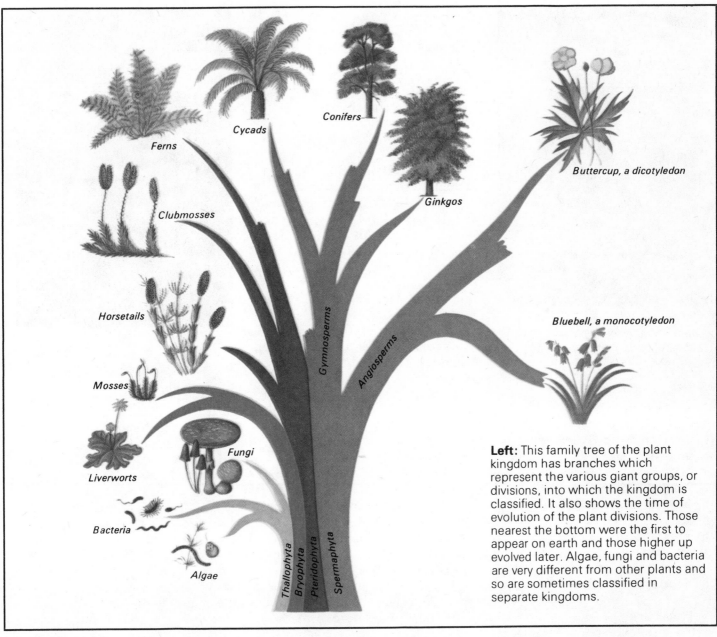

Labels on figure: Ferns, Cycads, Conifers, Ginkgos, Buttercup, a dicotyledon, Clubmosses, Horsetails, Bluebell, a monocotyledon, Mosses, Fungi, Liverworts, Bacteria, Algae, Gymnosperms, Angiosperms, Thallophyta, Bryophyta, Pteridophyta, Spermaphyta

Left: This family tree of the plant kingdom has branches which represent the various giant groups, or divisions, into which the kingdom is classified. It also shows the time of evolution of the plant divisions. Those nearest the bottom were the first to appear on earth and those higher up evolved later. Algae, fungi and bacteria are very different from other plants and so are sometimes classified in separate kingdoms.

who knows what details to look for. These details are usually those of the flowers of the various plants mentioned.

Division and kingdom

Even a non-botanist, however, could at once say that camellias and mangosteens are related in at least one way. That is, they are both plants with flowers, and so are distinct from such plants as ferns, which have no flowers.

All flowering plants taken together are classified in a very large plant group called a division. Other divisions include those of mosses, liverworts, horsetails,

clubmosses, cycads, ginkgos and conifers. These can all be seen here.

But even divisions are not the largest groups. All the plants mentioned so far may be put together in a group called the plant kingdom. This includes all flowering and non-flowering plants.

Having worked through to the largest of plant groups, we can now classify the camellia fairly completely. The only necessary extras are a couple of technical names for order and family:

Kingdom: plant
Division: flowering plants

Order: Theales
Family: Theaceae
Genus: *Camellia*
Species: *japonica*
Variety: *Abundance*

Other kingdoms

Algae and fungi are sometimes included in the plant kingdom. So also are those even smaller organisms, the bacteria.

The traditional reason for this is that these forms of life were once seen as distinct from animal life. Algae, fungi and bacteria are now more usually classified in separate kingdoms, distinct from both animal and plant kingdoms.

Fungi

Above: Moulds quickly form on a rotten apple. The many white threads make up the mycelium of the fungus plant.

Fungi have no green chlorophyll to make their own food. This means that they must feed on other plants or animals, dead or alive.

Fungi living on dead material are called saprophytes. This could be anything from neglected food to a dead tree. Those which attack living things are called parasites. Some toadstools attack living trees. Garden plants, like roses, also suffer from fungus growth.

Reproduction

Fungi produce spores, not seeds. These are minute and are produced in enormous numbers. In its short life the giant puffball may produce as many as seven thousand million spores.

Because of these high numbers of spores and the ease with which they travel through the air, they can settle almost anywhere. If the food is then suitable, and there is enough moisture, the spore will germinate.

A spore sends out a fine thread, called a hypha. This branches through the food to form a white, fluffy layer looking like cotton wool. This is called mycelium, and is the actual fungus plant. Mush-

room growers call it "spawn". It can be seen on mouldy food, in leaf mould, and under the bark of dead trees.

Out of the mycelium grows the fruit body, called a sporophore. This stage is familiar to us as the toadstool we find in a wood, or the mushroom we gather in a field.

Moulds and mildews

Fungi are divided into three main groups. Most of the microscopic kinds belong to the phycomycetes, or moulds and mildews. Moulds are saprophytes and grow on dead material, including our food. A common example is the pin-mould (*Mucor*), seen on neglected cheese, bread and fruit. The mycelium sends out rounded containers on branches, called capsules. These contain the spores, and look like pin-heads.

Mildews attack living things. One of these, called *Saprolegnia*, lives in water and attacks fish, including goldfish. Another mildew is found on rose leaves.

Although they can be harmful, some of these minute fungi have proved of great benefit to man. One of these is *Penicillium*, which contains the valuable drug, penicillin. It fights germs and has saved many people's lives.

The second group of larger fungi are called the ascomycetes. Inside the sporophore are tiny containers, called asci. Each ascus

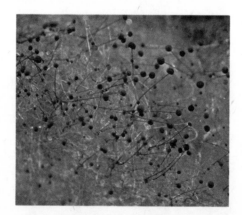

Above: Pin-mould or mucor, growing on a carrot. The picture shows clearly the fruit bodies, or sporangia, from which the spores are set free.

Above: In a wood, you will often see bracket fungus like this growing on trees. Spores are set free from the pores on the underside of the fungus.

contains eight spores. These fungi include the cup fungi, or pixie cups, which grow mostly on the ground. Others, more club-shaped, are called earth-tongues.

Another group, called morels, form a cap on the stalk which has a honeycombed appearance. Morels can be eaten. Perhaps the best known variety are the truffles which are considered great delicacies, and used for making paté. They are rounded fungi which grow underground. In the past pigs and dogs were trained to sniff them out.

The last major group of fungi are the basidiomycetes. Four spores are contained on each basidium (spore-carrying cell). The basidia develop on a ripe layer of the sporophore—where exactly they develop depends on the type of fungus.

Agaric toadstools

Agaric toadstools are well known basidiomycetes. They have a ring of gills underneath the cap. The cap grows on a stalk and resembles a miniature umbrella. Spores are shot from the basidia which line the gills, and are blown away on the wind. A spore may then germinate and become a new fungus plant. Toadstools are most common in woodlands, where the air is moist and there is plenty to grow on.

Some of these agarics, called *Amanita,* are poisonous, even deadly. One of these, the death cap, causes up to 90 per cent of deaths from fungus poisoning, and the familiar fly agaric which has a scarlet cap with white flecks causes sickness. And yet, some *Amanitas* can safely be eaten. So, if you do go gathering wild fungi, never eat a toadstool without being sure which kind it is. This is especially important when gathering mushrooms which resemble the death cap. There are minor differences to look for. *Amanita* toadstools have a ring on the stalk, a cup around the base, and the gills are always white. Mushrooms have only a ring, and the gills are pink at first, turning black with age.

The parasol mushroom can also be eaten. Its cap is scaly and can grow to the size of a dinner plate.

Other edible mushrooms are the wood blewit and the grisette. The oyster mushroom, which as its name suggests looks like an oyster, grows on dead and fallen trees.

Bracket fungi make up the Polyporaceae (many-pored) family. A common example is the birch bracket which lives on dying birch trees. Under the bracket are tiny holes through which the spores pass.

Some toadstools also have pores under their caps instead of gills, and belong to the Boletaceae family. They look solid in appearance, and have thick stems. A favourite species eaten by many Europeans is the *Boletus edulis.*

Other toadstools have spines under their caps and belong to the Hydnaceae family. One example is the coral fungus, which is pure white and has long hanging spines.

Stinkhorns have unusual shapes and all of them produce an unpleasant smell. The bright red cage fungus is a typical example. Stinkhorns start as an egg, then a stalk emerges with a hood of smelly slime full of spores. This attracts insects which feed on the slime and pick up and carry off spores on their legs.

Old wives' tales

There are many strange beliefs and legends about toadstools, especially about the cause of mushroom rings seen in fields.

In fact, the answer is simple. As the mushroom mycelium or spawn spreads outwards new mushrooms appear in a small ring. When they are picked or die off, the soil is improved by the mycelium so that a rich layer of grass appears. On the inside a similar layer appears, and in between lies a layer of poor grass. This gives the appearance of a circle. Some rings are very old and may be hundreds of metres across.

One of the most important functions of fungus plants is the way in which they help to break down dead leaves and other material. This helps to enrich the soil.

Above: The head of this maize plant has been attacked by a parasitic fungus called a smut, which is why it looks blackened. Smuts can be serious and may infect a whole crop of cereals.

Oyster mushroom
Grisette
Cage fungus
Lactarius volemus
Morel
Fly agaric
Parasol mushroom
Wood blewit
Yellow stalk toadstool
Boletus mushroom

Above: These drawings show some examples of the wide variety of larger kinds of fungi. The fly agaric is poisonous, and is commonly found growing in birch and pine woods.

Algae

Algae are the simplest forms of plant life, and have neither flowers nor roots. They occur wherever there is any moisture, on land, in fresh water and in the sea. They are usually coloured green, but some are more blue-green, and yet others brown or red. Whatever their colour, all seaweeds contain chlorophyll which helps them to make their own food.

Algae vary in size from microscopic one-celled plants to large seaweeds. One of the world's largest plants is a long oarweed found in the Pacific, which grows to 200 metres. A common one-celled alga is called *Pleurococcus*. It forms the green, powdery growth on tree trunks, walls and gate posts, and is easily spread by the wind.

Other minute algae live in fresh water. They drift about in huge numbers as part of the plankton, and are a valuable food supply for pond life. *Euglena* is a tiny, pear-shaped alga with a whip-like tail, or flagellum, which helps it to move through the water. *Volvox* is globe-shaped and consists of a colony of cells which slowly revolves through the water.

Some algae grow cells end to end which join up into long threads. *Cladophora*, or blanket-weed, is a many-threaded plant which sticks to rocks and stones, and may choke the water. In ponds, puddles and ditches a green scum is formed by *Spirogyra*. It feels slimy if you touch it.

Diatoms and desmids are one-celled algae which have a hard cell wall made of silica. Countless numbers of their fossils have turned into a rock called diatomite. This is mined and used for insulation, as it does not burn.

Diatoms have many shapes. During spring and summer they multiply in vast numbers in the sea. They are the main source of food for the krill on which whales feed.

Reproduction in algae

Algae reproduce either by breaking off pieces which continue to grow, or by means of zoospores. A cell in the filament (thread-like body) of *Spirogyra* will divide into these spores which then swim away and grow into new threads.

Sexual reproduction is also quite common among algae. In the one-celled pond alga, *Chlamydomonas*,

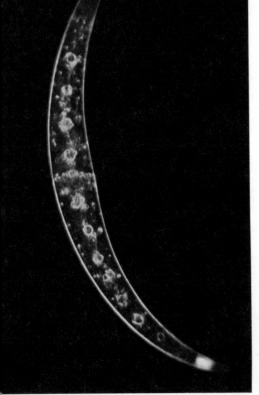

Left: *Closterium* is a diatom resembling a new moon in shape. It has a hard wall of silica.

Below: The blue-green algae grow in threads. You often see them growing on aquarium glass.

Right: The dense layer of algae is attached to the stones of a weir.

two separate plants (called gametes) swim together and join up to form a cell called a zygote. This then divides into "daughter" cells which are set free.

In another pond alga, the *Oedogonium,* actual sex cells are produced. Male cells swim away from one plant to find another plant containing egg cells. The male cells fertilize the female cells and a new plant is ready to grow.

Apart from growing on stones and other plants, algae will also attach themselves to the shells of snails and mussels. One of their most unusual homes is on the hair of the South American sloth which spends much of its time hanging upside down in trees.

Seaweeds

Seaweeds are the larger forms of algae. There are about 600 kinds around the shores of Britain alone. A seaweed usually consists of a blade or leaf-like frond, a stalk, and an organ called a holdfast. This is used to cling to stones, rocks, shells and breakwaters. Seaweeds are slimy to touch. The "slime" is a protective barrier against drying out in the sun when the tide is out.

Seaweeds are divided into four groups according to their colour—green, blue-green, brown and red. Some, especially the blue-greens, have not changed for millions of years.

A common green seaweed is *En-*

teromorpha. It consists of thin strands which cover the mud high up the shore. The sea lettuce looks much like the true lettuce. Both these seaweeds form slippery layers, especially at river mouths.

Along rocky shores the brown seaweeds, called wracks, are the most common. At the top of the beach is the channel wrack. It may turn black and brittle if not washed by the tide, and dries up in the sun. Half way down the beach is the knotted wrack which has large, single air-bladders on its fronds. Lower down still is the bladder wrack. It has pairs of smaller bladders which help to float the seaweeds when the tide is in.

At very low tides other brown seaweeds can be seen. These are the long oarweeds or tangles which form dense, underwater forests.

The red seaweeds are usually smaller than the brown ones, and can be found in rock pools, or in deeper water. On a sloping, rocky beach the green seaweeds are mostly at the top, and the browns and reds nearer the bottom.

Some seaweeds reproduce by breaking into separate parts. Others put out runners. Most seaweeds have separate male and female organs on separate plants. Their male and female sex cells unite to produce spores which then grow into new plants. In bladder wracks the sex cells are produced in hollow chambers near the tips of the fronds.

Uses

Seaweeds have many uses. Farmers gather them from along the beach and spread them on the land as fertilizer. Some types are used in paper-making. Others that contain a glue-like substance are put into jellies to make them set.

Right: Rocky shores are often left covered with seaweed when the tide goes out. Many shore animals find shelter among seaweed fronds. Seaweeds are classified by their colour, size and shape. They are among the oldest kinds of plants on earth.

187

Lichens and mosses

Above: Lichen growing on damp ashwood in Scotland.

Below: A lichen seen in cross-section showing its algal and fungal parts.

Almost everyone can recognize lichens growing on a country wall. Country people are also familiar with the lichens which sometimes festoon the branches of trees.

Lichens

Lichens are hardy plants which can live in the very small amount of soil they find in these places. However, they are sensitive to fumes from factories and motor vehicles, so do not grow so well in town.

One of the most common plants in the cold northern tundra is reindeer moss. This is mis-named, as it is a lichen and not a moss. But, as its name implies, it is the principal food of reindeer. Reindeer moss is also one of the larger, upright, branching forms of lichens known as fruticose lichens.

Other forms are the foliose lichens, which are also branched, but flatter, and the crustose lichens, which we know as flat, crusty patches on walls and tombstones. Some lichens can even grow down into stone, by secret-

ing a substance which dissolves the stone.

Lichens are really not one kind of plant, but two. The body of a lichen is composed of a mass of fungal hyphae, or threads, which hold many cells of an alga.

The relationship between the fungus and the alga in a lichen can be viewed in two ways. Only the alga can produce its own food by photosynthesis, but the fungus "steals" some too. In this case, the fungus is regarded as a parasite on the alga. The other view sees the two plants as living together in symbiosis, where both plants benefit. In this case, the fungus is seen as protecting the alga and supplying it with moisture, thus enabling the alga to live in places it would otherwise find too hostile.

Lichens can reproduce themselves by soredia, which are one or more algal cells surrounded by fungal threads. The fungus may also produce spores, which must, however, settle near algal cells if they

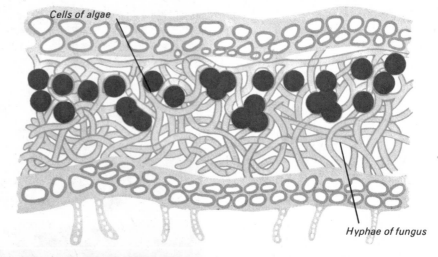

Cells of algae

Hyphae of fungus

are to develop into lichens. Lichens grow very slowly—at most they increase by only one or two centimetres a year.

Mosses, liverworts and hornworts

These little plants live in damp places. Liverworts flourish only

Left: Lichens prefer to live in places where the air is unpolluted by vehicle fumes. Gravestones in churchyards are often encrusted with lichen growth.

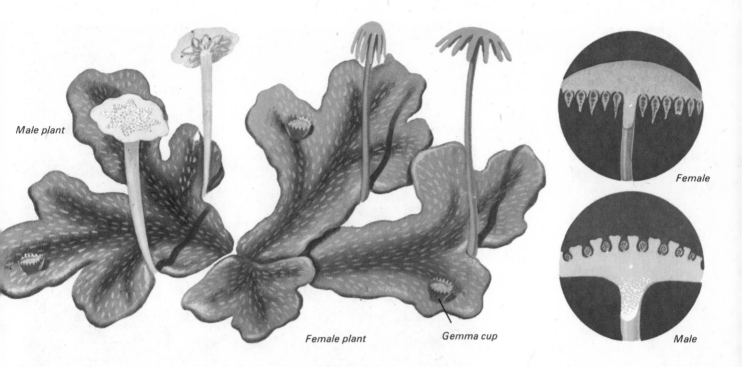

Male plant

Female plant

Gemma cup

Female

Male

Above: Liverworts are plants that live in or near water. They reproduce asexually by buds called gemmae.

The sex organs of liverworts are borne on separate plants. One produces sperms, the other eggs.

Above: These two enlarged drawings show the male and female structures of the liverwort plant.

where water is plentiful, in bogs and on the banks of streams. Hornworts, which are very similar to liverworts, include tropical species that grow on damp tree bark.

Liverworts and hornworts appear as flattish, strap-like green plants with a narrow stalk climbing upwards. In liverworts this stalk carries a cap, which is absent in hornworts.

Mosses also have this general appearance but their green parts are more leaf-like and are often raised higher above the soil.

None of these plants has true roots. They are anchored to the soil by simple, rather root-like rhizoids.

Their reliance on water gives a clue to their history. They were among the first plants to attempt life on land. Like frogs and newts, they have never become really independent of water, needing it particularly for reproduction.

Also, the water and food inside their bodies is largely passed about from cell to cell, as in algae. Higher plants use a complex system of vascular tissues.

Reproduction

Reproduction is similar in mosses, liverworts and hornworts. The male sex cells are sperm-like. In mosses, these are produced in special organs on the leafy parts. When released, a sperm swims in the surface moisture on the leaf until it reaches a similar type of sex organ containing an egg. Fertilization then takes place.

The fertilized egg then divides and multiplies until it produces a stalk. This stalk can be considered as a second type of plant growing out from the leafy green plant, from which it gets its nourishment.

Under the cap at the upper end of the stalk, asexual spores are formed. When released, these are carried away on the wind and so the moss is distributed. If an asexual spore germinates in the soil, it first grows into an alga-like protonema. This later develops into the leafy green plant which bears the sex cells.

Liverworts and hornworts have similar life-cycles, except that in some liverworts the sex organs are found at the tops of the stalks, not on the lower leafy parts. Sperms

and eggs are made on separate stalks, so fertilization can take place only when the plant is covered in water and the sperms can swim to the eggs. Seaweeds reproduce in a similar way and the flattish, lobed leaves of liverworts strongly resemble small seaweeds.

Some liverworts and mosses also reproduce asexually by means of gemmae. These are small packets of cells which leave the parent plant and float away on the wind. If a gemma settles in a suitable place, it grows into an adult plant.

Above: Like liverworts, mosses have female sex organs called archegonia, and male sex organs called antheridia.

Ferns

Plants first began to live on land more than 400 million years ago. They needed to develop new structures to cope with their new conditions of life and to make them independent of surrounding water.

Their most important need was an internal system for the storage and movement of food, and water containing mineral salts. With such a system all living parts of the plants could be nourished.

Vascular system

What plants developed was a system of mainly woody tubes called a vascular system. The tubes transport water and at the same time add strength and rigidity to a plant. This in turn enables a vascular plant to grow to a larger size than is possible with the non-vascular liverworts and mosses.

The very first vascular plants were the psilophytes. Only three species of this ancient group of plants are still living today, and even they are rather rare in warmer parts of the world.

The best known of these, *Psilotum,* has a horizontal underground stem, or rhizome, but no roots. It has forked branches coming out of the rhizome. These bear tiny, scale-like leaves, as well as sporangia which release spores during reproduction.

Clubmosses and their relatives

Clubmosses are small creeping plants. Some look like larger mosses, some like miniature pine trees, but a third group, the quillworts, are water plants which look more like onions or garlic.

Like psilophytes, clubmosses reproduce themselves with the aid of a single type of asexual spore. Spores are contained in sporangia which lie in the club-shaped parts of the plants, from which they get their name.

Clubmoss relatives, like the various species of *Selaginella* and the quillworts, have two types of spores. These are called, respectively, megaspores or big spores, and microspores or small spores.

Microspores give rise to male sperms while still on the plants. Megaspores similarly give rise to female eggs. In some cases, eggs are fertilized while still on the parent plant and may even develop into embryos there before dropping off the parent. This of course resembles the type of reproduction that occurs in the highest of plants, the seed plants. These include flowers, trees and grasses.

Horsetails

As with clubmosses, the horsetails of today are the few survivors of a once great group. Three hundred million years ago, many different kinds of horsetails grew as large trees in the coal swamps.

The 25 species that have survived until today are all woody plants a metre or less in height, growing from underground stems. They are seen most commonly as hedgerow or meadow plants, or as garden weeds. Other species still live in swamps and bogs.

The part most people are fami-

Above: Tree ferns, which live high up in the tropics, grow ten metres or more high and are the largest of all ferns.

Below and **right:** Hard ferns and the buckler, bladder and hart's tongue ferns are all of small to medium height.

Right: Clubmosses and their relatives are all small creeping plants. They reproduce by spores. The two types of spore produced by *Selaginella* bear some resemblance to the pollen and ova of higher plants. This might indicate how these higher plants evolved.

Bladder fern

Buckler fern

Hart's tongue fern

Fir clubmoss

Selaginella

liar with is their sterile shoot which makes food by photosynthesis, but does not produce spores. These shoots have an unmistakable appearance. They are upright, green, jointed stems from which whorls of slender green branches spring, more or less horizontally, at regular intervals. Spores are formed at the tips of more short-lived, fertile shoots.

The rhizome, upright stem and branches all bear scale-like leaves. The whole plant feels hard and rough because of silicon deposits in its outer layers.

Ferns

Ferns are the most successful plants of their group. They have by far the most species and these are more widely distributed. They also take many different forms.

In temperate glades and woodland, such ferns as bracken are common plants. In tropical forests, ferns range from the size of trees to filmy, fragile plants that look rather like mosses. Other tropical forest ferns include many epiphytes that perch on the branches and trunks of trees. Some small ferns are water plants with trailing roots.

Another way in which ferns are different from their relatives is that they have large, compound leaves. The way in which these leaves uncurl in the spring is most typical. All fern stems arise from underground rhizomes.

Woody and other vascular tissues are well developed in rhizomes and stems, enabling ferns to grow to a large size—some tree ferns are ten metres or more in height.

The spores of most common

Right: The sterile shoots of horsetails are a common sight on waste ground but the fertile, spore-bearing shoots are less often seen. Horsetails once included large trees living in the coal swamps of prehistoric times. The trees died and fossilized to become coal. Modern horsetails are only two metres or less in height.

ferns are borne inside sori which can be found in rows on the underside of the leaves or fronds.

Reproduction

Ferns, horsetails and clubmosses all reproduce in a similar way. As with mosses and liverworts, this involves an alternation of generations, where plants which bear asexual spores alternate with plants that bear sperms and eggs.

In contrast to mosses and liverworts, however, it is the spore-bearing plant of ferns and their relatives that is the largest and most obvious stage in the fern's life-cycle. This is known as the sporophyte. A fern or horsetail plant, for example, is a sporophyte.

The plant that bears sex cells, or gametes, is tiny. It is called the gametophy. This develops in the soil from an asexual spore, and bears either sperms, or eggs, or both.

When a sperm fertilizes an egg, the fertilized egg divides and multiplies until it has grown into the adult sporophyte. The complete cycle of a fern is shown on page 181.

Spores

Fertile shoot

Sterile shoot

Conifers

Conifers, as the name suggests, are trees which produce cones, not flowers. Their leaves are thin and needle-like and usually stay on the tree all year round.

Conifers include the largest, oldest and tallest living things on earth. The giant sequoia of California can live for well over a thousand years. The redwood tree is the tallest, measuring up to 111 metres. Another tall tree is the Douglas fir which can grow up to 60 metres.

The needles, or leaves, of a conifer cut down the water loss because of their slender shape. This is especially important during winter when the ground is frozen and water cannot be taken out of the ground.

The conifer belt

Conifers can withstand more severe weather than the broad-leaved trees and so grow successfully high up on mountains. A conifer "belt" stretches right across Canada, northern Europe and Asia. The dominant conifers in these regions are spruce and pine.

Many conifer plantations have been planted by man. These are easily recognized because the trees are always planted in rows. Plantation trees are cut down when fully grown. Conifers can grow in places where the soil is poor, and many plantations are now growing on what were once bare mountain slopes, heaths and moorland.

Unlike broad-leaved trees, conifers grow very regularly and have a definite shape. Each spring a fresh shoot grows out of the top, and the side branches grow equally to form a new ring of branches. The straight centre trunk provides smooth timber which can be cut into planks, floorboards and furniture, or used for making posts and ships' masts. The wood, called deal in the trade, is softer than the hardwood of broad-leaved trees. It can

Right: A variety of conifer needles. Some needles grow in bunches, while others grow separately.

Below: These three conifers are the Scots pine, native of Britain, the Norway spruce, or Christmas tree, and the American western red cedar.

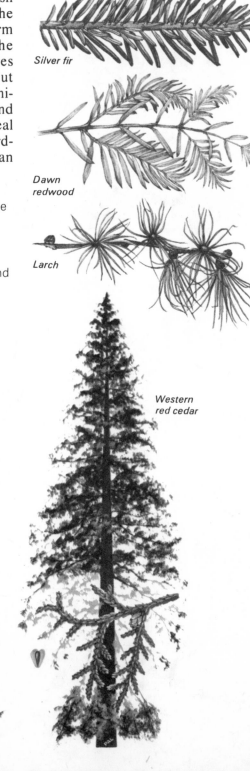

White pine

Cypress

Silver fir

Dawn redwood

Larch

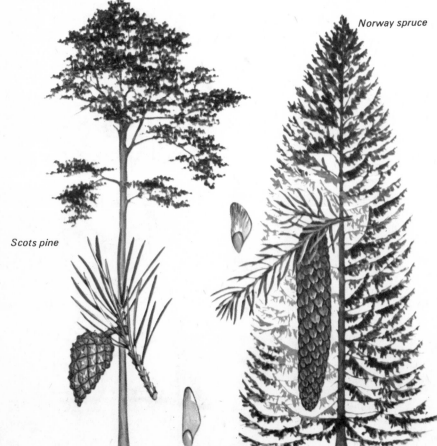

Scots pine

Norway spruce

Western red cedar

also be pulped for making hardboard and newspaper.

Conifers contain oils and resins which protect them in cold weather, and also seal up any wounds. Resin is used in soap and disinfectants, and for making turpentine. Some timber, like cedarwood, is hard-wearing and is used to build sheds.

Conifer foliage

It is possible to identify a conifer by its needles. Those of the spruce, yew and Douglas fir grow separately. Pines, cedars and larches have their needles in groups. The pines have two, three or five needles together. Larch and cedar needles grow in bunches. Hemlocks have single needles of different lengths, while cypress needles are closely packed around the twigs.

The bark of conifers is smooth at first, then divides into patches or furrows. Some bark contains a substance called tannin, which is used in treating leather.

Life in coniferous forests

A conifer wood is dark and gloomy because there is a continual cover of leaves. On the ground is a carpet of needles which decays slowly. The soil is acidic. A conifer wood is mostly a silent place, with few animals, since there are few sources of food apart from the seeds of the cones. There are far fewer flowers than in an oak wood, because it is too dark for them to grow. Only toadstools and some kinds of insects find coniferous forests good places to live in.

Because of the oil content in conifers they can easily catch fire. It is usually in coniferous woods and forests that serious outbreaks of fire occur, and sometimes these fires are very difficult to bring under control.

Right: Tall Douglas firs tower towards the sky. In the foreground of this picture is a broken and dying tree. Normally, a fully grown Douglas fir reaches a height of over 60 metres.

Life-cycle of a conifer

A conifer starts life as a seed inside a cone. Cones are made up of tightly packed scales or bracts. On each bract in a female cone the seed develops without a covering. Conifers are called gymnosperms, which means "naked seeds". In flowers the seeds grow inside a covering called the ovary or fruit.

Male and female cones

Male and female cones grow on the same tree. In spring the males appear in small clusters near the tips of the branches. They shed clouds of golden pollen which is carried by the wind to the female cones. Colour and scent are not necessary, since cones, unlike flowers, do not need the help of insects.

The pollen fertilizes the female egg cell inside its egg chamber or ovule. The female cone then closes up to give the egg cell time to develop into a seed. This may take two or three years.

Seed dispersal

At first a female cone is coloured green, blue or red. When fully ripe it turns brown and woody, and the seeds drop out. They have papery wings so that they float in the wind. In the yew and juniper the seeds have a soft, fruit-like covering. Birds eat the seeds and their coverings. Later the seeds pass out of the bird's body unharmed, and so the seeds are dispersed.

Cones open in dry weather when seeds can be scattered. They close in wet weather when the seeds would be washed straight onto the ground by rain and overcrowd the parent tree.

A baby conifer germinates and grows into a seedling at a rate of about 30 centimetres a year until it is about five years old. A pine tree is mature in about 60 years.

Transport system

Inside the trunk new growth continues in the ring of living cambium cells just beneath the bark. These divide continuously to form rings of cells on both sides. The

The circulation system of a conifer

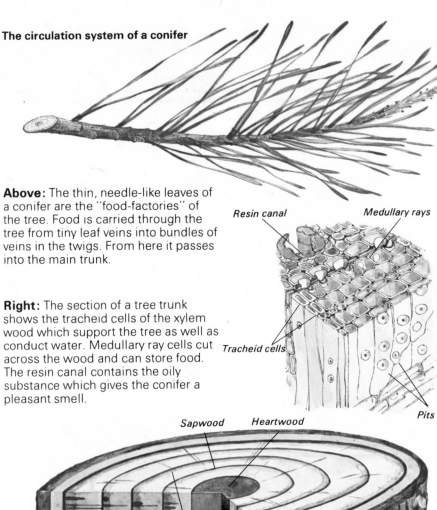

Above: The thin, needle-like leaves of a conifer are the "food-factories" of the tree. Food is carried through the tree from tiny leaf veins into bundles of veins in the twigs. From here it passes into the main trunk.

Right: The section of a tree trunk shows the tracheid cells of the xylem wood which support the tree as well as conduct water. Medullary ray cells cut across the wood and can store food. The resin canal contains the oily substance which gives the conifer a pleasant smell.

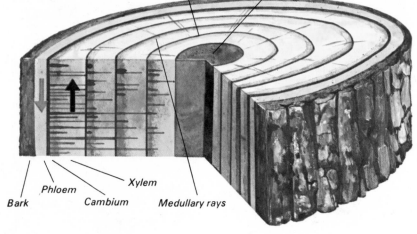

Above: This section of a trunk shows the rings of sapwood (xylem) with the heartwood at the centre. In between are the living cambium cells which divide on both sides to increase the size of the tree.

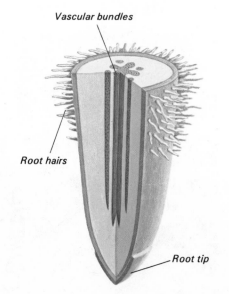

Left: This root section shows the bundles of vessels which join up with the xylem and phloem layers in the trunk above. Water is taken in by the root hairs. The root tip has a protective covering for pushing through the soil.

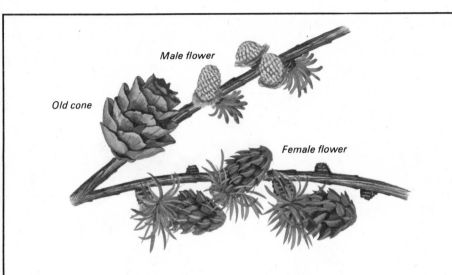

Above: Larches produce male pollen-producing cones. The wind blows the pollen to the young female cones, where the egg cells become fertilized.

A lot of pollen is produced because much of it never reaches a female cone. After fertilization, the scales on the cone open out to release the seeds.

Spruce

Pine

Cones eaten by
a crossbill

outside rings form the phloem which carries food (sap) downwards. The inner rings or xylem draw up water from the roots.

Since the cell division in the cambium slows down in winter, and speeds up in spring, the xylem cells look different. The result is the annual rings which can be seen on a cut log or tree stump. The number of rings give the age of the tree.

Xylem is largely composed of dead cells which support the tree and conduct water. This is called the sapwood. In the centre the darker wood, or heartwood, is empty of water and is the main support of the tree—its inner "skeleton".

Xylem wood consists mainly of long cells, or vessels, called tracheids. They have tiny openings or pits in their walls so that water can pass freely from one cell to the other. Medullary rays cross the tracheids like spokes in a wheel. It is these rays which give the wood its pattern, or graining.

The xylem-phloem circulation of sap and water starts in the leaves and passes right down to the roots. Root hairs draw in water from the soil which passes up the xylem vessels to reach the leaves. The water, plus carbon dioxide from the air, mixes with chlorophyll to make food. Sunlight provides the energy for this process. Food is then carried by the phloem cells to various parts of the tree where it is needed for growth.

A home for wildlife

Coniferous woodlands, whether natural or man-made, cannot support as many different species of wildlife as broad-leaved forests. This is because less light filters through the dense conifer foliage, so fewer plants can grow on the forest floor, and therefore fewer animals can live there.

However the spread of plantations can even help to increase the numbers of certain rare species of animal. In Britain, for example, wildcats and pine martens are found in much greater numbers than even a few years ago.

However, the vast, natural coniferous forests of northern Europe usually harbour more animals and birds than the plantations. In addition to the marten and wildcat, the occasional brown bear can be found. Even wolves still exist in remote areas. Europe's largest woodpecker, the black woodpecker, nests in conifers and another striking bird, the waxwing, makes its home there too.

Top: The crossbill twists off the bracts on a cone with its scissor-shaped beak to remove the seeds.

Above: A red squirrel will nibble off the bracts down to the middle column.

195

Broad-leaved trees

Trees are taken very much for granted, yet they are among the most important living things on earth, not only to man but to a great number of plants and animals.

Through the ages humans have depended on trees. They burned the wood to provide fuel for cooking and warmth, and they also built wooden homes, carts and furniture. Man made use of wood as far back as the Stone Age.

About 8,000 years ago man became a farmer. This was when the vast forests began to dwindle as he made room for his homes, his crops and animals. In much of the world today, these forests have been ousted by farmland, cities and roadways. Here and there are small woods and parks, together with remnants of the great forests. In other places where trees have been felled and not replaced by new seedlings, the land has turned into man-made deserts.

The reason for this is that trees protect the land. The roots bind the soil and the leaves above give shelter from the sun and wind. The falling leaves add to the richness of the soil. Take away the trees and the soil dries. It is either washed or blown away.

Woodland wildlife

Broad-leaved or deciduous trees, particularly oak woods, support the most varied forms of life. The oak grows to become a massive tree with a dense, rounded head of strong, twisted branches. Clusters of leaves grow at the branch tips. In May the hanging catkins, full of pollen, attract the bees. In autumn, acorns are gathered by squirrels and deer. At one time wild boar and farm pigs roamed the oak woods to fatten on acorns.

Below the oak tree is a lower layer of smaller bushes and trees, such as crab apple, hazel and hawthorn. These provide more food for animals and birds. Flowers such as bluebells, anemones and primroses grow on the ground. Ivy, wild roses and honeysuckle cling to

Broadleaf foliage

False acacia

Alder

Willow

Holly

Sycamore

Horse chestnut

Above: These leaves, apart from the holly, are deciduous and belong to broad-leaved trees. The alder, willow, holly and sycamore are simple leaves. The acacia and horse chestnut leaves are compound.

the trunk and branches.

Most woodland flowers bloom in spring when there is enough light before the leaves on the trees close in. The flowers set their seeds and continue to make their food until autumn. This is when the toad-stools take over, appearing on the leaf mould, dead branches and tree stumps.

Birds nest among the branches of an oak tree. Owls and woodpeckers make homes in holes in the trunk. The squirrel builds its drey in a tree fork, and bats may roost in a hollow. A deer finds shelter under the old oak. Woodmice scurry about among the fallen leaves, and may have a store of food hidden under a log. Badger setts are even built between the roots.

By day the butterflies fly around the tree, and caterpillars feed on the leaves. At night it is the turn of the moths and beetles, which are hunted by the bat. Weasels and stoats are day hunters. The fox and owl wait for darkness. Deer and rabbits feed by day, and badgers and woodmice at night.

Under the leafy woodland floor live countless numbers of woodlice, spiders, beetles, centipedes and slugs. These make up the "litter fauna" which do useful work as "dustmen". They feed on the fallen leaves and branches and bind them into the soil.

Food chains

The wealth of life on and around a tree can be linked together into a food chain. It starts with the plants. These provide food for insects, slugs and beetles. They in turn are food for the tiny shrew and various songbirds. At the top of the chain are the owls, hawks and foxes.

Even as a tree rots away into powder, it is putting food back into the soil ready to be used by new trees.

Myths and legends

Because of their value to mankind it is not surprising that trees have been worshipped. They were the first churches before buildings were used. The Druids of the Iron Age worshipped the oak and the rowan, and the mysterious mistletoe. The Christmas tree and yule log have long been used in ancient rituals.

Above: This old oak tree may be hundreds of years old. It shows some of the plants and animals which use it for food and shelter. A barn owl is roosting on a branch. A red squirrel is climbing up to its drey. A woodmouse is looking for food among the fallen leaves. Toadstools live on the tree as well as in the leaf mould. A patch of moss grows around its base. The green powdery growth on the bark is caused by algae.

197

Life-cycle of a broad-leaved tree

Broad-leaved trees are called deciduous. They shed their leaves every autumn in countries with cold winters, and rest until spring.

During winter the leaf buds are developing, then as the weather warms up, they open. All summer the leaves are busy making food with the help of the green chemical chlorophyll. Food passes along the leaf veins to be stored in the tree. As autumn arrives the leaf stalks are sealed off and the leaves change colour, then drop off. This is the season of beauty when trees are covered in brown and gold,

especially the beech and maple trees. Once the leaves are shed, the tree rests for the winter.

Some trees have brightly coloured flowers to attract insects which pollinate them, as in the hawthorn and horse chestnut. Others have loose, hanging catkins pollinated by wind, as in the birch and hazel.

Autumn is the time when the fruits are ripe. Since they cannot move on their own they are assisted in various ways. The fruit of the oak (the acorn) falls from its cup to the ground, and may roll a

few yards. So do chestnut, "conker" and hazel nuts. However, if all the seedlings took root too close to the parent tree, overcrowding would result. This is where animals can help. Squirrels gather acorns and bury them some way off. Woodmice store beech nuts and other seeds. Dormice collect hazel nuts. Sometimes they forget where the nuts are hidden, so new trees grow up well away from the parent tree.

Soft fruits are eaten by many animals and birds. The pips or seeds inside can pass through their

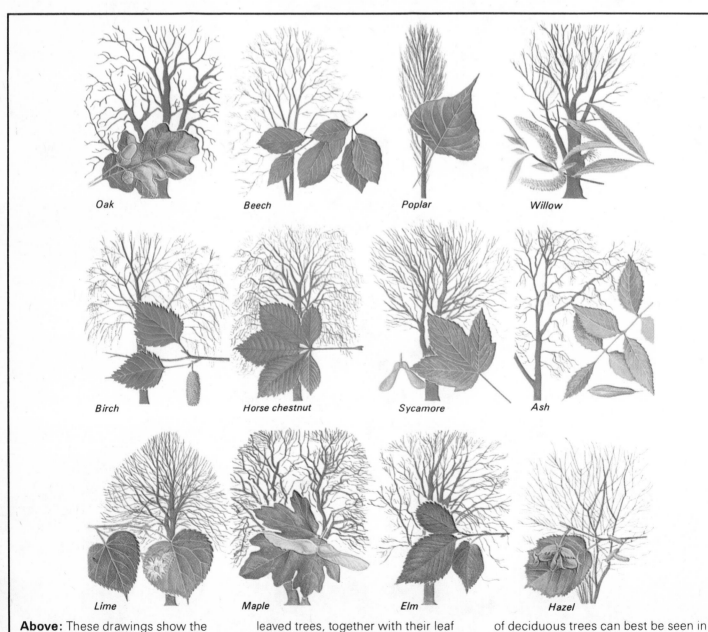

Oak   Beech   Poplar   Willow

Birch   Horse chestnut   Sycamore   Ash

Lime   Maple   Elm   Hazel

Above: These drawings show the winter outlines of a variety of broad-leaved trees, together with their leaf shapes. The branch and twig structure of deciduous trees can best be seen in winter after the leaves are shed.

bodies unharmed with their droppings, so spreading new trees.

Many tree fruits have wings and are blown away by the wind. Examples are the sycamore, lime, hornbeam and ash. The tiny seeds of poplar, birch, willow and elm are so light that they are scattered far and wide. Man even has a hand in spreading seeds and fruits. Over the centuries, many fruits which originated in the East have been introduced to other regions. Citrus fruits like oranges, lemons and limes were originally brought to the Mediterranean from Persia.

Germination

The fallen fruit of a broad-leaved tree lies dormant on the ground throughout the winter. So long as it has soil to grow in, and is not discovered by an animal it will germinate. Broad-leaved trees are dicotyledons (*see page 202*), so two seed leaves will appear as the root takes hold. In general the trees with short lives grow the fastest. A birch tree may become mature in about five years, and produce catkins. An oak may take ten to 15 years to produce acorns, and live for up to 500 years before it dies.

Soil and climate

Trees grow best wherever the soil and the climate is right. Hardwood trees like mahogany and teak prefer the warmth and dampness of a rain forest in places like tropical Africa, Asia and America. In the Mediterranean region the trees are largely evergreen. In western Europe the main trees are broad-leaved and deciduous, losing their leaves in winter. The temperate climate suits them best. The beech grows best in a light soil, especially a chalky one. Ash grows in limestone areas, and alder and willow in damp places along river banks and beside lakes. Oaks like a heavy clay soil.

In a beech wood there is little undergrowth because of the heavy shade during summer. The beech leaves grow horizontally, filling in the gaps so that little light gets

through. The fallen leaves decay very slowly so that the soil is poor.

An oak wood is quite different. Here the light can penetrate, and the leaf mould makes a rich soil. As a result there is a thick undergrowth of flowers and shrubs.

Ash trees grow their leaves late in the season, so there is plenty of light for a thick layer of shrubs to grow. On the ground the flowers are largely replaced with mosses and ferns which do not mind shady places. Marsh-loving plants grow alongside the alder and willow.

Some trees seem more at home in the open countryside or on the edges of woods. These include the elm, hawthorn and hazel.

Right and **above right**: Autumn is the season when trees can be said to show their true colours. The green chlorophyll decomposes and the leaves turn to their natural colours of yellow or red.

Below: Some deciduous woods, like this oak wood, have a rich variety of flora (flowers) and fauna (animals).

Flower families

The flowering plants form the most highly developed group within the plant kingdom. They range in size from small herbs to shrubs and trees.

There are three kinds of herbs (non-woody plants). Annuals grow, flower, set seeds and die in one year. Biennials grow in one year, and flower and fruit in the next. Perennials last for a number of years.

Those herbs which survive through one year and into the next die down to an underground organ in which food is stored. In a tulip this is a bulb, which is made of tightly packed leaves. A crocus has a corm, which is a swollen underground part of its stem. An iris has a rhizome, which is a horizontal stem below ground, from which fresh plants grow each year.

Flowering shrubs and trees are more permanent, since their trunks and branches are made of wood. This gives them support and allows them to grow bigger than herbs. The rose bush, the hawthorn shrub and the oak tree, all flowering plants, remain standing throughout life. Only the leaves and fruit drop off.

Seed-leaves

Flowering plants are divided into two main groups—the dicotyledons and the monocotyledons. A cotyledon is a seed-leaf containing food. It appears soon after a seed germinates, and provides the plant's food when it first starts growing. As the root is formed the first true leaves appear.

In the dicotyledon plants (*page 202*) there are two seed-leaves. The true leaves come in various shapes—round, oval, willow-leaved, heart- and palm-shaped. Their veins are branched.

In the monocotyledons (*page 206*) there is a single seed-leaf. The true leaves are long and sword-shaped, and the veins are parallel.

Parts of a flower

Flowers are composed of different parts which form in a tight spiral,

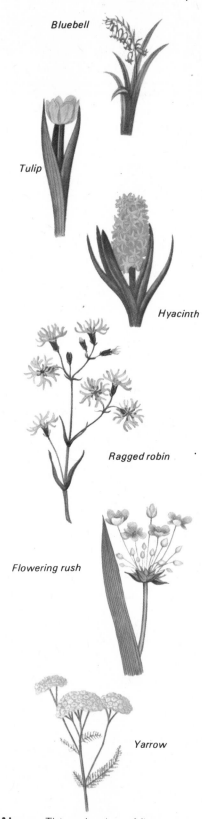

Bluebell

Tulip

Hyacinth

Ragged robin

Flowering rush

Yarrow

Below: This cross-section of a buttercup flower shows its different parts. The sepals are for protection. The coloured petals and the nectaries attract insects for pollination. Stamens contain the pollen, and the carpels the egg cells, which will develop into seeds.

Petals

Pollen

Stamens

Carpels

Sepals

Nectaries

Seed box

Above: This selection of flowers grow in very different places. The bluebell prefers a shady corner in a wood. The tulip and hyacinth are garden flowers whose ancestors grow wild in Asia Minor. The ragged robin likes damp surroundings, while the flowering rush stands right in water. The yarrow grows by the roadside.

one behind the other. This structure can be seen clearly in the regular shape of a field buttercup.

On the outside of a flower head is a ring of sepals which form the calyx. They are usually coloured green, and give protection to a flower during the bud stage. Inside the calyx are the petals, forming the corolla. They are often brightly coloured. Some flowers also have glands called nectaries which produce a sweet, scented honey substance. The flower's colour and scent help to attract insects which pollinate it.

In the centre of a flower are the sex organs. Male organs consist of stamens, made up of anthers on stalks. Anthers contain the pollen which is shed when the anthers ripen. The stamens surround the female organ, or ovary. This is made up of carpels, either joined together, or separate. Inside a carpel is the ovule, or seed-box, which contains the egg cell. If an egg cell is fertilized by a pollen grain, it turns into a seed.

Flower families

Botanists look at the number of sepals, petals, stamens and carpels each flower has in order to group them. For example, in the buttercup family, or Ranunculaceae, there are five sepals, five petals, and many stamens and ovaries. The family also includes the anemone, clematis and columbine.

Another common family, the Cruciferae, includes the wallflower, stock, shepherd's purse and many of our vegetables, such as the cabbage and turnip. Each member of this group has four sepals, four petals, six stamens, and two carpels joined together to form one ovary.

The rose family (Rosaceae) consists of flowers with five sepals, five petals, several rows of five stamens, and many carpels. Apart from roses, the family includes fruit trees, such as the apple, pear and plum, hawthorn trees, sloes, brambles and many wild flowers.

The pea family (Leguminosae) has an irregular shaped flower of five joined sepals, five petals, ten stamens and a single carpel. The fruit is a pod which contains the seeds, and splits open to release them. The bean, gorse and clover, sweet pea and acacia tree are all members of the pea family.

The Compositae form a very successful and widespread family. Small flowers are gathered into a flower head, as in the dandelion, daisy and thistle. Each seed has a tiny parachute and is carried away on the wind.

Some families have tight bunches of flowers in the shape of catkins. Male and female catkins usually grow on separate trees. The male ones are brightly coloured like the pussy-willow catkin of the sallow, and the "lambs' tails" of the hazel. Its catkins hang down loosely from the trees and are pollinated by the wind. Willow catkins stand more upright and are insect-pollinated.

The Umbelliferae or "umbrella" flowers grow in clusters on stalks which resemble the ribs of an umbrella. A common example is the cow parsley found along the hedgerows.

Century plant

Poinsettia

Most flowering plants produce flowers at the right time for pollination, but not all plants flower at the same time.

Left: The century plant can take up to a hundred years to flower.

Above: The Mexican poinsettia is kept as a pot-plant, and can be made to flower at different times of the year.

Honesty

Above: Honesty is an unusual plant, because it is both annual and biennial.

Dicotyledons

The flowering plants are called seed-plants, because they reproduce from seeds. In lower plants, such as ferns and mosses, reproduction is by means of minute spores.

A seed is more complicated than a spore, and develops from an egg cell inside the female ovule. The egg cell is fertilized by the male pollen grain.

Once fertilized, the egg cell begins to divide to form a tiny embryo. Other cells, called the endosperm, help to feed the embryo as it grows. The wall of the ovule protects the embryo in the early stages before it germinates.

By the time the seed is freed from the parent plant it has divided into various parts of a young plant. At one end is the shoot, the plumule, which is surrounded by the seed-like leaves, or cotyledons. At the other end is a minute root called a radicle.

Some seeds are formed in separate ovules, as in the buttercup and grasses. Others are contained in a compound ovary, as in the bean family. The peas we eat are the seeds inside a single container, the pea-pod. The pod is the ovary, called the fruit.

Two kinds of buds develop along the stem of a growing plant. One is a leaf-bud which lengthens out above the main stem, or forms a side branch. The other is a flowering bud which opens into a flower which will eventually produce the seeds.

Dicotyledons vary enormously in size, from small, annual herbs, to huge, spreading trees. The flower parts come in numbers of two, four and five and the leaves have various shapes. They are supported by a midrib with side branches. The flower is pollinated with the help of wind and insects and, more rarely, with the help of water.

Insect pollination

Insects play an important role in pollination. They are attracted by colour and scent and search for the nectar. Since the nectar and pollen

are well inside the flower, the insect has to find a way in. A flower like a buttercup or wild rose has a wide open flower and can easily be reached by insects with short tongues, such as flies and beetles. Other flowers are bunched together into flower heads forming a flat platform-like surface on which insects can walk. This is typical of the members of the Umbelliferae family (*page 201*).

In a tubular flower, such as the honeysuckle and primrose, only long-tongued insects can reach the

Left: The dahlia is a member of the Compositae family.

Below left: Antirrhinum is more popularly called snapdragon. It is a member of the pea family.

Below: This blaze of colour is created by two types of flower – the morning

glory and the oleander. Morning glory is a climbing plant. Oleander is a greenhouse shrub.

Top right: Dandelions spread rapidly on waste ground.

Below right: Dock grows by the wayside.

the stamens downwards so that they touch the back of the bee. The bee is dusted with pollen which is then transferred to another flower.

Underwater plants

Some flowers actually live under water. In ponds the hornwort has minute flowers in the angles of its leaves. Pollen is freed and spread through the water to reach the female flowers. Other water plants have flowers which float on the surface or stand above it, such as the water lily and water crowfoot. In these cases insects pollinate the flowers in the usual way.

As with pollen, the seeds and fruits also require some help in spreading from their parent plant. Fruits with feathery parachutes or wings are carried by the wind. Those with hooks cling to the fur of passing animals. Fleshy fruits are eaten by birds and animals, and the seeds or pips inside pass through their bodies and may be dropped well away from the parent. A few fruits, such as those of the water iris, are carried by water. The coconut can be carried for many kilometres across the sea, to be washed up on shores far away from the parent tree.

Where plants live

Flowers, like animals, are adapted to different surroundings. Some, like the primrose and bluebell, can grow in woods in shady places. The cowslip prefers a more chalky soil in the open. Heather grows in acid soils on moorland. Mountain flowers have to endure the cold and long winter, and reproduce in a short summer season.

Along the coast are flowers which can withstand the salt spray. Those living among rocks have deep roots to penetrate into the cracks to reach water.

In deserts and sand-dunes where water is scarce, flowers have thick, hairy or curled up leaves to cut down the loss of water. Cactus plants store water in their stems, and succulents in their leaves.

nectar. Some flowers, like the honeysuckle and tobacco flower, give off scent towards the end of the day when the air is still. This attracts the night-flying hawk moths. They hover in front of the flower, reaching in with their long tongues, in the same way as hummingbirds do.

Flowers of the pea family, such as the garden snapdragon, have a lower petal which acts as a landing platform. A bee settling on this causes it to drop, and this levers

Grasses

The family of grasses (Graminae) are all flowering plants. They grow wild almost everywhere – in Antarctica, on the tops of mountains, along the seashore, even in deserts.

Grasses are among the most successful plants, and are often the first to appear on waste ground, or after a fire, or on footpaths and brickwork. One of the few places where grasses find it difficult to grow is in tropical forests.

There are some 35,000 different kinds. Grasses have hollow, rounded stems with swollen joints from which side branches grow. The leaves are lance-shaped with parallel veins, as in other monocotyledons (*see page 206*). At the base, the leaves fit around the stem.

Grasses spread by means of runners, like the strawberry plant, or by a rhizome, or underground stem. Rhizomes help to bind the soil together and form a turf. This is especially important in loose or sandy soil which could be washed or blown away by rain or wind. The marram grass and sand couch grass along the coast keep the sand dunes together.

Grass flowers

The flowers of grasses are not brightly coloured, since they are wind pollinated and do not need the help of insects. The flower head consists of many flowers gathered in bunches or spikelets. They vary a great deal in appearance. Some heads are tightly clustered,

Left: Rice is the staple food of many people throughout the world.

Below: The wheat fields of North America cover vast areas of land.

as in the foxtail and Timothy grasses. The head of the brome grass is open and the spikelets hang loosely. Within a spikelet are small clusters of between one and five flowers, within a pair of bracts called glumes.

Each separate flower has its own bract, called a flowering glume, or lemma. This has a bristle on its tip, the awn. It shows up well in the wild oat and barley grasses. Around the actual flower is another protective bract – the palea.

Each flower has three stamens and a single ovary. The ripe stamens hang loosely and shake in the wind. Pollen is blown onto the ovary which has on it a feathery style to catch the pollen. The seeds which are produced are also scattered by the wind, and are blown over a wide area. If soil conditions are correct they will germinate.

Varieties of grasses

One of the commonest grasses is the cocksfoot. It has a branched flower head, with egg-shaped clusters of purplish spikelets, and may be found growing in grassy areas and waste grounds. The foxtail has a long and cylindrical flower head, and is more a meadow grass. So is

Below: This photograph shows the head of the cocksfoot grass with the pollen-laden stamens hanging loosely in the wind. The pollen is blown onto the styles of the ovaries, inside which the seeds develop.

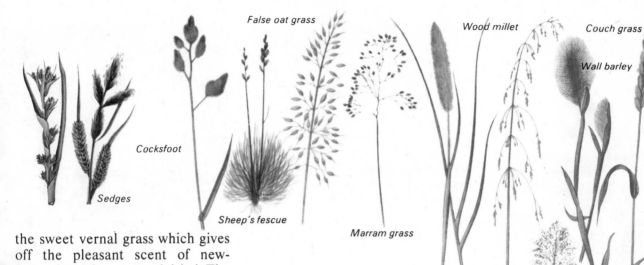

False oat grass

Wood millet

Couch grass

Wall barley

Cocksfoot

Sedges

Sheep's fescue

Marram grass

Wavy hair grass

Common bent grass

Purple moor grass

Timothy

the sweet vernal grass which gives off the pleasant scent of new-mown hay when cut and dried. The soft brome grass has many short-stalked, downy, egg-shaped spikelets.

Along pond and river banks the tall great water grass forms a dense cover for waterfowl. It has spreading flower spikelets and rivals in size the tall reed which can grow up to nearly four metres.

The great water grass has large, feathery flower heads, and grows in marshland. Reeds have been used for centuries in thatching.

Around the coast are large stretches of the cord, or rice grass. This has a slender flower head of unbranched spikelets. Like the marram on sand dunes this important grass helps to bind the soil along muddy shores, and has been planted in many places to protect the coast.

The sheep's fescue grass grows on dry soils on hillsides and on areas of chalk and limestone. As its name implies it is a food crop for sheep. Such sheep pastures also contain the upright brome grass.

A very distinctive grass is the quaking grass which is easy to spot. The triangular spikelets hang on slender stalks, and shake in the wind.

The patches of purple which you often see in the acidic soil of moorland are actually purple moorgrass. Other kinds of grasses are able to live in poor soil too, such as the tufted hair grass and the mat grass.

The summer season is short up in the mountains. Here, the vivi-parous fescue has adopted an unusual method of reproducing. Instead of flowers it grows leafy bulbils (a kind of small bud) on the spikelets. These fall off and take root to form new grasses.

In shady woodland there are few grasses. Two which do grow are the wood millet and the wood melick.

A tall and important grass which originates from Africa is the bamboo, which can be up to three metres tall. The canes have many uses. Bamboo thickets are a favourite haunt of the Indian tiger. In south-west China the giant panda feeds on bamboo shoots.

Growing crops

Of all the world's plants the grasses are the most vital source of our food. As far back as the Neolithic period (New Stone Age) the first farmers started growing food from wild grasses. From being wandering hunters men could then settle down in one place to plant and harvest their crops. Today, from these original wild grasses, we have developed cereals such as wheat, barley, oats, rye, millet, rice and maize.

One disadvantage of a primitive crop was that, like grasses, the ripe seeds scatter. As a result of careful cross-breeding, modern cereals now have tight heads so that the grains do not fall out and can be more easily reaped.

Monocotyledons are one of the

Bamboo

Above: The bamboo is the tallest among this variety of grasses. Sedges belong to a different family in which the male and female flowers are on separate spikelets.

Monocotyledons

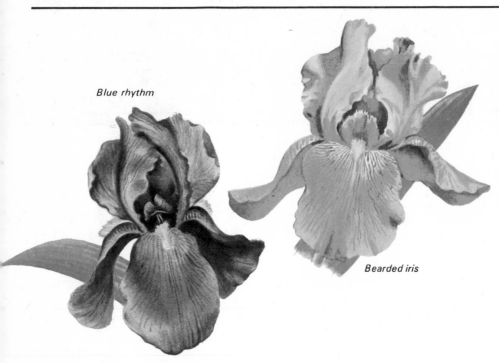

Blue rhythm

Bearded iris

two main branches of flowering plants, in which there is only one cotyledon, or seed-leaf, attached to the embryo. The true leaves on the plant are mostly long and narrow and have parallel veins. Dicotyledon leaves, on the other hand, are usually broad with complex veins.

As with all flowering plants, the embryo monocotyledon plant grows inside the ovule. The embryo is fed from the endosperm, or food store, contained in the ovule. This food consists of fat, starch and protein.

The ovule eventually changes into a seed which has a hard, outer coat called a testa. The seed then detaches itself from the ovary, and the ovary in turn changes into the wall of a fruit. The fruits with the seeds inside are then dispersed.

Whereas the plumule in a dicotyledon is curled as it breaks through the seed coat, that of a monocotyledon remains straight. In order to protect it as it pushes through the soil, the plumule is covered with a hard sheath.

The majority of monocotyledons are herbs (plants without woody stems) and grasses, including sedges and rushes. A few grow to tree size.

The coconut palm can grow very tall, and is one of the few monocotyledons to contain wood. Pam-

pas grass may grow to well over two metres high, and a form of American bamboo up to eight metres. Another palm, the date palm, is unlike most trees because it does not grow side branches. When a leaf falls off it leaves a scar. Palm trees do not grow in thickness, only upwards. If the top is cut off the plant dies.

Lilies and irises

Lilies and irises are well known monocotyledon families, commonly grown in gardens. The lily family contains flowers such as tulips, daffodils and hyacinths. Many kinds of lily that are now familiar to us have been introduced from abroad and were bred from wild flowers. The bluebell or wild hyacinth is a familiar woodland lily. Such flowers grow from bulbs, and a carpet of bluebells is a common sight in the spring.

The Amaryllidaceae is a family closely related to the lilies. There are about 1,000 species in the family, including the onion and its relatives – garlic, leeks and shallots. The snowdrop and the daffodil are probably the best known members of this family.

In the iris family, the ovary is usually below the other flower parts and there are only three stamens.

Above: There are about 2,500 different lilies. The lily family includes hyacinths and tulips.

Above left: Irises are striking garden plants. These two bear the names blue rhythm and bearded iris.

Early purple orchid

Bee orchid

Lady's slipper orchid

Above: A beautiful spread of daffodils is a sure sign of spring.

Below: The coconut palm is a valuable plant. Some use can be made of almost every part of it. Its fruit contains food rich in oil and protein.

Palms

The tall coconut palm is a familiar sight along tropical coasts, even on remote islands. The fruit which is covered with a husk floats on water, and can travel great distances on ocean currents. It can float for up to four months and colonize other coasts. Coconut palms grow mainly near the sea, since a coconut will not germinate unless it is soaked first.

The coconut palm is a valuable plant, and provides fibres from the husk and the tree itself for making mats and ropes. The milk of the nut is rich and nourishing. The shell can be made into bowls and ornaments.

The date palm originates from North Africa and can grow 33 metres tall. It usually grows in oases in desert country. The flowers grow in huge bunches of up to 10,000, and are pollinated by bees.

Bamboo

Some warm parts of the world are treeless but full of bamboo forest. Bamboos spread rapidly by underground stems. The young shoots can be eaten as food, and the older canes made into furniture. A bamboo produces flowers very rarely and there may be gaps of 20 years between flowering. The Japanese mandrake blossoms only once,

Above: The lady's slipper orchid has the largest flowers of all the European species. Once quite common, it is now very rare in many parts of Europe.

after a hundred years' growth. It is almost impossible to believe, but bamboos all over the world produce their blossom at the same time. Once a bamboo shoot has flowered it dies, but the underground part still continues to produce new shoots.

Orchids

Orchids are among the most beautiful monocotyledons. They are grown in special greenhouses, and worn for decoration. The tropical orchids grow mostly on trees and rocks. Orchids are pollinated by insects.

Much smaller sized orchids which grow in the ground are found in countries with a colder climate, like North America and parts of Europe.

Very small, light seeds are produced by orchids so that they can be borne on the wind easily. This is important for the epiphytic types of orchid which live in trees.

If you find an orchid growing wild, do not dig it up, because it will die. This is because orchids can only grow successfully if their roots are associated with a special type of fungus.

Habitats of the world

The raw materials of life are simple – water, oxygen, carbon dioxide and a few minerals. Using the sun's energy, a plant can make living cells from these materials. And wherever they exist, plants will grow. But nothing in the world lives alone. Plants need insects to pollinate them and insects need plants for food. Other animals eat the plants and insects and are in turn eaten by bigger animals. The animals excrete waste matter that helps to fertilize the soil. Everywhere, plants and animals form communities in which they depend on each other.

The type of community which grows in a particular area depends on the raw materials in that area. Different areas contain different minerals, as well as varying amounts of sunlight, water, oxygen and carbon dioxide. These things, together with the temperature, decide what plants can grow there. Plant-eating animals come to find the sort of plants they eat; they also have other needs, such as shelter and water. Meat-eating animals follow the plant-eaters. Gradually the different species settle into a balanced community.

Climatic regions

If you go from either of the poles to the equator, you will travel through every sort of climate from very cold to very hot. These bands of different temperature are the main climatic regions of the world. At the equator there is everlasting summer, and day and night are of equal length. If there is plenty of rain here, a forest will grow. If it is dry, then it will be a desert. Moderate rainfall encourages grass to grow. At the poles it is cold all the year round but a little less cold in

Left: Every landscape we see has its own kinds of life. The four pictures here show contrasting landscapes from different parts of the world. Signs of life are visible in all of them, with the exception of the desert. Yet it too supports some kinds of plants and animals.

summer. The amount of daylight changes a lot with the seasons. It is hardly ever dark in the short summer, but in the middle of the long winter the sun is barely seen.

Between these extremes are the areas, like North America, Asia, and Europe, which we call temperate. They have warm summers and cold winters, a climate suitable for woodland.

In every region there are oceans, rivers and lakes. The range of different watery habitats is as great as the dry land ones. The same things influence life in the water as on land – temperature, light, oxygen, carbon dioxide and minerals.

Micro-habitats

Within the large climatic regions of the world there are many smaller habitats, such as woods, marshes, heaths and villages. Very small ones – single rotten tree trunks, tiny ponds, cottage lawns – are called micro-habitats. Even in the oceans there are micro-habitats like coral reefs and lagoons, rock pools and sunken wrecks. Just as the micro-habitats form part of larger habitats, so the larger ones grade into one another. The edge of a forest contains features of both the forest and the grassland beyond it. Estuaries, where rivers run into the sea, are places where fresh water and salt water combine and so they contain several, slightly different habitats.

Niches

There are countless different places where plants and animals can find a corner to live the kind of life which suits them. These are called niches. The living things that occupy them have become adapted to their particular niches over millions of years of evolution. They are adapted to make the most of the climate where they live, but they are also adapted to live together with all the other species in the same habitat.

So a habitat does not just mean a place. It also means the plants and animals which live there.

Plant succession

The only places in the world where there is no plant life at all are where it is absolutely dry. Without water, there can be no life. But even the tiniest amount of water offers a chance to live.

In the very beginning, life came from water. Then there was no soil at all. Soil is a complicated mixture of organic and inorganic substances that has been built up over millions of years from the death and decay of living things and the weathering of rocks. The soil began to build up in the water, where the first organic substances were.

Our planet is now covered with soil. Even places where nothing grows today have been fertile at some time in the past. So many changes of climate have happened during the earth's history that almost every bit of land has at some time been a forest.

Water, then, is the key to life. If we could water a desert, plants would begin to grow there because there is already some organic material – some soil – mixed in the sand. It is also true that the growth of even the smallest plant can begin to change the environment.

Lichens and mosses

There are some completely new and soil-less environments such as bare rock on a mountainside or newly exposed rocks after an earthquake. On bare rock, or on the roof of a new house, there will be water, light, and minerals, but no organic food. The first plants to take hold here are the lichens. They grow very slowly, using every scrap of organic food they can find. They use the mineral salts in the rock under them. Lichens are a combination of two completely different kinds of plant – an alga and a fungus. It is this combination which enables them to survive where nothing else can.

Mosses are primitive plants that have no roots. They can survive in damp places with very little soil. Sometimes they are found where lichens have already been growing

Above: Slagheaps like these are hills of loose earth and rocks. If the right kinds of grasses are sown there, they can be made safe from landslides.

Right: This wood is a stable community with a rich variety of life.

Below right: If woodland is destroyed by fire, the process of succession has to begin all over again.

for some time. As the mosses die, they make a kind of shallow soil where other plants can root.

Bare sandy places show a different kind of succession. There are two problems with sand. It does not hold much water and it is also easily disturbed. The pattern of sand-dunes in a desert or on the seashore is constantly changing as the sand is blown about.

Grasses are the first plants to get a foothold on sand. Their seeds are blown there by the wind. Grasses can manage with very little water; their wide-spreading roots cover the surface of the soil and help to hold it down. The more grass that grows before the sand is blown

Above and **right:** To plants, our buildings are just another habitat to be colonized like any other rocky place.

from under it, the better its chance of covering enough ground to hold it against the wind. When grasses have covered a dune or slope, they hold it together in a net of roots. The longer they live there, the thicker and deeper the layer of roots and dead grass becomes. It retains moisture and so provides a place for other plants to take root. In fact, the grasses live on very little and they leave more organic material than they use.

Plants that become rooted among the grass still have to cope with exposure to wind. They therefore usually grow close to the ground or are tough and wiry. But with each new plant that grows there, the environment becomes richer until there is enough soil and moisture to support trees. In areas of low rainfall, the trees are short and scrubby and the grass still remains. But where there is enough rainfall to support a wood, the grass dies through lack of light and a new community is formed. It is a strange fact that the first plants to colonize a new area tend to make it more suitable for other plants and less pleasant for themselves.

When a completely new place,

Left: Pasture like this will remain the same as long as cattle graze there. If the cattle go away, it will probably go on to become a wood like the one in the picture above.

like bare rock or sand is colonized, the process is called primary succession. If an existing community is broken up, for example, a field ploughed or a forest felled, the re-growth of plants there is called secondary succession.

Three stages

The three main stages of colonization have also been given special names. The first – lichens or tough grasses, according to whether they are on rock or sand – is called the pioneer community. Next come several short-lived stages – mosses, herbs, low shrubs; these are called the seral communities. Finally the climax stage is reached. This is the community which will stay there, renewing itself as long as conditions remain suitable for it. The pioneer and seral communities cause conditions to change just by being there. The climax community is the stable end of the line – or at least as stable as anything in nature can be.

The climax community may be stable, but it does not stand still. If, for example, it is a wood, trees are dying and falling every year. New trees grow in the spaces they leave. Plants and animals use the dead wood, fallen leaves, nuts and fruit for shelter and food. It is because the cycle of life and death is balanced that the community can continue to exist.

A fine balance

Any upset in this balance can cause the community to fall apart. In very dry seasons some trees die. The ground is then exposed to wind and weather and may dry out so much that it is fit only for grass. Forest fires may follow a drought; the land will be sterilized, just like a needle in a match flame. The slow process of succession then has to begin all over again.

So the process of plant succession is not once and for all. It continues in small ways on the edge of deserts, rivers and sea shores all the time. Ground is forever being gained and lost, and regained.

North Pole

The North Pole is the second coldest place in the world. The reason why it is warmer than the South Pole is that it is mainly sea. Sea water is salty and freezes at a lower temperature than fresh water. Even under the winter ice the Arctic Ocean can keep moving.

Cold water holds more oxygen and carbon dioxide than warm water. Even though the Arctic Ocean is terribly cold, it is a very rich source of food. Plant plankton lives on the large amounts of carbon dioxide and oxygen in the water. Animal plankton (krill) therefore has plenty of food. Krill is the basis of most ocean life, providing food for fishes. Mammals of the Arctic Ocean are large and there are a surprising number of them. Seals feed on the fish, and polar bears feed on both seals and fish. The most spectacular mammals of all, whalebone whales, feed entirely on krill.

There is a big difference between summer and winter in the Arctic Ocean. In the summer, the sun shines constantly on the sea, allowing the plant plankton to carry on with photosynthesis nearly 24 hours a day. It grows and multiplies very fast, and so does the krill that feeds on it. At this time of year, all the creatures

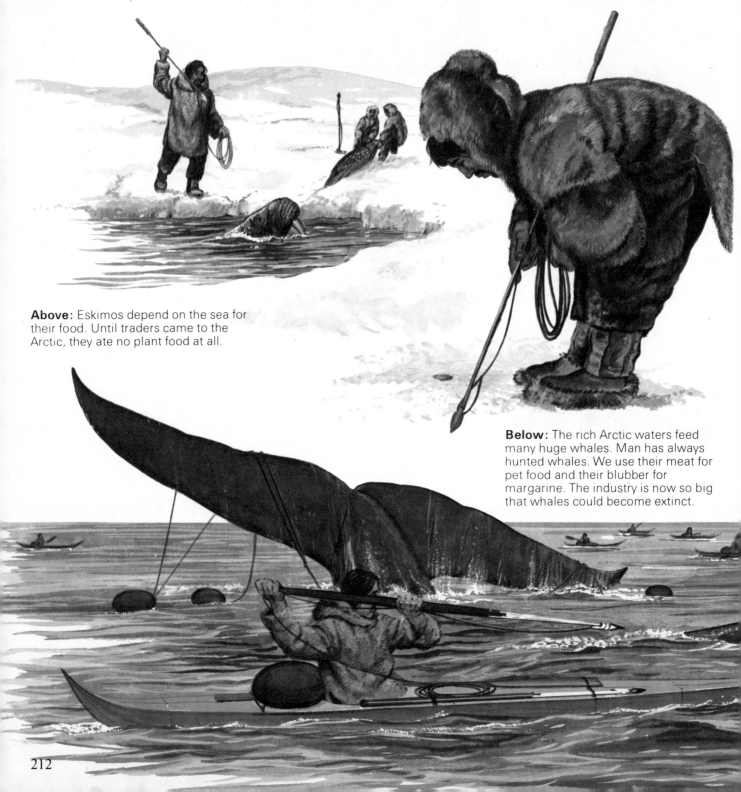

Above: Eskimos depend on the sea for their food. Until traders came to the Arctic, they ate no plant food at all.

Below: The rich Arctic waters feed many huge whales. Man has always hunted whales. We use their meat for pet food and their blubber for margarine. The industry is now so big that whales could become extinct.

suited to living in the chilly water have plenty of food. The cold-water fishes, squid, seals and whales, and polar bears can eat as much as they want. But in the dark days of winter, when the hours of sunlight are short, the surface of the ocean freezes into a solid sheet of ice metres thick. The seals that stay have to make holes in the ice where they can get their noses out to breathe.

Many fishes and larger animals travel south to the open waters of the Atlantic Ocean. Plant plankton cannot breed under the ice because there is not enough light, so krill becomes scarce and the whales move away to other feeding grounds. The polar bears split up in the winter. Males travel south to better hunting grounds, leaving pregnant females behind. The females dig a den in the snow and sleep until the cubs are born in December.

The Arctic grassland is called the tundra. It was covered in ice until about 20,000 years ago. Tundra is found in the far north of Europe, Asia and North America. Life there is similar in all these areas. Because the climate is so hard, there are only a small number of species of plants and animals in the tundra. The ones that do live there depend very much on each other. The food chain is very simple, for there is no room for competition where the Arctic conditions alone are hard enough

to bear. Any break in the food chain very quickly affects the other members of the chain. The most important plants are the lichens; the species that grow in the Arctic are sometimes called reindeer "mosses". They grow over the rocky ground where nothing else can survive. Tough grasses also grow where there is enough soil for them, and dwarf willows live in some sheltered places. These plants feed the large caribou of America and the reindeer of Europe. Lemmings and hares also feed on them. Wolves in turn feed on caribou and reindeer; snowy owls and foxes feed on the lemmings and hares.

Arctic hares

The larger animals like caribou, reindeer and wolves travel around, northwards in the summer and south in the winter. They sometimes go as far south as the coniferous forests of the taiga (*see page 220*). Small animals cannot travel so far. They have to be able to survive the winter. Arctic hares grow a white coat in winter. This helps to camouflage them in the snow and also to keep them warm because white surfaces give out less heat than dark ones. The Arctic foxes also become white in winter. They never hibernate, but can curl up, wrapped in their thick tail, in a snow burrow and sleep safely when the air outside is as cold as −50° centigrade.

Above: Polar bears are predators that live on the Arctic ice. A polar bear waits here by a seal's breathing hole until the seal comes up for air.

Lemmings

Snowy owls and foxes depend on lemmings for food. If lemmings become scarce the foxes and owls also begin to die. When lemmings are abundant, they eat up so much of the scarce vegetation that they have to travel in search of more. It is not true that lemmings deliberately drown themselves. They are good swimmers and can easily cross rivers on their travels. But if they come to a large lake or the sea, they set off to swim across and eventually die of exhaustion.

Below: Arctic hares live in the northern tundra; they are the main food of lynxes. In the north, they are always white, but southern hares are grey in summer and turn white in the winter.

South Pole

The Antarctic land mass is the largest continent in the world. It is also the coldest place in the world. Ninety per cent of the world's permanent ice is found there, lying up to four kilometres deep in the centre of the continent, where the temperature goes as low as 88° centigrade below zero. (The lowest temperature in the Arctic is 40° centigrade warmer than this.)

Antarctica is actually a frozen desert. Literally a desert, because the water is frozen so hard that, for all the use living things can make of it, it might just as well not be there at all.

There is soil under the ice, because until about five million years ago this continent was quite warm, with forests and grassland, lakes and rivers. But the land that does stick up out of the ice – the tops of mountains – is constantly eroded by frost and icy winds.

Nearer to the coast, where snow falls and there is some water, there are some small forms of life. Lichens manage to get a foothold on rocks, and some mosses and algae can also manage to survive. The only plant-eaters are a few insects no bigger than gnats, which are preyed on by tiny mites. In some places on the coast, there are mats of the primitive plants, but only two flowering plants grow on the mainland, and everything grows very slowly.

Antarctic waters

The cold ocean is the true home of Antarctic life. The seas surrounding the mainland contain the richest ocean life in the world.

Right: Elephant seals, Adélie penguins, and chinstrap penguins (far right) come ashore to breed. The bull elephant seal (he may be six metres long) collects a harem of cows. Pups are born in October and November. Adélie penguins spend the winter on pack ice and breed between October and March. Chinstrap penguins are hardly ever seen in the winter, but they come to breed in the same places and at the same time as the Adélie penguins.

There are islands, too, where seals and sea birds breed. Although there are not many different species of plant plankton in this cold ocean, they breed incredibly fast in the long summer days. The waters of Antarctica actually produce about 20 per cent of all the food in all the oceans of the world. The diatoms that make up the plankton feed tonnes of krill. Squids, fishes, birds, seals and whales all depend on the plankton for food.

Ice continues to dominate the scene, even at sea. In winter, the surface of the sea freezes solid, breaking up in spring to leave floating pieces of ice called floes. Where the ice floes grind against the rocky coast, nothing can live. But underneath this level, where warm water flows in from other warmer seas, sponges, sea anemones, sea urchins and starfish, and even corals, live on the rocks. The algae which have grown there in the summer help to keep these animals going through the winter when the thick ice overhead keeps out sunlight and prevents plants from growing. The ice helps to keep the sea warm, too, protecting it from the much colder air outside.

Seals and birds

Ross, Weddell, and crab-eater seals live all the year round on top of the ice. Leopard seals, which hunt fish and penguins, spend some time on the ice. Emperor penguins breed on the winter ice, while other penguins breed in summer on islands but spend the rest of the year on the sea ice. Many flying birds roost on the ice though they too breed on islands.

The birds of Antarctica are nearly all sea birds. Their thick waterproof plumage helps them to keep warm, and they feed mainly

on plankton and fish. Skuas prey on the penguins, harassing the colonies of breeding birds and stealing eggs and chicks.

All Antarctic mammals live in the sea. There are 12 species of whale and six of seals. Squids form an important part of the diet of these mammals, which also eat fish and plankton. Killer whales hunt seals and even other whales.

Because the Antarctic seas are so rich in food, man is seriously considering how he can make use of it. International treaties help to protect the whales, seals, and penguins while scientists work out how best to harvest the sea.

Right: Arctic terns breed in the far north during the Arctic summer. Then they fly south to enjoy the plankton of the Antarctic summer. They are growing their breeding plumage just as the Antarctic terns lose theirs.

Mountains

Above: Herds of chamois, the most agile four-footed mountaineers, spend summer high in the mountains of Europe and Asia. They winter down in the woods, and grow a dark winter coat for camouflage. Young ones walk as soon as they are born.

The main mountainous regions of the world are the Himalayas in Asia, the Rocky Mountains in America, the Alps in Europe, and the Andes in South America.

At the foot of a mountain, life is much the same as in the lowland regions. The tops may be permanently covered in snow. Between these two extremes are different zones, depending on height above sea level, where different plants and animals live.

The higher up a mountain we go, the colder it is. Every 300 metres

Left: Some chinchillas still live wild in the Andes. They were hunted for their warm soft fur and nearly became extinct, but are now bred on farms.

up, the temperature falls by nearly 2° centigrade. As well as becoming colder, the air gets drier. Winds hit exposed slopes, which are periodically washed by torrents of rain and scoured by glaciers and falling rocks. The steeper the rock face, the less soil it will collect.

Zones and seasons

One way of looking at mountains is to divide them into horizontal zones. At the bottom there is soil and vegetation giving cover and food for many animals. Above, as the air becomes colder and drier, trees become smaller giving way to grassland or, in tropical areas, to bamboo. In the Andes, there is a misty region above this, called the cloud forest, where more trees grow. Here many strange kinds of amphibious animals and plants live. At the foot of steep rock faces, where boulders fall, the ground is disturbed too often for permanent vegetation to get established. The rock faces them-selves contain soil only in crevices and may be permanently frozen higher up.

In the Alps, Rockies, and north Himalayas, the seasons also have an effect. Snow and ice cover much of the mountains in winter, but wherever the snow melts, even for the shortest season, there is some kind of life. Small wiry plants, rooted in crevices, flower briefly while they can, and lichens and mosses cling to rocks. Primi-tive insects like springtails have been found high in the Alps, pro-viding food for small spiders. Butterflies ascend the slopes in spring, attracted by the showy flowers.

Ways of survival

Soil collects on rocky ledges, allowing plants to take root, and wherever there are ledges the sure-footed mountain creatures will come in search of food. Many of the large plant-eaters of the Alps and Rockies are sheep and goats. They have hooves adapted for gripping rock and ice and manage

to survive on scrubby vegetation and tough grasses. Their coats become thick and warm in winter. The South American mountain grazers are llama, alpaca, and vicuña. They have hollow hairs which make their coats very warm. Chinchillas, wild rodents of the Andes, have feathery fur which is very warm and soft. The Alpine rodents, marmots, dig deep burrows in which they hibernate sometimes for more than half the year. Pikas, American relatives of rabbits, build haystacks of dried grass to eat during the winter.

Birds, however, can travel a long way without the problems of climbing. Birds of prey, like eagles, can build their nests high on crags – probably the only thing that has allowed some of them to survive man's interference – and hunt over the mountainsides, easily spotting small prey on the bare slopes. A few Alpine birds, like the ptarmi-gan, stay high up during the winter, but most birds come down to the trees when the snow falls.

Life high in the mountains is in a very delicate state of balance.

Right: Springtime on the mountain. A mouse has come out of hibernation; flowers bloom and butterflies visit them. The sharp-eyed marmots are ready to bolt into their burrows on seeing an eagle.

There are so few species able to cope with the hard conditions that each is vitally important for the survival of the others. The fragile Alpine plants, buried under snow and ice for so much of the time, are already at the limits of existence. It is here that careless interference by man can so easily tip the balance and cause their extinction.

Deciduous forests

Many trees growing together make a wood. Trees need a lot of water and woods can only grow where there is enough rain. Different types of woodland – evergreen, deciduous, or tropical – grow in different climates.

Deciduous woodlands, made up of trees like oak, beech, and alder, shed their leaves in autumn. They are found in temperate regions. These are places like Britain, where the cool winters and warm summers are of about the same length.

Even if the soil is wet, it is too cold in winter for the tree roots to get the water out of it. Deciduous trees avoid this problem by resting, without any leaves, until the soil becomes warm again in spring. When the leaves fall, they decay and make the soil fertile. While the trees are bare, light can get through to ground level.

Apart from fungi, which can grow in dark places, most of the lower vegetation of a wood reaches its growing peak early in the year before the trees have put on enough leaves to cut out the light. We find carpets of aconites when the winter is barely over, and blue-bells in early spring. Plants like ivy and honeysuckle climb up the trees to reach the sunlight.

How they grow

Different kinds of trees have their own style of growth. Beech trees are shallow-rooted and tall. They take a lot of nourishment out of the surface soil and keep out light even in winter. But their seeds – the beechmast – are an important food for mice, birds and squirrels. The crevices between their roots make homes for small animals, too.

Oakwoods grow on heavy clay soils. Their long roots take food from deep down and, when their leaves fall, this is deposited on the surface, making it very fertile. But again, old oak forests are too dense to allow much undergrowth other than brambles and primroses.

The trees themselves, then, have to be the main source of food for woodland animals. We know that over 200 species of animals depend on oak trees – these range from the gall wasps living in the leaves to woodpeckers eating insects that live under the bark.

Under the ground, earthworms pull down decaying leaves. Mice and voles on the ground pick up beechmast, acorns and other seeds. Mice, voles and worms are hunted by shrews, stoats, weasels and badgers. Squirrels live up in the trees, feeding on nuts and fungi. They are hunted by polecats.

Different birds nest at different levels – pheasants on the ground, warblers at bramble height, rooks in the treetops. The main predatory bird of woodlands is the owl. Tawny owls, flying silently at dusk, feed mainly on mice and voles.

A tree population

Not many food chains in woods are as simple as this, though. Even in the leaf litter, tiny invertebrates hunt and are hunted. Every fallen tree trunk contains its own complex population of ants, woodlice, centipedes and smaller invertebrates, each species playing its part in breaking down the dead wood and extracting new life from it.

As well as the cold in winter, the animals of the wood may need to guard against water-loss. The leaves keep the air under the trees damp in summer and in winter slugs and worms burrow deep under litter. Hedgehogs and badgers, which feed on them, must hibernate because their food supply is now too well hidden to get at. The leaf-eaters have nothing to eat in the winter; caterpillars usually spend winter as pupae. Seed-eaters like squirrels depend on stores they have made during the autumn. Their stores last longer if they spend a lot of the time asleep. With the trees bare, and many animals asleep or hidden, a winter wood is a silent place compared with the busy days of summer and autumn.

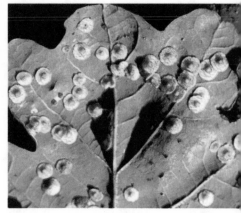

Above: Spangle gall of the *Cynips* wasp.

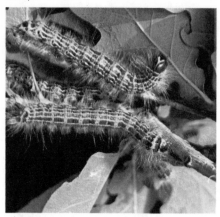

Above: Caterpillar of the buff tip moth.

Above: Galleries made by beetles which carry Dutch elm disease.

Above: The oak-apple gall of *Biorhiza* wasp. The pins show holes where the young wasps crawled out.

Above: Leaf miner insects feed inside leaves.

Above: Beech tuft fungus lives on lower branches.

Above: This bracket fungus feeds on living trees.

Oak

Beech

Below: This centipede lives in beech leaf litter.

Above: Woodlands give food and shelter to many different species. They all depend on the trees for a living, from the leaf-eaters to the fungi growing on tree trunks, roots and dead leaves. The multitude of plant-eating insects provide food for meat-eaters — birds, mammals and other insects. Everything in the wood is closely connected.

Left: Fly agaric, a fungus found in many kinds of wood.

Evergreen forests

Just south of the Arctic Circle, the world is encircled by a band of evergreen forests. It is called the taiga and extends north to the tundra and south over much of Canada, Russia and northern Europe. The climate here is not as cold and dry as the Arctic and allows evergreen trees to grow. Snow and ice can easily slide off their shiny needle-shaped leaves, and their flexible branches do not break in strong winds.

There are also boggy areas in the taiga, too wet for trees, where most of the other plants live. It is always dark under the trees, because they bear leaves all the year round; only mosses, lichens, and fungi survive in shade. Shrubs and green herbs grow around the bogs, and water plants grow in them.

Animals of the taiga, then, depend on coniferous trees, lichens, mosses, swamp plants and a few herbs. Many of the larger plant-eaters feed mainly on herbs and shrubs, while seeds support most of the smaller ones.

Pine needles rot very slowly, making an acid soil. This is not suitable for larger animals, though many small invertebrates live among the fallen twigs and needles.

Problems of survival

One of the main problems for a mammal in a cold climate is keeping warm. They all have thick warm fur. The wolverine's fur has the advantage of repelling moisture – Eskimos use it to line the hoods of their parkas. Some plant-eaters, like squirrels and mice, are small. Their bodies lose heat quickly and when winter comes they cannot eat fast enough to make up for the energy their bodies radiate. These small mammals hibernate. They eat enough food in summer and autumn to build up a store of body fat. They may also gather a larder full of seeds. Then they can spend all or most of the winter asleep. Mammals that do not hibernate tend to grow especially large in cold climates. This is an advantage in keeping warm, because their bodies then have a smaller radiating surface per kilo of weight. But it brings its own problem. A big animal needs more food. This is

especially true of plant-eaters, whose food is not as energy-rich as meat.

The big plant-eater of coniferous forests is the elk – called a moose in Canada – which is the largest deer in the world. Elk have big splayed feet and can walk safely over the swamps. In the summer they feed on herbs and water-plants, especially water-lilies. They manage on tree bark and hard shrubs in the winter, when they travel in herds for protection against wolves.

There are many birds in evergreen forests. The grouse feeds on herbs and many of the smaller ones live on the seeds of conifers. The crossbill is a finch whose beak is beautifully adapted for breaking open pine-cones. Insect-eating birds such as titmice have a rich supply of food. Many insects inhabit these forests, boring into wood, feeding on the year-long supply of leaves and scavenging under leaf-litter.

Carnivores have to be very fit and active. The largest carnivore in the world, the Siberian tiger, lives in the cold northern forests of

Above: Wolves roam the forests, constantly travelling on in search of game. They cover a territory which takes them weeks to patrol. The biggest ones, such as timber wolves, live farthest north.

Russia. Weasels and stoats hunt small game on the ground while pine martens and their relatives pursue squirrels and birds in the trees. Some squirrels have a flap of skin between elbow and knee, which they can stretch out into a sort of wing to glide from one tree to another. This saves precious energy and helps them to escape from climbing predators.

Larger plant-eaters travel widely, northwards in summer and southwards in winter, closely followed by the carnivores that prey on them.

Below: Summer in a Canadian pine forest. The snow and ice have gone, fungi grow under the trees, bracken and greenery on the woodland edge. Food is now plentiful and animals gather strength for winter.

Temperate grasslands

Grass usually grows in places where there is not enough rain to grow trees. Sometimes even when there is enough rain there are no trees because the soil is too well drained. Sandy or chalky soil does not hold water for long so is often covered with permanent grassland.

The grassland of many parts of Europe and America is not like this. There is enough rain, and the soil is rich and fertile. The grasslands here would turn into woodland if they were left alone. Grazing animals and the work of farmers prevent trees from growing. The grazing animals trample the soil so young trees cannot get well rooted. Farmers burn stubble fields and keep their hedges neatly trimmed. Fires can also begin naturally in some places. They can be started by lightning, or by two dry sticks rubbing together in the wind.

The grasslands of temperate places like Europe and North America are very important for producing our food. We eat many grasses such as wheat, oats, rice, barley and rye. These have been cultivated for so long that today they have much bigger seeds than the wild grasses they once were. We also feed our cattle, pigs, and poultry on the seeds and leaves of grasses, and get meat, eggs and milk from the animals. Grass is a rich food and supports many species of wild animals.

Enormous herds of bison and buffalo used to roam across the grasslands of North America and Europe. They are nearly extinct now, and have been replaced by our own cattle. We have also domesticated some of the wild sheep and goats that feed on grass.

Rats and mice

Small mammals like rats and mice eat grass seeds. We regard them as pests when they eat our grain, but they are really only taking advantage of the super-grasses we have created. Harvest mice build nests among long, strong grass stalks. Our cultivated wheat fields were perfect places for them to live until the combine harvester was invented. Now they have had to return to the reed beds where they probably lived before the wheat

Above: We have taken natural grasslands like the one below and used them to grow grain for food.

Below: Some of the animals that live on temperate grassland.

fields were planted.

A temporary habitat
In the normal order of plant succession, grassland is a fairly temporary habitat. The small animals which feed on grass would once have had to make the most of it for a few generations before moving on. Grass provides the kind of soil where many other plants, including trees, like to grow. In some American woodlands, the burrows of prairie rodents have been found underneath fully-grown trees, showing that once the woods were open grassland. Forest boundaries are always changing. Dry weather kills trees, and sometimes it is so dry that forest fires start. Afterwards the grass is first to return, later followed by new trees.

Grazing animals prevent the growth of trees and keep the grassland going. Their droppings fertilize the ground and they themselves provide food for meat-eaters such as tigers, mountain lions and bears. The smaller grass-eaters like rabbits and rodents are hunted by small cats, stoats, weasels, owls and hawks.

Small animals living in grassland are often burrowers. There is nowhere for them to hide except under the ground. Many squirrels, called ground squirrels, live in burrows. These include prairie dogs and marmots. Even some birds burrow under the ground, like the burrowing owl in the picture. Grassland supports many birds. They feed on grass seeds, or the grass-eating insects, or on the small mammals. Budgerigars of Australia travel over the bush in great flocks, living on grass seeds.

Camouflage is very important for animals that live in exposed places. Most animals are coloured dark above and pale underneath. This helps to cancel out the light shining on their backs and the

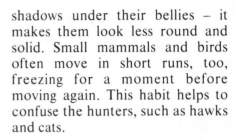

shadows under their bellies – it makes them look less round and solid. Small mammals and birds often move in short runs, too, freezing for a moment before moving again. This habit helps to confuse the hunters, such as hawks and cats.

Coyotes
Dogs are good at hunting in open country. The wild hunting dogs of America are the coyotes. Coyotes and foxes feed mainly on rodents. If too many wild dogs are killed by man, rodents can multiply and become a pest. On the other hand, wild dogs can become a nuisance if the rodents they normally eat are destroyed by man. When this happens they try to live by raiding chicken runs, making a nuisance of themselves and probably being shot by farmers.

The temperate grasslands are the most unstable habitats in the world. They are kept in a state of primary succession by a combination of such factors as grazing, fire and agriculture. Some of these things are natural and others have been created by man. The balance of nature here is very important to us.

A desert
In places where there is not much rain, the land can be turned into a desert by too many grazing animals, too many fires, or too much ground clearing. This has already happened in some parts of the United States, causing great hardship.

It is important to keep some trees and bushes in the grasslands. Where there are no trees at all, there is a risk that the soil may become too dry for a period and blow away. On the other hand, in places where the rainfall is high – where we get the richest crops – the grassland can turn to forest if the balance of grazers, rodents and hunters is not right. We must take great care of our grasslands, for our lives depend on keeping a healthy balance of nature there.

Savanna grasslands

Between forest and desert, where there is not enough rain for trees, we find grasslands. The hot grasslands of Africa, South America, and Australia have different names – veldt, pampas, bush – but they are all dry, exposed places. Grasses have matted roots which cover the soil surface and help to keep in moisture. Their narrow, spiky leaves do not lose moisture easily, and their flowers are pollinated by the winds.

Plant-eaters

The large plant-eating animals of these grasslands have stomachs which can digest the grass. They roam across the plains feeding on grass leaves. The tender growing parts of grass plants are low down inside the tough old stalks, so they are not damaged by the grazing animals. The grazers can feed and the grasses can continue to grow, fertilized by their droppings, in an almost complete cycle. This relationship between grazers and grass is well known to farmers, who use cattle to turn grass into meat and milk.

African grasslands are the home of antelopes and zebras. They have been hunted by man for meat and skins, but some still remain. Other meat-eaters also feed on them, such as lions, cheetahs and hyaenas. In this wide open country the grazers are constantly alert to danger from hunters. Their young can stand almost at birth and must be able to run with the herd soon after. Living in a herd also gives them protection. Each animal in the herd is less of a target than if it lived alone. At the same time, the hunters do not get much chance to hunt by stealth because they are so easily seen. Dogs and hyaenas hunt in packs; they can cooperate to bring down even something as big as a wildebeest.

Right: A scene near water in African grassland. Trees provide food for giraffes and termites, and shade for many creatures. Two dung beetles are rolling away their ball of dung to bury and eat it.

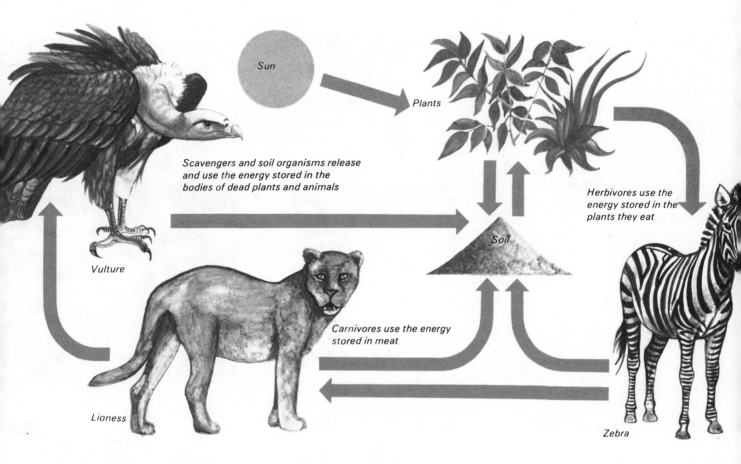

Scavengers and soil organisms release and use the energy stored in the bodies of dead plants and animals

Sun

Plants

Herbivores use the energy stored in the plants they eat

Soil

Vulture

Carnivores use the energy stored in meat

Lioness

Zebra

The two big cats of African grasslands are the lion and the cheetah. Lions are unusual cats because they live and hunt in groups. The lionesses hunt as a team, isolating an animal from the herd in the way that a sheepdog will cut out a sheep from a flock. Cheetahs do hunt alone, but more like a dog than a cat. With their long legs and rough feet they rely on speed to catch their prey instead of stalking it like most other cats.

Sometimes herds of impala are found grazing near a group of baboons. The impala get some protection from the aggressive baboons. In return the baboons are helped by the impalas' keen sense of danger. A single baboon cannot fight off a lion but, if they get enough warning, a group of males together can usually chase a lion away.

Some other big grass-eaters are the flightless birds – ostriches in Africa, rheas in South America and emus in Australia. They can all run very fast, and have long necks and sharp eyes for spotting danger.

There are also small seed-eating birds and grass-eating insects. Locusts occur in enormous numbers when conditions are right for them. Grass is a rich source of food for the creatures that can digest it. Many of the creatures of tropical grassland, however, depend on the big grazers. Birds such as oxpeckers live entirely on the external parasites of cattle. Dung beetles feed on cattle droppings, and many scavengers feed on dead grazers.

Patterns of life
Different creatures are active at different times of day on the flat grassy plains. Hippopotamuses keep cool in rivers and water-holes during the day. They emerge to graze at dusk, leaving the water for other creatures that come to drink at night. Most activity is seen at dusk and dawn, for the heat of the day is too much for many animals.

Meat-eaters of the plains follow a set order in feeding on a kill. An animal may be killed and partly eaten by a group of lions. Later hyaenas may find it and take their

Above: Plants get energy directly from the sun. All the animals use some of this energy to live, and pass on the rest to the next link in the chain. Their body wastes fertilize the soil for plants.

share. Finally the specialized scavengers, such as ants and vultures, will arrive. Even among vultures there is an order of feeding. Last to arrive is the lammergeier, which breaks open bones by dropping them and then feeds on the marrow inside them.

As grasslands are dry places the rivers and water-holes are very important to larger animals. They also provide small areas of slightly different vegetation. Trees grow near the water; their leaves feed the long-necked giraffes and their trunks are eaten by termites. Some birds nest in them, like the weaver-birds in the picture, and they give shade from the sun.

The balance of grazers, hunters, leaf-eaters and scavengers is very important in hot grassland as it is in temperate grasslands. The land itself will suffer if this balance is upset in any way.

Deserts

A perfect desert, with dry air and no rainfall, will have nothing living in it. When we speak of deserts, we really mean places in which the average rainfall is under 125 millimetres a year. This could be a region where no rain falls for a number of years, but where there is a torrent of rain once in a while. Or it may be a place where there is an occasional sea mist at various times during the year. Where there is water life of some sort will survive.

The scarce plants of desert lands have roots that go very deep or spread very wide. The widely-spaced cacti are at war with one another – their roots are engaged in a struggle for possession of the soil. They give off chemicals that slow down the growth of other cactus roots and so guard their own precious water supply.

Most of the time, cacti keep water to themselves and wait for more. They store it in fat, spongy stems with a waxy waterproof skin. Very little is lost by evaporation. The leaves, through which other plants lose water, are reduced in cacti to dry spines – very useful for keeping away animals that may steal their water. The green stem carries out photosynthesis and, when rain comes, bears short-lived flowers.

Extremes of temperature

Because the air is dry, the sun's rays strike the desert soil with all their power. But at night the same dry air allows the heat of the day to escape. So deserts can become extremely cold when the sun goes down. The animals that live there must cope with these extremes of temperature as well as the water shortage. Many mammals shelter from the sun in deep underground burrows. Most desert mammals have large eyes, showing that they are nocturnal, and carnivores have very big ears. In the wide wastes of the desert it is important, especially for hunters like the kit fox, to be able to hear small creatures some distance away.

In the desert there is not enough water, therefore not enough food, to support many animals in any one area. The desert rodents often have very long hind legs; they can cover a great distance in a short time by leaping along like little kangaroos. Some species, such as the jerboa, can even manage without drinking; they can somehow save all the water their bodies need from the process of digesting the seeds and tubers they live on. This involves complicated changes in body chemistry to turn wastes into harmless substances.

Below: The American desert. A roadrunner chases a sidewinder snake; a scorpion waits for a pocket mouse; a kit fox digs for kangaroo rats; a chuckawalla shelters while a vulture flies overhead.

Because they need such a large territory to provide enough food – for example, a desert mouse may need two hectares – desert mammals have a problem when it comes to finding a mate, because they live so far apart. Many small desert mammals, like the pocket mouse and kangaroo rats in the picture, have a tuft of hair at the end of their long tail. This is used for silent signalling between the animals; a noisy mouse would soon be eaten by the alert fox. The fox, too, has a long fluffy tail which can be used as a parasol.

Left: After a fall of rain, the desert becomes a garden overnight. Plants that live here can grow rapidly when rain comes, making food that keeps the animals alive through the next drought.

Birds, reptiles and insects

Birds do not thrive in deserts but large ones like the vulture can fly a long way to find carrion. The roadrunner in the picture hunts reptiles. Of all vertebrates, reptiles are probably best suited for desert life. They can survive for a long time without eating and they can swallow a large meal at one go. The sidewinder snake moves on loose sand by throwing its body along sideways in a continuous corkscrew movement, leaving characteristic tracks over the dunes.

Some invertebrates manage to survive in deserts. Large scorpions prey on small creatures. The scavenging beetles are mainly oil beetles and darkling beetles. They have round bodies with thick wing-cases fused together, sometimes with an air space underneath them. These adaptations help to prevent the beetle's body drying out and keep it cool.

Flowers of the desert

Where there is a seasonal fall of rain, many desert plants are adapted to take full advantage of it. The same chemicals that cactus roots make to prevent other roots growing are also present in their seed coats. This saves them from germinating if there is not enough rain to wash the coat clean. When the rainfall is heavy, the seeds can germinate and grow enough to set them up for a long period of drought.

Other plants lie in the sand as seeds. If they are not found and eaten by rodents they can germinate and flower rapidly when rain comes, leaving seeds to wait for the next rainfall. Tumbleweed is a plant which can become almost dry yet still live, growing whenever it becomes wet.

All this growth, together with the cactus flowers, can turn the desert into a green place, bright with flowers, almost overnight. The small animals survive on the products of this brief season until the next rain.

Tropical forests

Cauliflorous flower

Liana

Strangler fig

It is always summer in the rich mixed forests that grow between the Equator and the Tropics. The main requirement of a tropical forest is rain, for without it the jungle would become a desert.

Whether the hot regions of the world get enough rain to grow a forest depends on physical geography. In much of Central and South America, western South Africa, and the Pacific region, there are over 130 millimetres of rain a year – enough for the enormous tropical trees. They form the structure of a great living city, dark and wet on the ground and light and airy in their crowns 50 metres up. The only limit to the height of

forest trees is whether they have enough strength to stand. Some types of tree have natural buttresses to support them. Others, like the lianas, use nearby trees to give them support.

In the tightly-packed tropical forest it is the tallest trees which get the most light and grow ever taller in the constant battle for sunlight. This means that the forest floor is very dark because, although many trees are deciduous, they do not all lose their leaves at the same time. There are always some trees flowering, others fruiting, and some resting. Vegetation under the trees is sparse. It may look thicker than it is because the ground-floor plants have to grow huge leaves to collect what light they can, but they are very fragile.

Small plants of the forest are mainly epiphytes (plants that live on other plants). They grow up in the trees, rooted in humus in the forked trunks of the jungle giants. Members of the pineapple family, as well as orchids, live this way. Each species has its own level above the ground.

Life in the forest
The forest animals are nearly all climbers. There are tree frogs, snakes, monkeys, squirrels, tree porcupines and of course the birds. Each species occupies its own level in the trees. Even different mosquitoes, which breed in pools of water trapped by leaves, live at different heights, some in the tree tops and others on epiphytes lower down. Life is stacked up in the forest like a tall block of flats.

The ice of recent Ice Ages did not reach the tropical regions of the earth. The animals and plants here have not been sorted out by the snows and glaciers which

Left: A slice of rain forest, showing the plants that live at different levels. Strangler figs get their name because they often kill the trees they climb. Lianas are trees that have lost the power to stand. Other plants grow in humus on trees.

reduced numbers of species to the north and south. Life has changed so little in these warm wet regions that some interesting relationships have been able to develop between different species. Sloths, which spend their lives hanging from – or slowly moving along – branches, belly upward, cannot walk on the ground. They have green-coloured fur. The colour comes from algae living in special grooves in the hairs. There are even insects that follow the sloths around, feeding only on their algae.

Colour and sound

High up in the treetops many of the flowers are small. They can be pollinated by the wind. But under the canopy of leaves the air is still and dark. This is where the gorgeous tropical flowers are found. They are large and brightly coloured, attracting the insects and hummingbirds that pollinate them. Flowers visited by hummingbirds are often red, which is the colour birds see best. Birds of the forest are also brightly coloured, though they are not easy to spot between the dappled light and deep shadows. Many birds and animals like monkeys are extremely noisy. They use sound to communicate where sight is difficult.

There is an abundance of food for plant-eaters. Leaves, flowers, fruit and seeds can be found all the year round. Some species eat only unripe fruit, while the messy eaters like parrots leave rich scraps for scavengers. Some monkeys eat only leaves. Fruit-eating monkeys

Below: Creatures of the forest. Bright birds, butterflies, monkeys and snakes move among the foliage. A leopard lies in wait on a branch. It may drag its kill up into a tree to keep it safe from other meat-eaters.

live where rivers let in enough light for fruiting vines to grow.

Carnivores include a large number of cats. Together with raccoons, tayra and grison martens of South America, and genets and civets of Africa, they are expert climbers. On the ground there are skunks. The forest is not an ideal habitat for dogs but one species, the bushdog, does live in dense South American forests. Bushdogs have very short legs and hunt ground-living rodents for food.

There is food in rich tropical forests for any creature that can find a place to live. In the everlasting summer, the leaves in one square metre of forest can supply more than 80 million joules of energy in a year; that is enough energy to keep a one-kilowatt fire burning for 22 hours. It is not surprising that thousands of species of animals live there.

Ponds

Ponds and lakes vary from tiny puddles to huge expanses of water so big that it is difficult to see across them.

The two things they all have in common are that the water is not salty and that it is fairly calm.

Water is a natural place for a great variety of plants and animals to live. Millions of years ago, life began in water. Plants and animals on land constantly have to seek water to survive. In ponds and lakes, water is freely available to the creatures that live in it.

Obtaining oxygen underwater

The main problem for aquatic life is to get enough oxygen. Still water does not collect much oxygen from the air. Nearly all the oxygen in a pond comes from the plants that grow in it. These plants are not the ones which grow with their stems or roots submerged, but those which have their leaves under the water, too. Only a few species of higher plants, such as Canadian pondweed, grow entirely submerged and contribute oxygen. The real oxygen producers are the algae – small relations of seaweeds. Algae grow as a scum on the surface of the water, over stones, and on the mud. They also grow as masses of tangled threads in the water.

The amount of oxygen plants give out depends on how much light reaches them. Even then, water can only hold five per cent of the amount of oxygen that is present in air. It holds carbon dioxide far more easily. A pond which contains little oxygen and much carbon dioxide is said to be "stagnant". Rotting leaves or dead fish help make a pond stagnant, because the bacteria that break down dead matter give off carbon dioxide.

Only animals which need little oxygen can survive in stagnant water. One such creature is the tubifex worm. It is bright red, and the colour comes from its red blood, which contains the same oxygen-catching pigment, haemo-globin, as our own. There are very few invertebrates with red blood and all of them live in such circumstances that it is hard for them to get enough oxygen to survive. Another pond creature with red blood is the ramshorn snail, which is about the largest animal to be found in a muddy stagnant pond.

Many of the animals that live in water have gills to filter oxygen into their bodies. But, because there is not as much oxygen, even

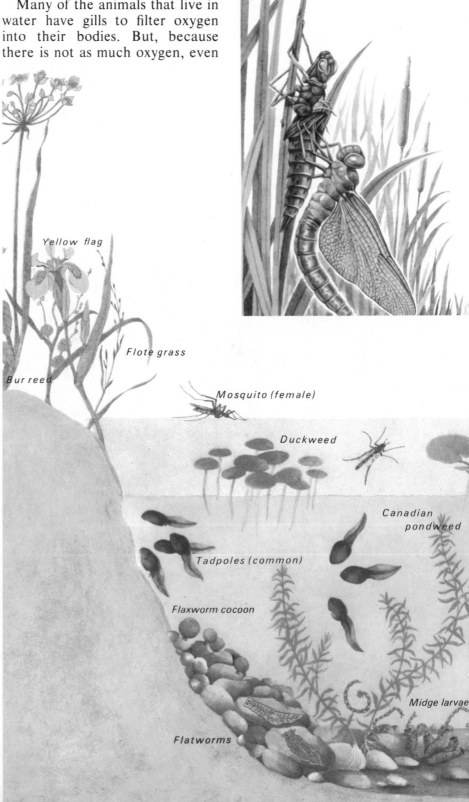

Below: Many flies breed in ponds. Here a dragonfly has just emerged from its nymph, which crawled out of the water a few hours ago.

Yellow flag

Flote grass

Bur reed

Mosquito (female)

Duckweed

Canadian pondweed

Tadpoles (common)

Flaxworm cocoon

Midge larvae

Flatworms

in healthy ponds, as there is in rivers, many pond creatures obtain oxygen direct from the air. Few fish live in small ponds. Those that do such as the carp family, which includes goldfish, can manage with very little oxygen. They sometimes come to the surface and gulp air to help them out. If you watch the surface of a pond in warm weather, you will probably see many creatures "coming up for air", including beetles, frogs, newts, and bugs such as backswimmers and water boatmen. A water spider gets its oxygen in a different way: it carries a bubble of air from the surface down to the bottom of the pond with it.

Most water-breathing creatures found in ponds are slow and sluggish. They do not use much

Below: The plants and animals on the left-hand side of the picture can only live in clear, oxygen-rich water. Those on the right can stand water with less oxygen because they are less active or have special ways of breathing.

Right: Pond life does not end at the surface. Some animals, like this kingfisher, depend on water life for food even though they live on land.

oxygen. The only fast-moving animals in the picture below are tadpoles, and they could not live in a stagnant pond.

The other factors which control life in still water are temperature and fertility. The depths of a large lake can be very cold indeed. Very little life can live there, even if the surface water is light and warm. The rate of decay on the cold mud at the bottom is often too slow to provide plant food. A deep, still loch can be as dead as a small stagnant pool, though for completely different reasons.

Many ponds and lakes contain a rich variety of plant and animal life, crossing and interlocking to make a tangle of food chains. Though a pond may seem to be enclosed by its surface, in fact the surface provides a place where there is all kinds of activity. Pond-

skaters walk across it, picking up tiny creatures for food, and fish are pulled out by birds such as kingfishers and herons, as well as human anglers.

Ponds are used by many insects for their growing lives. Larvae of midges, caddisflies, mayflies and huge dragonflies all grow to full size in the pond before taking to the air. Birds such as ducks live on the surface of the water and take out both plant and animal food.

The plants that grow in or around ponds or lakes are found in a regular order. Some, for example, waterlilies, grow with their roots in the mud and their leaves on the surface, putting out flowers into the air. Others grow with only their roots in the water, and still more grow in the damp rich soil at the margins of the water. Such plants provide homes for many more animals, often ones which also live in marshland, and these creatures also help to enrich the life of the pond.

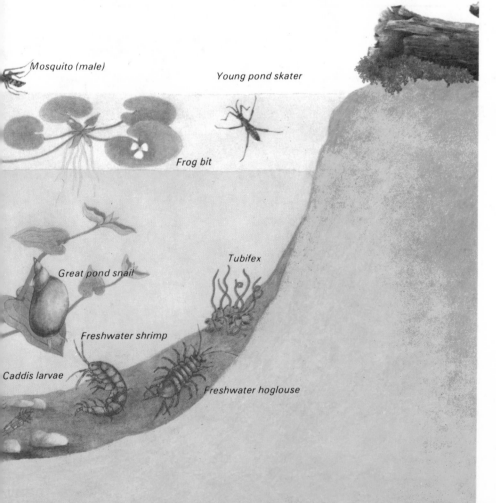

Mosquito (male)

Young pond skater

Frog bit

Great pond snail

Tubifex

Freshwater shrimp

Caddis larvae

Freshwater hoglouse

231

Rivers

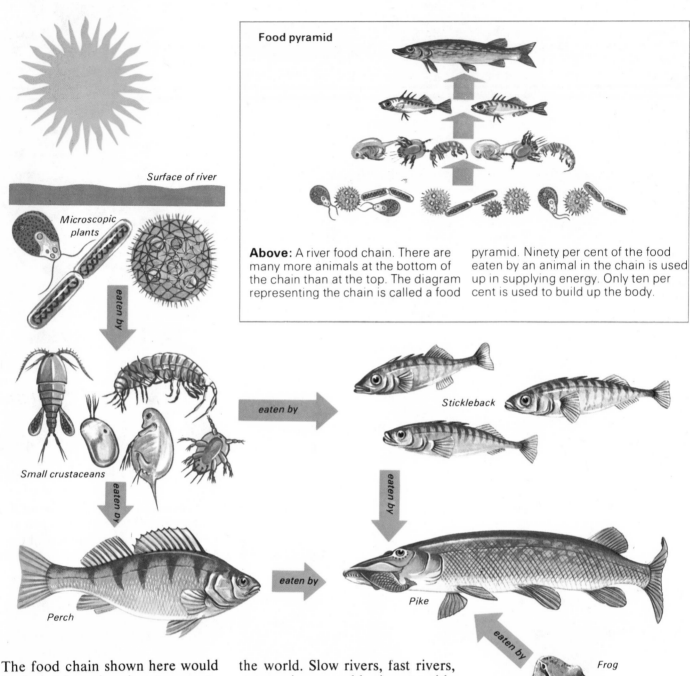

Food pyramid

Above: A river food chain. There are many more animals at the bottom of the chain than at the top. The diagram representing the chain is called a food pyramid. Ninety per cent of the food eaten by an animal in the chain is used up in supplying energy. Only ten per cent is used to build up the body.

Surface of river

Microscopic plants

eaten by

Small crustaceans

eaten by

Perch

eaten by

Stickleback

eaten by

Pike

eaten by

Frog

The food chain shown here would be found in a river in a temperate climate. Not too fast, not too slow, this river would have plenty of vegetation growing on its muddy banks. It would probably have a muddy bed, too, but the water would be clear except for the green stain of plant plankton in the summer. The light which falls on the water gives energy to the plant plankton, which is eaten in turn by the animal plankton. These microscopic animals are eaten by invertebrates and fishes. The pike feeds on other fish and birds also take fish out of the river.

There are rivers everywhere in the world. Slow rivers, fast rivers, warm rivers, cold rivers, wide rivers and tiny streams. A river less than five metres wide is usually called a stream. Rivers generally support a richer variety of life than ponds. This is because there is a better supply of oxygen in a river. A fast-flowing river can get a lot of oxygen from the air as it bubbles along. A slow-flowing river relies on plants for most of its oxygen but, because the water is moving all the time, it cannot become stagnant. The current keeps pushing carbon dioxide up to the sunny surface water where plants can make use of it.

Above: In a stream the pike is at the top of the food pyramid. It not only eats fish but frogs as well.

Tropical rivers

Rivers in hot countries do not hold a lot of oxygen, though there may be plenty of carbon dioxide to support plants. This is because oxygen does not easily stay dissolved in warm water. But the life of tropical rivers like the Amazon in South America is very varied. Many creatures live on the lush vegetation in the water, though they may be air-breathers. A relation of the whales, called the manatee, which lives in the Amazon and in the warm rivers of Florida, grazes on water plants. Amphibians are plentiful, too, spending their early life as water-breathers and emerging to become air-breathing adults. Many insects breed in water because there is such a rich supply of food there. They too emerge as air-breathing adults.

Tropical rivers are places where many animals come and go. They make use of the water and the rich vegetation it contains, but they never quit the land entirely. Similarly, some of the water-dwelling creatures prey on land animals. Piranhas, for example, generally feed on other fishes. But they can be attracted by splashing in the water and can devour a larger creature that has fallen in.

Creatures which live in the river also have to cope with periodic changes in water level. There may

Above: Tropical rivers have lush vegetation growing along their banks. This one in Ecuador is lined with trees, vines and low bushes Warm water also contains a lot of carbon dioxide, so many kinds of water plants grow in great quantities.

Below: Crocodiles live in tropical rivers Their greyish-green skin blends in with the muddy water. They have nostrils and eyes on bumps on their snout and head so they can breathe and see while their bodies are submerged. They lurk unseen in the water waiting for a thirsty animal to come down to the water's edge to drink.

be a rushing torrent or a slow trickle according to the time of year. This is especially true of tropical rivers, because of the rainy season.

Fast-flowing streams

A cold, fast-moving mountain stream is very different from a tropical river. It is very rich in oxygen, partly because of the fast current and partly because cold water can hold more oxygen. But there is very little vegetation; it would be washed away by the current. Animals, too, must be either very fast and active or very well anchored if they live in fast streams. Food chains in these waters are quite simple because not many species live there. Plants and the creatures that live on them can survive in deeper pools or on the side of a bend where the current is weaker. Fast-flowing water holds only a few fishes.

Young salmon grow in these oxygen-rich waters, feeding on whatever the water brings as they face upstream. When they grow too big to live on the small amount of food the river holds, they turn round and make for the sea. They grow to maturity in the sea and return to the rivers to breed.

Marshes

In low-lying areas, both inland and by the sea, the ground is often permanently wet. There are completely enclosed valleys, where the water runs down the hills but has no river to take it to the sea. There are places which are so flat that, although there may be many rivers, the water flows out more slowly than it comes in. And there are the wide stretches of muddy sea shore we call salt marshes. The soil in all these places is always waterlogged. The plants that live in these areas all have their different problems.

Acid bogs

In freshwater bogs and marshes, one of the problems is the same as in stagnant ponds. Dead plant material rots very slowly when it is covered by a layer of still water. Instead of breaking down into soil, it becomes the fibrous spongy stuff we call peat. Peat is often very acid. Not many plants can live on acid soil, because it does not contain the right minerals for growth. The bog moss, sphagnum, may be the only thing growing in a very acid bog. Two other plants that can live in moss bogs are bladderwort and sundew; they get the nourishment that they cannot find in the soil from the bodies of insects they trap in their leaves.

The fens

Flat marshy ground with many rivers and lakes is very different from mossy bogs. The water there does move, even if very slowly. If the soil is not acid, these kinds of marshes offer a rich environment for any plant and animal life that can use it. The Fens of England and the vast Everglades of Florida in America are examples of this kind of marsh.

Much of the environment is aquatic; the plants and animals in the water are the same as those that live in shallow lakes and slow rivers. Plants that grow on the mud are often grasses, like reeds, and ones with rhizomes, like yellow

flag. Their tall leaves and flowering stems provide food and cover for many animals. Snails can find their own level, some on the wet mud and others enjoying the damp air among the leaves. They are eaten by glow-worms.

The largest mammal that lives among the reeds is the capybara; it grazes along river banks in Central and South America. Another South American rodent, the coypu, has been brought into Europe.

Where reed beds have been growing for a long time, their dead leaves build up until they make areas of fairly firm ground. Many other plants can take root here. Tussock grasses raise even higher patches of ground where birds can nest. If reed beds, tussocks, and other plants have raised the ground high enough above the water, even trees can begin to take root.

The marsh will now begin to break up. Deeper rivers will run among islands of higher ground, which will become firmer as it is better drained. Marsh grasses, then, can be regarded as the first step towards the land becoming wooded.

Where drainage is not good enough, the marshes remain. They are rich in humus and can be wonderfully fertile ground if they are treated sensibly. The Everglades were for a long time thought to be useless for agriculture. Now better understanding of ecology has made it possible to turn the marshes into good farmland. The land is being drained carefully and some of the minerals the water has washed out are being replaced.

Salt marshes

Salt marshes are quite different. The main problem facing plants there is the salty water. It is hard for plants to extract fresh water from salty water. They can only get it out very slowly. Many salt marsh plants are adapted to store whatever water they do get, and may look very much like desert plants, with their fleshy leaves and stems and tough skins.

Down on the salty mud, eelgrass lies limply, floating when the tide is in, and samphire stands erect on islets. Along the landward shore of the salt marsh, sea rushes grow. Between them there is a definite series of different plants, some growing just above the water-line and others higher up. Each plant lives in a narrow zone of the shore, helping to turn the mud into higher ground that suits the next plant up. Even on high ground where the sea does not soak up into the soil, plants like sea pinks and sea lavender may be splashed by salty spray, so they must be able to stand salt water for a short time. Animals keep pace with the plants. There are sea worms, molluscs and crabs on the mud, and insects among the erect plants higher up.

Below: Tussocks rise up out of the marsh. They are sedges which make dry homes for insects and birds.

Below right: Dragonflies are common in marshy areas.

Sandy shores

Sea shores are where two completely different habitats meet. If you come from the land, the shore is the end of the land; if you come from the sea, it is the edge of the sea. Plants and animals from both places live here, each at the limit of their own environment.

For land life, living on the shore raises salt problems. Even quite a long way inland, stormy winds from the sea can carry salt in the air. The kind of land plants which grow near the sea have to be able to stand some salt on their leaves. Plants which live right on the coast, on cliffs and sand-dunes along the shore, may even have their roots in salty soil. They need to store as much water as they can, because it is hard to get water out of salty soil, and so they sometimes look like desert plants. The strong sea winds would also dry these plants out if they were not adapted to hold on to water.

Down towards the sea, dunes give way to sandy beaches. There may be shingle washed up by the sea. Shingle beaches are probably the most difficult places to live. The stones are shuffled by every wave of every tide, making it hard for anything to escape being uprooted or crushed. But some things do live here—a few plants can grasp the shingly beach tightly enough to hang on and, further down, a few little insects and salt-water crustaceans scavenge among the stones.

For all the forms of life that live on the edge of the sea, waves and tides are their greatest problem. The moving water would wash away anything that was not firmly attached or embedded, and the tides leave them out of water for periods of time. So sea-dwelling plants and animals that live on the shore-line have to be adapted to live in air sometimes.

Living among the sand

Sandy shores do not provide a great deal for living things to hang on to. The sea creatures of sandy shores often have to burrow into the sand to keep themselves safe from the waves, and from the air when the tide is out. There is not a great deal to eat in the sand, either, so the animals of sandy shores are often burrowing filter-feeders. They keep most of their body under the sand, putting out tubes or tentacles to collect plankton when the tide washes over them, and withdrawing completely into the sand at low tide. Molluscs like clams and razor shells live like this, and so do many kinds of worms.

Crabs are found scavenging on all types of shores, but the ones on sandy shores are quite small. They

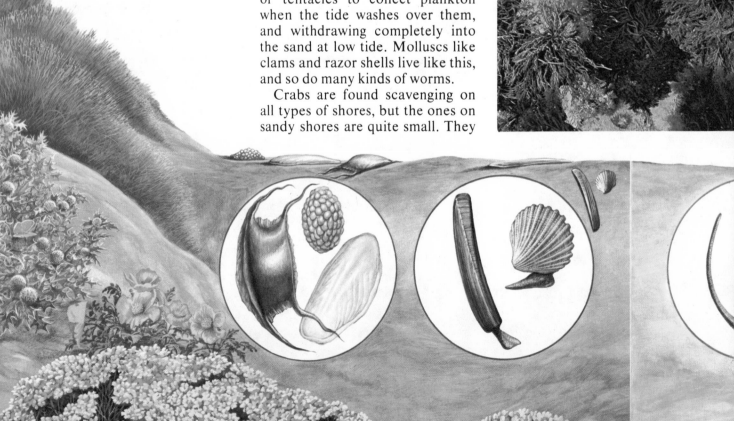

Above: The limestone cliffs at Marloes, in Pembrokeshire, tower over the beach, which is littered with fallen rock. This is a point along the coast where the sea currents sweep round a corner of land, wearing away softer rocks into sand.

Left: Seaweeds need rocks to hold on to. They do not grow on sandy or muddy shores.

Below: Some of the things you may find on a sandy beach. Razor shells and cockles burrow under the sand high on the shore. Worms live lower down, and crabs scavenge between sea and shore. In the shallows there are flatfishes and more molluscs. The tide carries fish eggs in flotsam up to the high tide mark.

pick up bodies of creatures stranded by the tide, and can often bury themselves in the sand—backwards—very quickly when danger threatens. A number of sea birds feed on the crabs, worms and molluscs of the shore. They often have long beaks for probing deep down in search of their buried prey. Most long-beaked shore birds feed in muddy water, however.

Riches in the mud

Muddy shores are richer in food than sandy shores. They occur where the sea moves more gently, leaving smaller particles behind when the tide goes out. Usually, muddy shores slope very gently and stretch over vast areas. A lot of the small particles left by the sea are food particles. This makes muddy shores rich in food for the kind of creatures which scavenge on the bottom or burrow in search of organic matter. The only sign of life when the tide goes out may be the little coils of mud left on the surface by burrowing lugworms.

These burrowing creatures are an important source of food for many species of birds. Avocets have long beaks which curve upwards for combing through the mud for shellfish and worms. Sandpipers move across the beach in great flocks, searching for food.

Mixed habitats

Some shores are a mixture of sand and shingle, or sand, shingle and rocks. These are the richest places in terms of the number of different species that live there. All of the plants and animals living between the high and low tide levels are limited as to where they live, and the kind of life they lead. So, any one type of beach only has the kind of life which is perfectly adapted to it. Between shingle and sand, and between sand and mud, there are an enormous number of different habitats. The exact size of the particles making up the beach can be so important to the worms and molluscs that they will only be found at a particular level. The other thing that decides what level they occupy is how long they can survive out of water. Living things lower down the shore do not have long to wait before the water comes back. Nearer the high tide mark, plants and animals may spend more time out of the water than in it.

For sea creatures, the shore is really just a continuation of the sea bed. But living on the shore brings special problems which occur nowhere else in the sea. All of the shore creatures have relations which live in other places on the sea bed. Most of them also have relations on land and in fresh water, for if animals can manage to solve the problems of shore life, they are more than halfway towards solving the problems of land life.

A point to remember, when you are exploring a beach, is that not everything you find there is bound to actually live there. A lot of things are washed up by the tide. So make sure that what you find is really at home on the beach.

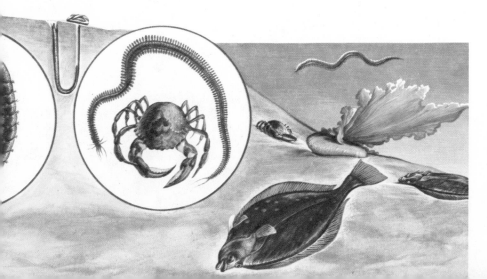

Rock pools and cliffs

Many animals live on the sea bed, some under deep water and others in shallow coastal waters. As we have seen, the plants and animals that live on the very edge of the sea bed, in the area between high and low tide, have special problems. They have to be able to cope with spending some time out of the sea. When the tide is out, they might be heated by the sun or drenched with freshwater rain. They must also be able to cling on tightly to stay at the level they prefer against the power of tides and waves.

Clinging to the rocks

Where the ocean meets a rocky shore, there is firm ground for plants and animals to hang on to. The wildest storm-lashed coasts may have only a few places for things to shelter, but most rocky coasts are rich in life.

On the rocks below low tide level we find red and brown seaweeds, sea anemones, sea urchins, and, in warm seas, corals. All these living things can just about manage to survive in the air for a short time. Red and brown seaweeds, mixed with green ones, are attached to rocks just above the low tide mark, which is where we also find mussels. Mussels anchor themselves to rocks with very strong threads; they can close their shells tightly so their bodies do not dry out when they are exposed to the air. Oysters have thicker shells than mussels and can manage to live out of water for a little longer. They live on rocks just above the mussels. Barnacles live here too. Mussels, oysters, and barnacles are filter-feeders. They strain microscopic plankton out of the water when the tide washes over them.

There are also plant-eating molluscs, like the limpets and periwinkles, which graze over the rocks scraping off the lichens that grow there. Limpets can stand being out of water for a long time. Each one wears away a little pit in the rock which fits its shell exactly. When the limpet has finished feeding, it comes back to its own pit and turns until its shell is sealed into the hole. There, it hangs on tightly, using its sucker-like foot and a very strong muscle.

The anchored seaweed shelters many of the smaller creatures. Seaweeds keep moist by producing a sort of jelly which holds a lot of water. Some small sea anemones and crustaceans can stay wet if they hide under the weed.

Rock pools

Things that live in rock pools do not often get dry. But they have another problem. If the weather is hot, some of the water may evaporate which will make the pool very salty. If it rains, the sea water in the pool may be diluted. So the inhabitants of rock pools have to be able to stand very salty or nearly fresh water.

Above high tide mark, the rocks are sprayed with salt water and washed by rain. This is a difficult place to live and usually only lichens can manage to survive

Below: Kittiwakes nest in colonies on cliffs. They feed on fish, molluscs and plankton from the surface of the sea. Their droppings cover the cliffs where they come year after year to breed.

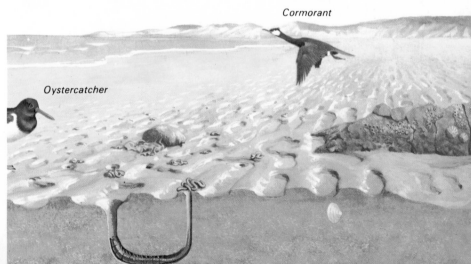

Cormorant

Oystercatcher

here. There are always the scavengers of the shore—like crabs—which roam around picking up dead creatures washed up or stranded by the tide.

Cliff birds

Sea birds, too, sometimes feed on carrion. They nest on rocks or cliffs by the sea. Cormorants choose flat rocks to build seaweed

Below: Some of the creatures of the shore. Crabs and starfishes live on all kinds of shores, the others are all found on rocky beaches. Dog whelks feed on other molluscs like mussels.

nests on, while sea ducks and kittiwakes nest on cliff ledges. These birds feed on fish and molluscs, and their droppings fertilize the cliff face so that plants can grow there. Sand martins are insect-eaters. They catch insects on the wing, like other martins do, but they hunt along the shore and build tunnel nests in soft cliffs. Peregrine falcons nest on cliffs in many parts of the world, where they feed on sea birds.

Here, where the ocean meets the land, there may be problems of adaptation, but there is always a rich food supply.

Below: High on the cliff, sea pinks and sea lavender flower. The rocky pools are home for some sea creatures, but other kinds live in the sand. Herring gulls feed on the rocks, oystercatchers probe the mud.

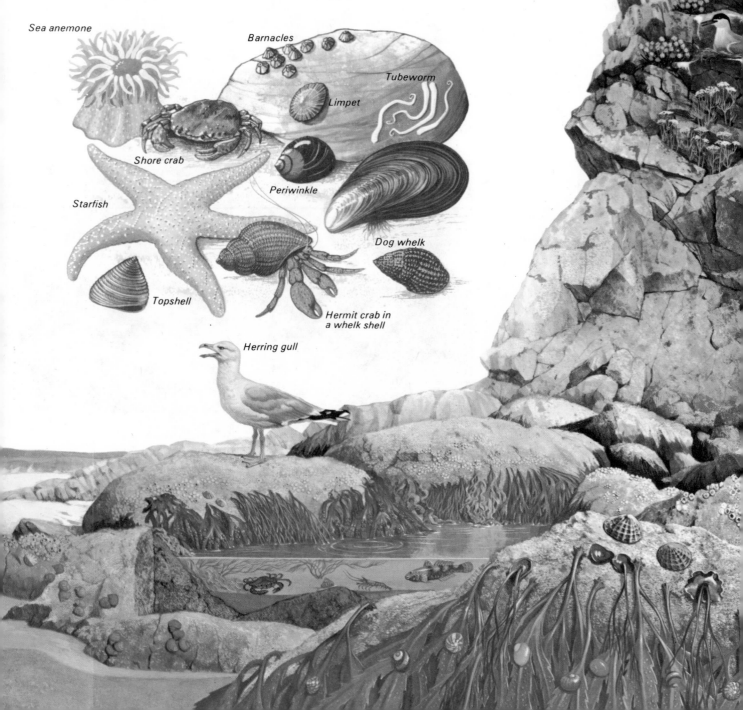

Sea anemone

Barnacles

Tubeworm

Limpet

Shore crab

Periwinkle

Starfish

Dog whelk

Topshell

Hermit crab in a whelk shell

Herring gull

Islands

Islands have fascinated biologists since Charles Darwin made his famous voyage to the Galapagos Islands. It was there that Darwin got the ideas that helped him to work out his theory of evolution. Not all islands are the same, of course. They are different sizes and have different climates.

Colonizing an island

Islands in the Pacific Ocean are especially interesting. They are made by volcanoes erupting from the sea bed. A volcanic island is either the top of a volcano itself or a platform of coral that has grown on top of a volcano that did not quite reach the surface. Coral atolls are left where a circle of coral has grown on the slopes of a volcano that then collapsed, leaving a ring of coral with a lagoon in the middle. The special thing about volcanic islands is that they spring up suddenly. One day there is no land, the next day there the island is—with nothing at all living on it. So the things that live on these islands must somehow get there from other places, often across hundreds of kilometres of sea.

Some plants and animals are more likely to arrive than others. Plants with seeds that are borne on the wind, are often found in remote places. Birds and insects can fly there. Some, like frigate birds, travel great distances over the sea; they often visit remote islands. Smaller birds and insects can be blown off-course by strong winds and, once having arrived on an island, cannot get off again. As well as the wind, the sea can carry living things to islands. Floating logs may travel a long way before they sink. They may carry seeds; a few stranded creatures like small reptiles could survive long enough on a floating log to reach land. Mammals cannot survive long without food and water; most mammals of remote islands are marine ones like seals.

When an animal does reach an island, the kind of soil, food, and shelter it finds there may not be what it is used to. It may also encounter no enemies or competition in its new home. These two things mean that animals have a chance to adjust to their new habitat without enemies to make life impossible.

The Galapagos finches

This is exactly what Darwin observed. He saw birds on the Galapagos Islands that were very similar to each other. They clearly had the same ancestors. But each type had a slightly different beak and lived in a slightly different way. There are actually 14 different species of finches on the islands that have evolved from a single species which was probably swept there by a great storm long ago.

The island itself puts limits on the kind of life that can survive there, in addition to the problems

Above: This species of sheep has been living for hundreds of years on a little rocky island called Soay, off the coast of Skye. We do not know whether the sheep were brought by crofters, or if sailors left them there as a food store. However they first arrived, they are now perfectly adapted to the hard life on this wet, windswept island. They may be very similar to early domesticated sheep.

Above: Coral islands are found in the South Seas. They are made from the limestone skeletones of millions of little anemone-like creatures that live in large colonies. The coral animals build their homes upwards towards the surface of the sea, but they cannot live out of the water. Many other creatures live among the coral branches and boulders.

Below: Triton trumpet shells up to 50 centimetres long live on Pacific coral reefs.

of getting there in the first place. As a general rule, the bigger the island, the more species it can support. This is because a bigger island can catch more rainfall. The more rain it gets, the wider the range of habitats it will contain.

A big island in a warm climate with plenty of rainfall will therefore have the most habitats. If the island is a long way from land, it may take a long time for the habitats to become occupied. If it is near the mainland, it may fill up quite quickly. A small island, with fewer habitats, will fill up much more quickly than a big one. Once an island is full, new arrivals must either defeat species already there or die themselves. So the rate of extinction of species on a fully-populated island will equal the rate of arrival of new species.

Some islands are not "new" land like the volcanic ones. They might be bits of the mainland that have been broken off by movements of the earth's crust. This has happened many times in the past. In these cases, the animals and plants that were there when it happened have been marooned. Ones that could swim or fly may have got back to the mainland, but the rest remained.

Evolution has been affected by the breaking up of continents. Australia is a very big island indeed. It contains nearly all the primitive mammals called marsupials left in the world. In most places, marsupials were defeated by more advanced placental mammals, but placentals did not evolve in Australia. There were many marsupials in South America until it became re-attached to the rest of America at the time of the last Ice Age; marsupials became extinct as soon as placentals came across the new Panama isthmus.

The same sort of thing can happen to small islands today, when man comes along with his own species of food plants and animals. It is happening on the island of Mauritius, where dodos once flourished.

Above: Giant tortoises live on the Galapagos Islands. They are large and slow, and feed on scrubby vegetation. The tortoises of each island have very different shell shapes. Those that live on islands without ground-level plants have a notch above their necks which allows them to browse on shrubs.

Above: It is no accident that coconut palms grow on remote islands. Their seeds are adapted for sea travel. The nut we usually see has a very thick, fibrous coat when it falls from its tree. This holds air, and enables the nut to float undamaged until it reaches land. These coconuts may have just fallen from above – or they may have arrived from a far-away shore.

The oceans

We have already seen that living things on land and in fresh water have many problems to overcome if they are to live there successfully. Most of the problems are connected with water. Life on dry land needs to be able to get enough water and freshwater life needs a high quality of water, with enough oxygen, carbon dioxide and plant food.

The teeming sea
The sea has none of these problems. It is where life began, after all, and the seas still contain many plants and animals that have had no cause to change their shapes or ways for millions of years. All the life on land and in fresh water has evolved from sea life, but thousands of living things have stayed behind in the sea. Whole groups of animals, adding up to more than 15,000 species, have hardly ever ventured out of their first comfortable home in the sea. They include sponges, sea urchins, jellyfish and corals.

The only animals in the sea that have any water problems are the fishes. All the invertebrates have body fluids that are at the same strength as sea water—they can let water in and out of their bodies without any trouble at all. Fishes have blood that is weaker than sea water, so they have to have kidney organs to keep their blood at the right concentration. Because of this, some scientists think that fishes could have evolved in fresh or brackish water and only later went back to the sea. If this is true, it would mean that just about all the vertebrates in the sea are recent arrivals. Nevertheless, fishes manage very well indeed in the ocean; they do not need to breathe air like other water vertebrates.

Plant life
Plant life in the sea can be just as primitive as the simplest animal life. The important plants of the oceans are tiny single-celled things

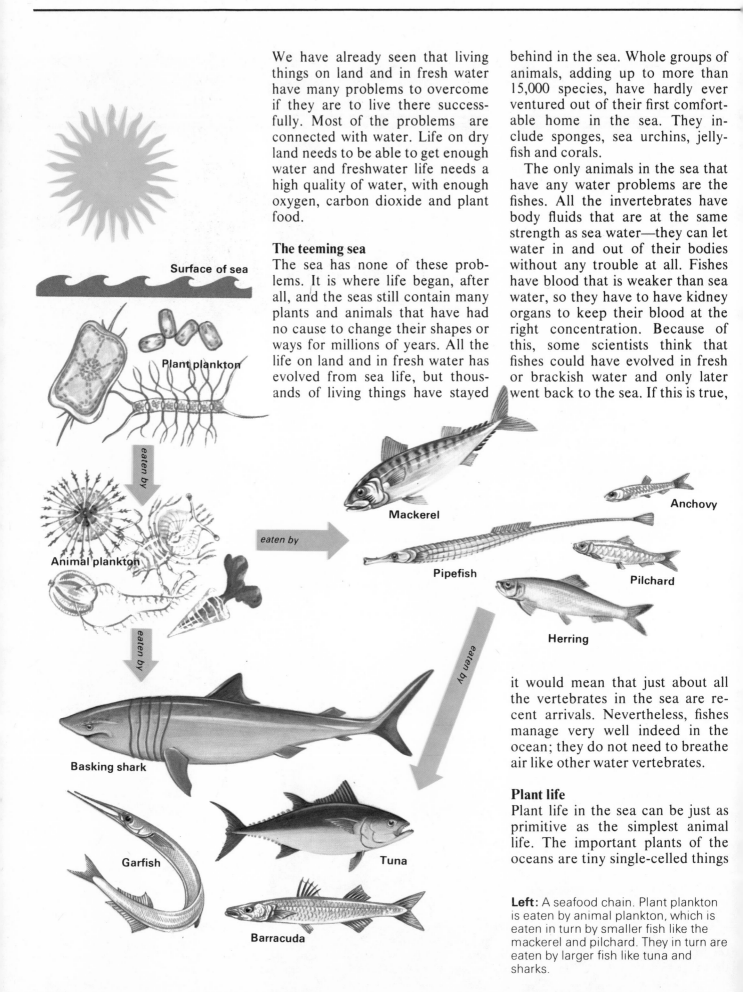

Surface of sea

Plant plankton

Animal plankton

eaten by

eaten by

eaten by

eaten by

Mackerel

Pipefish

Anchovy

Pilchard

Herring

Basking shark

Garfish

Tuna

Barracuda

Left: A seafood chain. Plant plankton is eaten by animal plankton, which is eaten in turn by smaller fish like the mackerel and pilchard. They in turn are eaten by larger fish like tuna and sharks.

Above: Red clown fish are covered with slime which prevents sea anemones from stinging them.

Right: Sea horses swim head-up, using their fins to propel themselves gracefully forwards.

like algae, diatoms and flagellates. They have probably changed very little since the earliest times on earth. Some algae have grown very large; they are the ones we call seaweeds. But it is the very tiny ones which provide most of the plant food in the seas.

The food chain on the left begins with tiny plants. They live near the surface of the sea, where they can get most sunlight. Tiny animals, animal plankton, eat these plants and provide food for bigger animals. Some of the biggest animals in the sea live entirely on the plankton, such as some sharks and whales.

There is practically no waste in the sea. A host of creatures live on the sea bed, picking up any scraps of food that sink down to the bottom. They themselves provide food for other more mobile creatures, and so the endless recycling of food goes on.

Corals

Tropical seas contain the great reefs of coral that grow in warm shallow water. Corals are animals that live in colonies, sharing the work of feeding, cleaning, and defence. Helped by algae that live with them, they build a lime skeleton which forms the basis of a whole community of living things. Seaweeds grow on the dead coral skeletons, together with sponges and other attached animals. The jungle they make provides food and cover for hundreds of other animals.

Molluscs may graze on algae, or strain food particles from the water, or even harpoon fish to eat with poison darts. Crustaceans like crabs and shrimps feed on anything they can find and are often eaten by the fishes lurking among the coral. Groupers, lion fish, and stone fish hide among the coral, waiting for unwary victims. Butterfly fish eat coral animals, picking them off delicately, while parrot fish bite off whole lumps of coral at a time.

Left: Lion fish have poisonous spines. They lurk among coral, hidden by their own spines.

243

Regions within the sea

The oceans are vast. They are all connected to one another, and together they cover more than 65 per cent of the earth's surface. Under the surface of the sea, there are as many different places to live as there are on land.

We can divide the sea into regions. It has three dimensions—up and down as well as sideways—and different plants and creatures live at different depths. In the surface waters, down to about 200 metres, which is as deep as sunlight can penetrate, there is plant plankton. Instead of being green—like land plants—sea plants are often red or brown. These colours help them to gather more of the weak light under the water. Animal plankton often lives mixed with the plant plankton, but some

tiny animals go deeper, feeding on dead plant plankton as it drifts down past them to the sea bed. The middle waters contain many meat-eating swimmers—invertebrates, fishes, and whales too. Many of these creatures keep to the same level in the water. We can use echo-sounding machines to find out where these levels are. Sometimes as many as six layers of living creatures can be found, each at a different depth. When it rains, the layers move towards the surface, and when the sun shines they go downwards. Some creatures come up to the surface at night.

Below: The midwater zone of the sea receives little sunlight. The fish that live there often have brilliant colouring and weird shapes.

Even the plankton in the upper layers travels up and down regularly every 24 hours.

Deep down in the ocean, more than 2,000 metres below the surface, are the cold dark depths of the abyss. Some meat-eaters live here, too. And under all the oceans, from the great abyss to the shallow waters round the continents and islands we live on, there is the sea bed.

The sea bed contains an enormous number of habitats—rocky, sandy, muddy, valleys and peaks, caves and forests of coral. Creatures scavenge all over the sea bed—even under the deepest oceans—and wherever there is a scavenger to eat, there will be another creature to feed on it. Molluscs live everywhere, crawl-

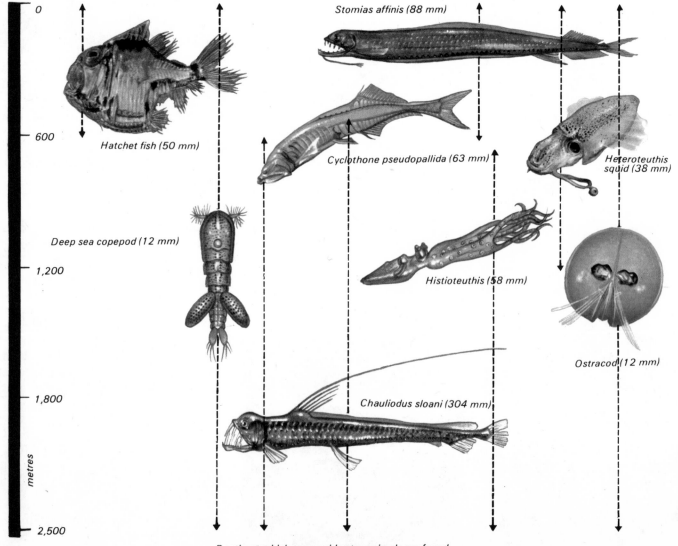

Depths at which some midwater animals are found

Below and **right:** The strangest sea creatures live in the cold, dark ocean depths, where men can only peer at them out of thick steel diving bells. The pressure of all the sea on top of a creature down here is enormous. Deep-sea fish have to push back against the water so hard, to avoid being squashed by it, that if they are pulled out of the depths where they live they will explode. This is one reason why we know so little about deep-sea creatures and how they live.

In the ocean depths food is scarce and light even scarcer. Some deep-sea fish have such enormous teeth and jaws that they are little more than swimming mouths. Some of them have enormous eyes, too, while others have given up trying to see and are completely blind. Many deep-sea creatures can turn some of their body energy into light. They flash signals to one another in the darkness, which is one way of avoiding being eaten by a potential mate!

The angler fish uses a little light at the end of its "rod". When curious creatures come to investigate, it snaps them up in its huge mouth. Many deep-sea carnivores feed on the tiny bristlemouths, which somehow find plankton to eat down there. Molluscs, including squids, live as deep as anyone has ever been.

Lantern fish

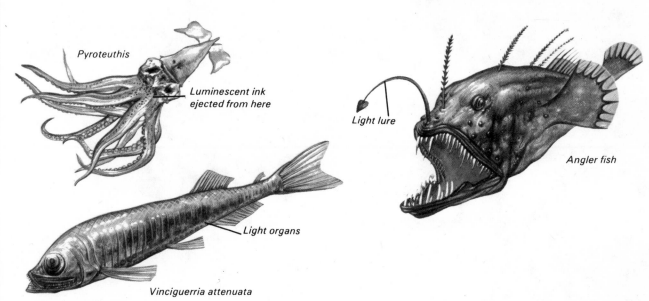

Pyroteuthis

Luminescent ink ejected from here

Light lure

Angler fish

Light organs

Vinciguerria attenuata

ing ones such as snails, and burrowing ones such as clams, as well as the swimming ones such as squids. Worms, too, of many different kinds, live in different places on the sea bed. Starfishes, sea urchins, sea lilies, and a host of other invertebrates crawl or cling to the bottom. Most of them have been given the names of land plants or creatures, but they have little in common with the land life they are named after.

Water moves between the oceans all the time. It is helped along by ocean currents. The Gulf Stream brings warm water to north-west Europe, and the Humboldt Current carries cool water along the west coast of South America. These currents make areas of different "climates" in the oceans they pass through. So as well as different oceans, there are different regions within the oceans. The currents also help to mix water from deep down with the surface water, by drawing it up, just as winds on land raise dust. This helps to bring minerals into the surface water where plant plankton can use them.

The currents that bring most nourishment to the surface are more often found in cold seas. It is in these cold seas, then, that most plant plankton is produced. Just as on fertile land, the plankton-rich cold seas support more animals. This does not necessarily mean more different kinds, just greater numbers. The great plankton-eating whales live in cold seas because they can only find enough to eat there. Whales have to go to warmer waters to breed, though, because baby whales are not born with enough blubber to keep them warm in the chilly feeding grounds. However, some inhabitants of cool waters hardly travel at all.

The balance of nature

Above: Factories are often built near rivers. Once, the river was used to transport materials and products. Now it helps to cool machinery and carry away wastes from the manufacturing processes.

Man is the only animal that can design and build his own environment. All the animals and plants on earth have evolved over millions of years to become adapted to their own particular habitat and lifestyle. Cold-climate mammals have thick fur coats, nut-eating mammals have strong front teeth, swimming mammals have webbed feet. Man has only his hands and brain—he makes warm clothing, nutcrackers and rubber flippers as and when he needs them. While other living things can only survive in particular habitats, man can create his own habitat anywhere. This is a tremendous step forward in evolution, and gives man a special responsibility.

Rapid change

It is true that all life is continually struggling for survival. Of all the different mammals that have ever lived on earth, only a tiny fraction are alive today. The others mostly died out because they were less successful than other species.

The most efficient mammal that has ever lived is man. If another creature bothers us—by eating some of our crops, taking our cattle, spoiling the appearance of fruit or vegetables—we can take instant action to solve the problem. We simply make war with machines and chemicals, which we can invent far more quickly than the victim can evolve an answer. Sometimes, as has happened with a drug used to poison rats, nature can answer the challenge. Many rats are now immune to the drug. They breed quickly, and creatures which breed fast can evolve fast.

Creatures at the top of food chains often have no natural enemies. This means that they do not have to have a fast reproduction rate because their babies have a good chance of growing up. Hawks are often at the top of food chains. We now know that some insect poisons can build up in the bodies of other animals—without killing them—which hawks eat. Peregrine falcons feed on pigeons in some places. The pigeons feed on farmland, and insect poisons on farm crops get into their bodies. Nearly 65 per cent of all the peregrine falcons in Britain died from the effects of insect poison before the connection was realized.

Pollution
But, more often, the damage we do is accidental. As a result of our own way of life, we pollute the air, the soil, and the water, without even noticing it.

The factory in the drawing has been built beside a river. It uses river water to cool its machinery, and may throw out wastes into the water. The river is very useful to the factory, but what is the factory doing to the river? If it puts poisonous wastes into the water, the result is obvious. But even warming up the water just a little can change the river. Warm water holds less oxygen, and is not such a good place for cold-water fishes, which will probably die and change the whole ecology of the river. If the factory puts the kind of chemicals that fertilize the water into the river, it may make weeds grow so fast that they use up all the oxygen, with the same result. The life of the river is so delicately balanced that any interference is bound to upset it.

In 1957, the River Thames in London was so badly polluted that it had no fishes in it at all. Work was begun to improve the treatment of sewage going into the river. After 20 years, there were 50 species of fish in the river, and now even salmon—which need a great deal of oxygen—have been seen.

Above: The lives of the animals which live in a river are very closely connected. Fish such as trout, sticklebacks and minnows, need clean oxygen-rich water. Frogs, too, breed in clean water. Pike feed on small fish and frogs, and so do kingfishers. Water voles feed on aquatic vegetation. None of them likes polluted water.

If we are absolutely selfish, we will not care what happens to the living things we share our planet with. But we must still realize how much we depend on nature. It has taken over 3,000 million years of evolution for man to arrive on earth. In the short time we have been here, we have begun to change the face of the earth. But we are just another kind of animal, in spite of all our skills and intelligence. We depend, like all other life on earth, on the soil, the air, and the water, and on a complicated web of other lives, for our food, our homes, our fuel, everything we have.

When the oil tanker *Torrey Canyon* ran aground off the Cornish coast, thick oil floated ashore all along the coast. The first effect this had was to kill thousands of sea birds. Detergents were used to break up the oil, and may have caused more damage to life than the oil did. Before the accident, the rocks were bare of weed **(left).** They were grazed by limpets. Today **(right)** the limpets are dead and weeds cover the rocks. Molluscs are very sensitive to pollution. The accident caused a major change in the environment.

Index

249

Index

Index

Acknowledgements

The publishers have made every effort to trace the ownership of all copyrighted material in this publication and to secure permission from the holders. Photographs have been credited by page number and position: (T) top, (C) centre, (B) bottom, and combinations, for example (TR) top right.

The publishers would like to thank the following:

J. Allan Cash: 37R 210T
Heather Angel: 37L, 43, 51T, 55L, 58B, 64T, 65T, 72T B, 74, 77L, 78TR BR, 79, 127, 170L, 180TL BL TR, 181, 184TL B TR, 185, 188T B, 189T, 190T B, 199T C, 202BL, 203TR, 210C B, 211CL BL TR, 218BC B, 219TL TR TC B BC, 234TR TL B, 235, 236-237T, 240B, 241T
Ardea: 42T, 53
Associated Freelance Artist: 220
Australian News and Information Bureau: 60T
British Museum (Natural History): 27
Bruce Coleman: 48, 49, 55R, 73, 75T, 93, 150B, 175TL, 186C, front cover TL
Gene Cox: 59B, 63C
M. Chinery: 90TR, 91, front cover BL
D Collins: 108-109
Ted Ellis: 218T TC
Peter Fraenkel: 174-175
Sonia Halliday: 186R
Brian Hawkes: 51B, 233B
Eric Hosking: 117
Imitor: 12L, 13B
P.A. Jewell: 240T
Pat Morris: 41, 62, 90B, 110, 116, 119BL TR, 124B, 125, 158, 193, 211TL, 238, 241B, back cover BR
National Trust: 234TL
N.H.P.A.: 40R, 75B, 119BR, 124T, 138-139, 144, 145T B, 150T, 204BL, 215, back cover CL
Natural Science Photos: 38R, 118, 129, 226-227, front cover TC
Maurice Nimmo: 199B
Novosti Press Agency: 12R
Photo Aquatics: 68-69
Popperfoto: 101TR
Royal Society for the Protection of Birds: 234BL
Seaphot: 64B, 78BL
Shell Photo Library: 63R
M.I. Walker: 58T, 59T
C. James Webb: 63L, 95B T
D.P. Wilson/Alison Wilson: 246-7
Zefa: 54, 140, 176R, 233T

Title Page: Tigress and cub
Endpapers: Giraffes

Contributors and Consultants
Neil Ardley
Linda Bennett
Barry Cox
Chris Gray
Dr. Keith Hyatt
Dr. Ray Ingle
Alfred Leutscher
Ron Taylor
Solene Whybrow